Trade and Fiscal Adjustment in Africa

Trade and Fiscal Adjustment in Africa

Edited by

David Bevan
Fellow of St John's College
University of Oxford

Paul Collier
Professor of Economics
University of Oxford

Norman Gemmell
Emeritus Professor of Economics
University of Nottingham

and

David Greenaway
Professor of Economics
University of Nottingham

First published in Great Britain 2000 by
MACMILLAN PRESS LTD
Houndmills, Basingstoke, Hampshire RG21 6XS and London
Companies and representatives throughout the world

A catalogue record for this book is available from the British Library.

ISBN 0–333–58585–2

First published in the United States of America 2000 by
ST. MARTIN'S PRESS, INC.,
Scholarly and Reference Division,
175 Fifth Avenue, New York, N.Y. 10010

ISBN 0–312–21464–2

Library of Congress Cataloging-in-Publication Data
Trade and fiscal adjustment in Africa / edited by David Bevan ... [et al.].
p. cm.
Includes bibliographical references and index.
ISBN 0–312–21464–2 (cloth)
1. Free trade—Africa. 2. Africa—Commercial policy. 3. Fiscal policy—Africa. 4. Structural adjustment (Economic policy)—Africa. I. Bevan, David.
HF2416.T7 1998
382'.096—dc21 98–11471
CIP

This book is printed on paper suitable for recycling and made from fully managed and sustained forest sources.

10 9 8 7 6 5 4 3 2 1
09 08 07 06 05 04 03 02 01 00

Printed and bound in Great Britain by Antony Rowe Ltd, Chippenham, Wiltshire

Contents

List of Figures

List of Tables

Acknowledgements

The CREDIT/CSAE Workshop on Trade and Fiscal Adjustment in Africa, held at St Antony's College, Oxford on 6–8 January 1992, from which the chapters in this book are drawn, was generously supported by the Overseas Development Administration, (now the Department for International Development). The Development Economics Consortium gratefully acknowledges this support.

Chapters 3 and 6 first appeared in the *Economic Journal*, and Chapter 11 in *The World Economy*; the publishers and editors are grateful to Blackwell Publishers for permission to reproduce copyright material.

Notes on the Contributors

David Bevan is Fellow of St John's College, University of Oxford.

Michael Bleaney is Professor of Economics, University of Nottingham.

Christopher Bliss is Professor of Economics, Nuffield College, Oxford.

Ngee Choon Chia works in the Department of Economics and Statistics, University of Singapore.

Paul Collier is Professor of Economics, University of Oxford and Director, Development Research Group, The World Bank.

Rodney Falvey is Professor of International Economics, University of Nottingham.

Norman Gemmell is Emeritus Professor of Economics, University of Nottingham.

David Greenaway is Professor of Economics and Pro-Vice-Chancellor, University of Nottingham.

Jan Willem Gunning is Visiting Professor of Economics and Director of the Centre for the Study of African Economies, University of Oxford.

Cha Dong Kim works in the Ministry of Science and Technology, Korea.

William Lyakurwa is Research Director, African Economics Research Consortium, Nairobi.

Oliver Morrissey is Senior Lecturer in Economics and Director of the Centre for Research in Economic Development and International Trade (CREDIT), University of Nottingham.

Nehemiah E. Osoro is Lecturer in the Department of Economics, University of Dar es Salaam.

Ritva Reinikka works in the African Technical Department, The World Bank.

Sadek Wahba works in the African Technical Department, The World Bank.

John Whalley is Professor of Economics, University of Western Ontario and University of Warwick.

1
Introduction

David Bevan, Paul Collier, Norman Gemmell and David Greenaway

African governments inherited at independence liberal trade regimes and fiscal conservativism: their economies were highly open and had very low inflation rates. By the mid-1980s most African governments had introduced a trade control regime which combined high tariffs and quantitative restrictions, usually associated with foreign exchange rationing (other than in the Franc Zone). In doing this, African governments were moving in the opposite direction from the rest of the world, which was engaging in global and regional trade liberalizations. Partly as a result of these contrary policy changes, a globally integrated economy is rapidly emerging, from which Africa is increasingly marginalized. Also, by the mid-1980s most African governments had increased fiscal deficits, financed partly by foreign borrowing and partly by domestic deficits. As a result, both international debt and domestic inflation had become serious concerns. The classic instance of these trade and fiscal trends is Nigeria. After an excellent economic performance up to the mid-1960s, by the mid-1980s there were severe trade restrictions, manifested in a spread between the official and the parallel exchange rate of more than 3:1, an accumulated fiscal deficit, with foreign debt at around $30bn despite oil revenue, and a domestic inflation rate that had risen from zero to over 40 per cent. In the process, growth had first decelerated and then become negative. Evidence has accumulated that, internationally, both high levels of import restrictions and high and variable fiscal deficits are detrimental to growth. The African growth experience is consistent with this evidence, and so it is a reasonable inference that a substantial part of Africa's slower growth is attributable to poor trade and fiscal policies.

From the mid-1980s, African governments attempted to restore open trade regimes and sustainable fiscal stances. Usually, these attempts were in the context of externally supported 'structural adjustment' packages, so

that donors had considerable influence as bargaining units and the transfers themselves had direct and substantial macroeconomic effects. The attempts have met with mixed success, in two senses. First, they have not always been sustained. For example, the Nigerian trade liberalization of 1986 collapsed in the early 1990s, although a further liberalization attempt began in 1995; similarly, the Ghanaian fiscal restoration of the late 1980s collapsed in the early 1990s. Secondly, althout6
h African economic performance improved somewhat following the trade and fiscal reforms, the recovery was usually modest. Hence, the history of trade and fiscal policy in Africa raises questions both in political economy, as to the motivation of governments, and more narrowly-focused questions relating to the design and efficacy of policy reforms.

These questions are the subject of this book. Each chapter is based on a paper written for and presented at two workshops of the Development Economics Consortium formed between the Centre for Research in Economic Development and International Trade, University of Nottingham, the Development Economics Research Centre, University of Warwick, and the Centre for the Study of African Economies, University of Oxford. The topic was discussed under three headings: trade liberalization; fiscal reform; and interactions between trade and fiscal reform. We consider these in turn.

Trade reforms

The trade liberalization chapters cover credibility, aid, and sequencing. Three chapters discuss credibility and its consequences. An analytic framework is set out by Collier and Gunning in Chapter 3, which is extended and applied to Kenya during the 1970s and 1980s by Reinikka in Chapter 5. Three necessary conditions are postulated for credibility: macroeconomic compatibility; time consistency; and the absence of systematic forecastability such as would arise were a government following an endogenous trade policy rule, tightening trade policy if the balance of payments deteriorated. Once incredibility arises, two types of portfolio response arise. First, as shown in the Calvo model, the anticipation of the imposition of trade restrictions provides a rationale for the hoarding of imports. Second, as shown in the Dixit model, temporary uncertainty provides a rationale for the postponement of fixed investment. In the context of credit rationing these effects interact: the reduction in fixed investment finances an increase in import hoarding, which could otherwise only be financed by the reduction in consumption. Reinikka applies a model to Kenya which includes borrowing constraints. She shows that there were episodes in which credibility was likely to be low, caused by endogenous trade policy in the late 1970s, and to macroeconomic incompatibility in the early and late 1980s. She then shows that these episodes gave rise to substantial speculative behaviour. Using data on inventories in bonded warehouses, total inventories, and import licences, she distinguishes between specific types of speculation and the expectations that generate them. For example, speculators will hoard licences if they believe that quantitative trade restrictions will be imposed but that the exchange rate and tariffs will stay unaltered. They will hoard in bonded warehouses if they believe that the exchange rate will be depreciated or foreign exchange rationed to the extent that licences will not be honoured, but that tariffs will not be raised, and they will store in unbonded warehouses if they believe that tariffs will be raised.

Falvey and Kim, in Chapter 2, discuss credibility in relation to the types of trade controls and in the context of the timing and sequencing of liberalization. They argue that if controls take the form of quantitative restrictions, and if the liberalization relaxes but does not abandon these restrictions, then speculators are unable to take advantage of the liberalization even if they are certain it will be reversed. This has repercussions for the relaxation of capital account controls which provide finance for speculation. If tariffs are reduced gradually then credibility is important, and becomes even more important if capital account restrictions are removed. By contrast, if quotas are relaxed gradually, then, because no speculative opportunities arise regardless of credibility, capital account liberalization does not carry the same risks. Hence, whereas the normal sequencing of trade liberalization is first to convert quotas to tariffs and then to reduce the tariffs, where credibility is a major problem as it is in much of Africa, there is a case for abandoning this sequence and instead directly and gradually relaxing quotas. Turning from the type of trade restriction to broader issues of timing and sequencing, they set up a trade-off between second-best considerations of efficiency and political economy considerations of sustainability. Following Rodrik, they argue that if liberalizations are very wide-ranging they may arouse so much opposition that they will lack credibility, but if they are not substantial they risk not being convincing. These propositions led Rodrik to advocate that liberalizations should be narrowly focused but deep. However, Falvey and Kim show that it is just such liberalizations that are most liable to generate allocative inefficiencies because of second-best effects. They also consider pre-announcement as a signalling strategy. This, again, is a case in which considerations of credibility might modify what is otherwise desirable. If pre-announcement is fully credible then there can in some circumstances be an efficiency gain. However, in the context of limited reputation pre-announcement is unlikely to be very credible. The implication of these papers is that incredibility can be very costly – indeed more costly than not attempting the liberalization – but that to both the consequences of incredibility and the extent to which a liberalization is incredible are within the control of the government.

Most African trade liberalizations have occurred in the context of foreign aid. Two chapters discuss the interactions between aid and trade liberalization. Morrissey in Chapter 4, focuses on bilateral aid. He shows that most of the bilateral aid programmes to Africa are implicitly or explicitly tied to trade with the donor country, this being particularly the case for France and Italy. The rationale for tying may be to maintain trade shares in countries with which the donor has a historically strong trading relationship. As such, it may not be explicit tying but will nevertheless lead to the persistence of trade patterns. Morrissey then argues that this persistence has the effect of inhibiting trade with non-donor countries, and most particularly with other African countries. Hence the massive transfers provided by bilateral donors may damage intra-African trade. Although some African trade would not compete directly with the output of developed countries, the manufactures of South Africa and Zimbabwe would be placed at a notable disadvantage. The policy of the European Union (EU) is interesting in that it both promotes and retards African regional integration. As a regional trading group it promotes the concept of regional integration through a special programme known as the Cross-Border Initiative. Yet this is combined with the tying of all its import support aid to the purchase of imports from the EU. The use of aid as a mechanism for maintaining the trade share of the donor also has repercussions for the credibility of trade reform. To the extent that governments are unwilling liberalizers, donor conditionality has been used in an attempt to induce governments to accept reform in exchange for aid. Even if the donor threat is fully credible, such conditionality runs the risk of being time inconsistent in that the aid is only temporary, so that policy may revert once the aid has been received. However, if recipient governments come to believe that donors are motivated by trade preferences rather than policy choices, the threat implicit in conditionality becomes even less effective.

In addition to its effects on credibility, aid has direct effects on the exchange rate and the money supply. Trade liberalization tends to worsen the balance of payments because it lowers the price level directly, and therefore the demand for money. An unaided liberalization therefore needs to be combined with either a policy that increases the demand for money (such as devaluation) or a policy that reduces the money supply. Collier and Gunning discuss this role of aid in Chapter 3. If aid is used by the government to purchase domestic money from private agents, then even temporary aid can, if it is large enough, achieve a compatibility without other offsetting policies such as exchange rate depreciation. However, while aid can thus be effective in maintaining compatibility, it comes at a cost to the real economy through the Dutch disease it induces. The use a simple computable general equilibrium model with gradual adjustment of the capital stock to show that export response is slower if the liberalization is aided. Further, resources may first move into the non-tradable sector and then move out again, with the implication that avoidable adjustment costs are being incurred. Finally, the import-substitute sector suffers an income loss, both as a result of the liberalization, which is unavoidable, and as a result of Dutch disease, which is avoidable. Hence, far from meeting the 'costs of adjustment', aid in fact inflicts additional adjustment costs on agents in the sector which is losing, while conferring benefits on other agents. The implication in these chapters is that aid has some serious negative effects in the context of trade liberalization, discouraging African regional integration, potentially undermining credibility, slowing export response and exaggerating redistribution.

The sequencing of trade liberalization is the main focus of Chapter 2, by Falvey and Kim. Their discussion on the liberalization of the capital account in relation to trade liberalization is closely analogous to that of the effect of temporary aid discussed by Collier and Gunning. Early liberalization of the capital account may induce a private capital inflow which finances consumption and reversed is subsequently, with resource allocation effects identical to those of a temporary aid inflow. There is, however, an important difference between aid and a private capital inflow through opposite implications for the money supply. A private capital inflow increases the supply of the domestic currency unless the central bank is able fully to sterilize it with sales of domestic debt which in the context of Africa is seldom feasible at other than prohibitive cost. By contrast, a public capital inflow, because it accrues to the government, can be used to reduce the domestic money supply. Hence, whereas the real effects of a capital inflow are invariant with respect to ownership, unless the owners have different expenditure preferences – as between tradables and non-tradables, the monetary effects change sign depending upon ownership. This is one reason why it might be defensible to accept aid during liberalization while not liberalizing the capital account. A second is that public capital inflows are likely to be less vulnerable to political and economic shocks than private capital. A third is that the sign of private capital flow in the early stages of capital account liberalization is unpredictable. In most of Africa this is probably not the case because even during inconvertibility private agents have been able to export capital illegally, so that only repatriation has been prevented. Convertibility thereby permits the repatriation of previous capital which has flown. However, there are occasional circumstances in which capital controls have been sufficiently effective that there might have been a pent-up demand for foreign assets. In Zimbabwe this may have been the case because of a long history of tight and effective foreign exchange controls, and in Zambia parastatal firms, which were widespread, may have felt obliged to comply with the exchange control laws even though evasion would have been feasible.

Whereas the above discussion of the capital account has focused on finance capital, there is also an issue of sequencing concerning inflows of fixed investment. Until trade is liberalized investment decisions will reflect the trade control regime. Again, Falvey and Kim show the distinction between tariffs and quotas to be central. However, their discussion treats the trade regime as being exogenous to foreign private investment. In practice in Africa, in the circumstances of changing trade restrictions, foreign investors may try to negotiate both trade liberalization on inputs and increased protection (or a slower liberalization) on outputs. In such an environment it may be best first to reach the new trade regime and to bind as many parts of it as possible before encouraging private capital inflows. Unfortunately, African governments largely failed to use the opportunity to bind tariff reductions at close to their actual liberalized levels afforded by the Uruguay Round. For example, Zimbabwe chose to bind its tariffs at levels far higher than those in fact applied.

Fiscal reforms

There are four fiscal chapters: two concerned with features of the tax system that might make reform desirable; and two with the characteristics of reform itself. Tax system in developing countries have a variety of unsatisfactory features, and this has generated a large literature, and indeed a very extensive programme of reform. However, the principal concerns of this work have been with the level of revenue generated by taxation, and its buoyancy; the size of the deadweight losses inflicted on private agents in the process of collection; and associated problems of administration and of ensuring compliance. The first two chapters focus on two other important issues which have been largely neglected: those of revenue volatility and distributional incidence.

Bliss, in Chapter 6, is concerned with the theory of revenue reforms in a country seriously constrained in its choice of revenue instruments by limitations in administration, information, or public probity. It is assumed that these restrictions are exceptionally severe, so that the only conventional tax instruments available to the government are tariffs. However, the government is also engaged in public production of non-tradable goods, and can set the prices of its outputs. The author extends his earlier work on the design of tariffs for revenue to relate optimal public enterprise pricing to the optimal choice of tariffs. It emerges that, since the government is constrained to generate tax revenue in a way that protects private producers (as a by-product of raising revenue via tariffs), it should generally also set the price of its own production at a level offering protection to the private sector. Since, in practice, many public enterprises are run at a loss, this suggests that a beneficial reform would often result from a lowering of tariffs, matched by a revenue-neutral raising of public enterprise prices and net surpluses.

Chapter 7, by Bleaney, Gemmell and Greenaway, examines the sources and consequences of tax revenue instability; its principal focus is on experience in Sub-Saharan Africa, but this is placed in a wider context. While this phenomenon is quantitatively important, and is widely understood to be a characteristic of developing country finances, it has been very little studied. The authors argue that there is ample evidence that revenue instability creates cumulative fiscal problems. There is an asymmetry between revenue booms and slumps, with expenditure adjusting readily, and indeed often overshooting in the booms, but being slow to adjust in the slumps. For whatever reason, governments do not appear to be efficient at smoothing their expenditure at an appropriate average level if their revenue is unstable. Countries experiencing high revenue volatility are not only faced with the direct consequences of this instability, but are also more likely to suffer from larger average fiscal deficits, inflation and indebtedness. There are also a priori reasons for expecting real tax revenues to be less stable in developing countries than in developed market economies. One is a consequence of the typical structure of their economy, which makes them more vulnerable to internal and external shocks, because of the greater importance of the agricultural sector and their greater dependence on exports of primary products whose prices are volatile. The other reflects the typical structure of taxation, which is weighted towards taxes on international transactions. This suggests that revenue would tend to be more volatile in developing countries than elsewhere and, within the developing countries, more volatile in poorer, more open economies. Calculations of the standard deviation of year-to-year changes in the ratio of central government revenue to GDP bear out this expectation, with Sub-Saharan Africa exhibiting far more volatility than developing countries on average. Using a sample of thirty-six developing countries (seventeen in Africa), the authors then investigate the correlation of revenue instability with the share of foreign trade taxes in total revenue, and with the share of domestic indirect taxes in non-trade revenues. Revenue instability turns out to be positively correlated with the former, as expected; it also turns out to be negatively correlated with the latter, which is less easily explained. For the African countries, openness and trade tax dependence are the major sources of revenue volatility; however, they do not explain all of the extra volatility experienced on the continent. While government expenditure also emerged as more unstable in these countries, this was entirely explained by the correlation with their (higher) revenue instability; however, it was not possible to draw any inferences about causality. This work has important potential implications for policy, both with regard to the design of domestic policy to reduce or cope with volatility, and with regard to the design of policy conditionality by donors.

Chapter 8, by Chia, Wahba and Whalley, examines the incidence of taxation in developing countries, using the Côte d'Ivoire as an illustration. Limited analytical attention has been devoted to the issue, although the question has been much discussed at a general and somewhat speculative level. The intuitions underlying these discussions are often informed by the types of tax incidence result obtained from studies of OECD economies. The authors argue that these results need to be heavily qualified before being transferred to developing countries in this way. First, these countries typically have narrow bases for each of the major taxes, so that incidence effects are concentrated more by socio-economic and sectoral groupings than by income range. Second, in a trade-restricted environment, changes in trade-related taxes may have large income effects. Third, with the large inter-household transfers typical of many African economies, there may be important transmission effects via induced changes in transfers, so that the overall incidence effects may be very different from those suggested by the distribution of endowments and changes in relative prices alone. The potential importance of these general points is then demonstrated in the context of the Côte d'Ivoire using a numerical general equilibrium model. This model has a rich structure, distinguishing fifteen production sectors –

seven tradable and eight non-tradable – and a set of households distinguished by socioeconomic group. An important distinction carried through the model is that made between formal and informal sectors; close attention is also paid to the existing structure of public finances. The authors use the model to carry out differential incidence calculations, where each major component of the tax system is replaced in turn by a broad-based sales tax, with the switch designed to be revenue neutral. Since the latter tax is roughly neutral distributionally, this exercise permits the distributional consequences of the existing structure to be assessed. It turns out that domestic indirect taxes are broadly neutral, while export taxes are regressive. Other components of the system have strong distributional effects, but these are very mixed: that is to say, they criss-cross the rich–poor spectrum of household mean incomes in complicated ways. There is no clear gradation from rich to poor, as is typical in the OECD studies. If inter-household transfers are suppressed, the pattern of incidence is very different, but it shares this general characteristic of non-monotonicity. The conclusion of the exercise is that the distributional effects of the tax system may be very substantial, that they need not accord at all well with the intuitions developed from OECD studies, and that any serious analysis of incidence must incorporate country-specific features.

Chapter 9, by Osoro, looks at the attempt to reform the Tanzanian tax system in 1992. It provides a wealth of fiscal data, and sets the reform in its historical and fiscal context. The background to the reform was the major shift in general policy orientation which began in the mid-1980s with trade liberalization, deconfinement, price decontrol, an active foreign exchange rate policy, and a shift in attitude to the private sector, recognizing its importance to the economy. Against this background, the 1992 reform also involved a major shift in emphasis. Previously, the accent in tax policy discussion had been on equity at the expense of efficiency; in the event, the tax system was poor at providing either, nor was it capable of generating adequate revenue. This meant that the government was left to rely very heavily on foreign sources of finance, for 45 per cent of the recurrent budget and 75 per cent of the development budget, a position likely to be exacerbated by the fiscal costs of financial reform. However, the 1992 reform was focused mainly on improving the efficiency of the system, and its potential revenue impact was always likely to be uncertain. It continued the process of reducing income tax rates that had started in 1986, but did not accompany this by improvements to the base, which was weakened by the exemption of allowances and fringe benefits that often far exceeded workers' basic salaries. As regards commodity taxes, the reform reduced rates, abolished or modified exemptions, and removed taxes on raw materials used by domestic industries to produce final goods. These changes were intended to improve efficiency, and also to increase revenue, partly by improved compliance, but mainly by the removal of the exemptions that had become very pervasive. Unfortunately, as the author stresses, discretionary powers to grant exemptions remained with the Ministry of Finance. In consequence, it was always doubtful whether the exemptions would be abolished effectively, and in the event this central feature of the reform was abandoned very rapidly. The attempted 1992 Tanzanian reform therefore must be counted as a demonstration of the potential primacy of political economic considerations as opposed to technical economic ones in this area. Effective reform requires that a sufficiently powerful and stable coalition of interests can be constructed to see the process through, and this was not achieved in Tanzania.

Trade and fiscal interactions

The final chapters are concerned with the interaction between trade and fiscal policies and outcomes, and with the consequences for each of attempts to reform the other. Both concentrate on the impact on fiscal outcomes of trade reforms, though once again they do so in somewhat different ways. Chapter 11, by Lyakurwa, examines the consequences of the trade reforms in Tanzania in the 1980s. It sets the scene for this by noting that the fairly conservative fiscal profile of the 1970s, with revenue and expenditure both running at around 20 per cent of GDP, was massively disrupted at the end of that decade by a number of shocks, including the war in Uganda. These had the consequence of inducing a sequence of very large deficits, but had other by-products in the composition of revenue. In particular, not only was the share of total indirect taxes very high (at 75 per cent of the total) and rising, but the domestic share in these was also high – 40 per cent of all revenues and 75 per cent of sales tax revenues. This reflected the very low share of trade taxes, which fell below 7 per cent of total revenue in the early 1980s. The major reason for this pronounced dependence on domestic taxes was that foreign exchange shortages limited Tanzania's ability to import goods, so limiting the amount of duties and sales tax that could be levied on imports. This effect was reinforced by the structure of the sales tax as a suspension system, with many goods used as inputs imported free of tax. This extreme compression had been somewhat relaxed by the end of the

1980s, with the recovery in import capacity, but with government accounting for 70 per cent of all imports, the effect on revenues was more muted. On the other hand, the effective taxation of exports was very high; not only were there direct export taxes, but also controls on producer prices and an overvalued exchange rate. The author stresses the link between fiscal and trade policies that runs through the exchange rate. Not only have excessive fiscal deficits been at the root of overvalued exchange rates, but these in turn shift value added away from the trade sector, where it is most easily taxable. However, devaluation, while relieving this problem in the long run, may not necessarily improve the fiscal deficit in the short run. In Tanzania, as elsewhere, the forced compression of imports was implemented by means of quantitative restrictions. One implication of this is that significant trade policy reforms may also reduce the fiscal deficit and inflation relative to weaker reforms; this is especially likely to be the case if quantitative restrictions are replaced with equivalent tariffs.

Chapter 10, by Bevan, examines similar questions, using a numerical general equilibrium approach with an illustration from the abortive Kenyan trade liberalization at the beginning of the 1990s. Relatively few studies have focused on the extent to which trade liberalization exacerbates the government's existing budgetary problems, or the converse. Yet this is a consideration which often makes developing country governments wary of embarking on a liberalization programme, and which can lead to the collapse of a programme once adopted. The importance of the joint structure of the economy and of the tax system in determining the fiscal outcome is stressed. In the case of Kenya, it appears that this joint structure made it likely that trade liberalization would be powerfully budget-enhancing, so that the government's fears that it would worsen the fiscal management problem were misplaced. There are a number of reasons for this, but the two major ones relate to the role of quantitative restrictions in controlling imports. First, this meant that relaxation of the trade regime involved losses to those private agents who had privileged access to import licences, not to the budget. Second, since the imports which were most severely quota-constrained also carried much higher tariff rates than those which were not, substitution within the bundle of imports following liberalization would tend to raise the effective tariff rate. It is also the case that the government would itself have benefited substantially as a spending agency from the relative price shifts following liberalization. Given this general result, the author then considers a variety of combined fiscal and trade reforms, all of which are designed to be revenue-neutral in the long run. Because of the favourable fiscal effects of a pure trade reform, these packages all involve a degree of fiscal relaxation. The dynamic properties of adjustment to the new equilibrium are then examined. In each case, the budget deficit initially deteriorates, because the relatively slow adjustment of wages and the price of non-tradables (relative to the domestic price of tradables) means that government expenditure is slower to adjust than revenue, and these are both lower (in dolar terms) in the new, less-distorted equilibrium. As a consequence, the short-run fiscal signals from a long-run neutral reform package are perverse; they include deterioration of the deficit, acceleration of the inflation rate, and possibly an investment collapse. They are likely to test the resolve of even committed reforming governments, and may call the credibility of the whole reform into question. One possible response is to design a temporary tightening of the fiscal stance to neutralize these short-run symptoms. However, this is a somewhat perverse response and may delay desirable adjustment. Another possibility is to negotiate a temporary enhancement in the aid inflow. Governments frequently argue for some accommodation of this type to help in the reform process. It is often argued that this type of temporarily increased aid will merely delay the adjustment, but the author's simulations suggest that it might have a more constructive role to play, offsetting the temporary fiscal deterioration without much harm to the rate at which reallocation of resources is achieved. By way of contrast, the fiscally conservative strategy of raising tariffs temporarily to a level 'equivalent' to the quotas that are being removed appears in the simulations to be profoundly problematic; it exacerbates the original misallocation, and does not necessarily help with the revenue problem. The implication of this analysis is that unassisted intuition may be very misleading, that a detailed specification of individual country characteristics is necessary for analysis to be useful, and that it may be particularly important to supplement a static analysis with a dynamic one.

It is widely accepted that the fields of trade reform, fiscal reform, and the interaction between them, are highly significant for developing countries, and that it is important that they be well understood. The chapters in this volume demonstrate that there are a number of important aspects of these fields which have, surprisingly, been little studied and are certainly not well understood. Together they constitute a substantial attempt to subject these matters more fully to systematic analysis. However these are large questions and much remains to be done.

Part I
Trade Reform Issues

2
Timing and Sequencing Issues for Trade Liberalization in Africa

Rod Falvey and Cha Dong Kim

Introduction

Since the 1970s there has been a shift in the trade regimes of many developing countries away from the inwardly-orientated, import-substituting policies that most had pursued since independence. In its place we now see attempts to improve growth performance, raise export earnings, and increase the efficiency of domestic industries by increasing their exposure to foreign competition. An important part of this realignment has been the adoption of programmes of trade liberalization. Most of the adjustment programmes undertaken in Sub-Saharan Africa (Africa) in the 1980s include elements of trade policy reform. These elements have been sufficiently modest, however, that African trade regimes remain some of the most restrictive in the world (Nash, 1990).

Several reasons have been suggested for this change in approach (Whalley, 1989). Undoubtedly it reflects some dissatisfaction with the results of import-substitution, and a desire to emulate the strong growth performance of the 'outwardly-orientated' NICs. International donors and lenders (such as the IMF and the World Bank) now often make their assistance conditional on some programme of trade policy reform. Developed countries have also begun to take more notice of developing country policies, particularly those of the more successful exporters, and have begun to press for reforms in industries or sectors of interest to developed country exporters.

While this change in the direction of trade policy might be said to reflect a general dissatisfaction with past performance, what triggers many liberalization programmes are balance of payments crises. Such crises seem unavoidable, given the policies adopted by many developing countries (Mussa, 1987). International transactions are subject to a wide range of restrictions, including taxes, tariffs and quantitative restrictions on commodity trade, exchange controls and, particularly in Africa, parastatal control over marketing channels. These restrictions partly reflect the basic import-substitution policy, but they also result from the government's inability to meet its expenditure targets without recourse to inflationary financing. In order to maintain the exchange rate, governments impose ever-tighter restrictions on international transactions, and the domestic currency rapidly becomes overvalued. The result is recurrent balance-of-payments crises, which are occasionally alleviated by devaluations and the temporary loosening of controls, only to reappear as government deficits continue. An important element of this scenario is that the real exchange rate, defined as the relative price of non-traded goods in terms of traded goods, remains above its equilibrium level – pushed there by the excess of domestic expenditure over income. This, combined with the assistance import-competing industries receive from the trade regime, results in a structure with a strong home market or anti-export bias.

When embarking on a programme of trade liberalization, governments face certain issues relating to the timing and sequencing of reforms. One immediate issue is whether trade liberalization should begin at once, or whether a programme of macroeconomic stabilization, if needed, is a necessary precondition for success (this issue is discussed in the following section). Several sequencing issues then follow. First, should both capital and current account transactions be liberalized simultaneously, or is there some preferred order of liberalization? Relevant here are both the expenditure effects of opening the domestic economy to world capital markets, and the implications of a more liberal foreign investment regime. Second, should quantitative restrictions (QRs) be converted to tariffs as an initial step in the trade liberalization programme, or should they be liberalized directly along with the tariffs? Third, what role, if any, is there for export incentives as part of this process, given an anti-export bias will otherwise persist until the reforms are completed?

Once these sequencing issues have been resolved, the question of the appropriate speed of liberalization arises. Should the reform be a one-shot change or a series of smaller, pre-announced changes? Here the main concerns are the implication of the speed of liberalization for government revenue, the adjustment costs imposed on the economy, and the credibility of the reform. Getting the timing and sequencing of reform right is important. Inappropriate timing and sequencing may raise doubts as to its sustainability and deter the private sector from undertaking the adjustments necessary to make the reform a success.

Initial timing

As noted above, the origins of many liberalization programmes can be traced to some balance-of-payments crisis for the country concerned. It is clear that if macro-stabilization is required (Wolf, 1986; and Mussa, 1987; discuss the appropriate macro policies), it would be pointless to embark on trade reform in advance: the trade reform signals would be swamped by the macro uncertainties. The question is whether it is appropriate and advisable to enter into programmes of trade liberalization and macro-stabilization simultaneously, or whether the government should put its macroeconomic house in order first.

There has been some debate on this issue. Wolf (1986) summarizes the arguments for stabilizing in advance. First, there is the conjuncture problem. Initiating trade and stabilization packages simultaneously means that the contractionary aspects of the stabilization programme tend to be linked with the trade reform (see also Michaely, 1986), so that, in the public awareness, trade reform becomes associated with unemployment and deflation. For the liberalization to be sustained it might be better to leave protection in place until the macro crisis is over.

Second (and related), is the notion that it is inadvisable to unite the political opposition to the stabilization programme, which, although widespread, is likely to be diffused and therefore relatively ineffective, with the more localized (but also more organized, vocal and effective) political opposition to the programme of trade reform. Both programmes are more likely to be sustainable if they are undertaken sequentially rather than simultaneously. Trade reform may be more credible if the macroeconomy is stable.

Third, the adjustment costs imposed on the economy by any policy package are likely to be positively related to the speed and extent of the changes in relative prices that economic agents are confronted with. The adjustment costs of the combined package are therefore likely to be higher than the sum of those associated with their sequential implementation, where the relative price changes generated by both are in the same direction.

Finally, aspects of the stabilization package will also promote trade reform: for example, by reducing the excess of expenditure over income, and therefore the real exchange rate, the stabilization policy itself goes some way towards reversing the anti-export bias implicit in the initial policy structure. Substantial real devaluations may make QRs redundant and easier to abolish (for example, Ghana, Nigeria and Zaire). Also, by reducing the significance of QRs the stabilization programme will increase the transparency of the existing pattern of protection, thereby providing a clearer basis for its subsequent reform.

Against these arguments in favour of delay, there are reasons for initiating a programme of trade reform at the outset. The adjustment costs associated with trade reform may pass unnoticed among those generated by the stabilization programme. One might as well obtain the efficiency gains from the trade reform as quickly as possible. Further, once the atmosphere of crisis has passed, it may be more difficult to build up the necessary political momentum for reform, particularly if the economy has just passed through a difficult stabilization period. One possible way around this difficulty is an early announcement of a programme of trade reform, which will not begin until after the macroeconomic crisis is over. The risk with this strategy is that it allows the political forces in opposition to gather strength. Lobbying for the status quo will gain momentum without the potential beneficiaries of the trade reform being able to identify themselves and to provide countervailing pressure.

On the question of the desirability of prior stabilization, Michaely *et al.* (1991) conclude (p. 280) that experience indicates no particular necessity to stabilize *prior* to liberalization, as long as the policies *accompanying* liberalization are appropriate to the macroeconomic situation. Trade liberalizations begun in crises have generally been deep and speedy, which may account for their success despite their inauspicious beginnings; but liberalizations have been slowed (Malawi, Kenya) or reversed (Zambia) by poor macro performance (Thomas and Nash, 1991).

Sequencing

The problem of sequencing arises where reform is envisaged for a range of policies in a variety of markets, but not all policies and markets are to be liberalized simultaneously. In which order should policies or markets be liberalized? If some markets are to be left distorted in the short run, will it be optimal to fully liberalize the others? Should any limited liberalization be gradual? The answers to these questions are closely related to the general analysis of the second-best, where the concern is with the implications of distortions in some markets for appropriate interventions in others. This observation alone indicates the difficulty of finding definitive answers. Here we aim to draw out the relevant considerations, recognizing that ultimately the optimal sequencing will be an empirical issue.

Capital and current accounts

Should trade (current account) liberalization come before, after or simultaneously with liberalization of the capital account? This question has received considerable attention in the literature. The implications of capital account liberalization can be viewed from two perspectives – expenditure (that is, allowing domestic residents to borrow and lend abroad) and output (that is, allowing foreign direct investment). These perspectives have generally been examined separately, a practice that will be followed here, beginning with the expenditure effects and leaving foreign investment for later.

Trade restrictions can inflict two types of distortion. At each point in time agents' choices with respect to the current commodity mix of consumption and production are distorted. But in addition there can be an intertemporal distortion in the allocation of expenditure over time if trade restrictions have different impacts on 'the cost of living' in different periods. One aspect of the debate over the sequencing of current and capital account reforms is concerned with this intertemporal distortion. The underlying issue involves the implications of restrictions in one account for the optimal policies in the other. The solution depends on the nature of the restrictions. If these are quantitative, then one need not be concerned in general about their interactions – that is, reform can proceed one account at a time. But if the restrictions involve tariffs or taxes, then, in general it will not be optimal to fully liberalize one account while the other remains restricted.

Suppose trade is subject to tariff restrictions. If these tariffs create an intertemporal distortion, then there is some intervention in the capital account that will be welfare-improving. For example, if tariffs have distorted expenditure in favour of the current period, then current saving is lower than optimal, and capital account interventions that discourage foreign borrowing (or encourage foreign lending) will be welfare-improving. The opposite intervention would be called for if the distortion was towards future expenditure.

The implications this has for policy reform can be illustrated by considering two alternative circumstances. Suppose the government has announced a programme of gradual tariff cuts. In addition to its effects on within-period resource allocation, such a programme, if it is credible, will distort expenditure in favour of future consumption when tariffs are lower, and lead to excessive saving in the current period. Unless some other distortion exists that results in too little saving in the current period, a small capital account intervention that encourages current borrowing will be welfare-improving.

Alternatively, suppose the announced reform programme is *not* credible, so that agents expect today's tariff cuts to be reversed in the future. Expenditure is then distorted towards current consumption, implying a larger than optimal current-account deficit and welfare gains from restricting foreign borrowing.

These examples illustrate two points. First, that full capital account liberalization may not be optimal if tariff reform is gradual. Second, that the appropriate direction of capital account intervention will depend crucially on intangible factors such as 'credibility'. General policy recommendations are therefore hard to come by, though one can see that governments concerned with the credibility of their trade reforms may be reluctant to liberalize their capital accounts during its early stages for fear of the current-account blowout that might result. A flexible attitude to capital account reform therefore seems appropriate.

If the trade restrictions are QRs, rather than tariffs, then similar intertemporal distortions result. Capital account interventions are *not* called for in this case, however, because such interventions are unable to offset the consumption constraint imposed by the QRs.[1] Thus gradual quota reform, credible or otherwise, yields no second best arguments for capital account interventions.[2]

The same considerations apply if it is capital restrictions that are lingering, and we are concerned as to the implications for trade reform. If these capital account restrictions are quantitative, then a small manipulation of traded goods prices will not weaken them. If, however, capital account transactions are taxed, there is some scope for trade interventions partially to offset the distortions so generated. The latter circumstances might, depending on the direction and magnitude of the capital account distortions, provide a case for gradual trade liberalization.

Aside from the second-best implications of restrictions in one account for reform of the other, there are concerns that differences in their speeds of adjustment – capital account adjustments are generally assumed to occur more rapidly than current account adjustments – could imply that simultaneous liberalization would lead to an avoidable reversal of resource flows. The basic argument is as follows (Edwards, 1986). Suppose that capital account liberalization leads domestic residents to borrow abroad to increase their present consumption. Part of the resulting expenditure increase falls on traded goods and is accommodated by a deterioration in the current account. The remainder falls on non-traded goods and leads to an increase in the real exchange rate, which eliminates the resulting excess demand partly by shifting resources away from the production of traded goods. A successful trade reform, on the other hand, requires a fall in the real exchange rate in general, or at least a shift in resources out of import-competing production, and possibly non-traded goods, into exportable production.

If the adjustments to these liberalizations were to occur at the same rate, so that there was a smooth adjustment of the real exchange rate to its new equilibrium level, there would be no problem with simultaneous liberalization. But the concern is that the capital account adjustment will dominate in the short run, and may even involve some overshooting given the 'rigidities' in some of the other variables. In this case we would observe a temporary increase in the real exchange rate, possibly inducing resource flows into the non-traded goods sector that are later reversed. This possibility had led to recommendations that the appropriate order of liberalization is the current account first, with the capital account liberalization being delayed until after the current account adjustment has gathered momentum.

Developing-country experience provides few lessons in this area, because few developing countries have liberalized their current and capital accounts simultaneously. Where capital accounts have been liberalized, there have been substantial early capital flows which have later been reversed, with the movements of the real exchange rate as predicted (Edwards, 1990). What the evidence does suggest is that appropriate movements in the real exchange rate are important for the success of the liberalization. In fact, Michaely *et al.* (1991, p. 218) conclude that an 'impact' decline in the real rate 'appears to be almost a prerequisite for survival of any liberalization policy'. The general view, based more on theory than experience, is that liberalization of the capital account should be held back until well into the process of tariff reform,[3] with a willingness partly to reverse the capital account reforms should it appear necessary for the substainability of the trade reform programme.

Quantitative restrictions and tariffs

Non-tariff barriers are more extensive in Africa than in any other region (Nash, 1990). There is a general presumption in the literature, which has been carried through into practice in Africa and elsewhere, that the initial stages of trade reform should see the removal of any QRs on imports and their replacement, if so desired, by tariffs. Several arguments have been put forward in support of this strategy (Michaely *et al.*, 1991; Bhagwati, 1987; Krueger, 1978). First, that the seemingly arbitrary yet inflexible nature of many quota allocation systems results in uncertainty for those producers dependent on imported inputs, machinery or parts. As a consequence, producers and consumers tend to overstock on imported products when they get the opportunity. Second, that QRs support the development and maintenance of domestic monopolies. Third, that, unlike tariffs, the rents associated with importing under a QR are typically retained by the license rather than going to the government. Rent-seeking and corruption in the allocation of rights to import often emerge as a result. The pattern of protection established by a QR regime is typically 'unknown, fortuitous and unplanned' (Michaely *et al.*, p. 131).

Converting from QRs to tariffs therefore has three main advantages. First, it makes the overall structure of protection more transparent and predictable. Second, the rents are transferred from the importers to the government, which may be an important consideration if the government is attempting simultaneously to balance its budget as part of a stabilization programme, or is reducing the general level of tariffs as part of its trade reform programme. Third, if the QR administrative machinery is also dismantled this should reduce the severity of hoarding of imported goods by domestic agents who doubt the liberalization's credibility. Finally, when protection is provided only by tariffs it is possible to announce a general programme of trade reform in advance, with producers having a clearer idea of how much their protection will be reduced at each stage.

But, given these well-known advantages, it is worth nothing that there are other differences between tariffs and QRs that are of relevance to trade policy reform. In particular the second-best implications of the two policies are quite different, as emerged in the discussion of capital and current account reforms above. Suppose trade is restricted by tariffs only. It is well known that the presence of a tariff on good *i* implies that free trade is not the optimal policy for good *j* in general. If goods *i* and *j* are net substitutes (complements) a tariff (subsidy) on imports of *j* will raise welfare. The optimal mix of tariffs therefore depends on the net substitutability and complementarity relationships among the goods. In general, as long as some tariffs remain it will not be optimal to completely remove the others.

This feature of tariffs tends to complicate the rules for gradual trade reform, if one aims at an improvement in welfare at each step of the process, in order to maintain the momentum for reform. Two general rules are known, however:

1. A proportional reduction in all tariffs will be welfare increasing.
2. The following adjustment in individual tariffs will be welfare improving:
   (i) a cut in the highest *ad valorem* tariff if this good is a net substitute for all other goods;

(ii) an increase in the lowest *ad valorem* tariff, including any zero tariffs, if this good is a net substitute for all other goods; and

(iii) a reduction (increase) in the tariff on a good which has a higher (lower) tariff than its net substitutes, and a lower (higher) tariff than its net complements.

Results (i) and (ii) form the theoretical basis for the popular 'concertina' approach to tariff reform, although little concern appears to be expressed over determining whether the net substitutes requirement is satisfied in practice. Of course, other formulae could be applied – the tariff-cutting formulae employed in GATT rounds for example – and in practice what may be important is to have some non-discretionary tariff-cutting rule, even though there is no presumption that it will necessarily result in a welfare improvement at each stage of the process.

In contrast, if the only trade restrictions are QRs on imports, the second-best implications are quite different. The existence of a binding quota on good i still leaves free trade as the optimal policy for the other goods (Corden and Falvey, 1985). Restricting (or promoting) imports (or exports) of other goods will not increase imports of i, and will not raise welfare. Unlike tariffs, a QR in one market does not spill over into other markets. This makes recommendations for quota reform straightforward. Loosening any binding quota will be welfare-improving. Unfortunately, this simplicity is lost once QRs are converted to tariffs.

Where trade is restricted by a combination of tariffs on some goods and QRs on others, then recommendations for piecemeal policy reform become more complicated. An equiproportional reduction in all distortions will raise welfare, and one can also show that if the quota-restricted goods are net substitutes for all other goods, then the rules for piecemeal tariff reform described above continue to hold. It is no longer true that the relaxation of any quota will necessarily be welfare-improving, however, because the presence of the tariffs does imply that some pattern of restrictions on the quota restricted goods will be optimal (see Falvey, 1988, for further details).

If QRs are to be converted to tariffs, then the most direct method is simply to impose explicit tariffs equal to the implicit tariffs generated by the QRs, and to dismantle the QR allocating and monitoring apparatus. The volume of imports will not change as long as there were no monopoly elements in domestic production or importation. Such a move will have income distribution effects, as quota rents are transferred from importers to the government, and while this redistribution may be desirable from a stabilization perspective, it is possible that it could threaten the sustainability of the liberalization. If so, then a more gentle approach would be to convert the QRs to tariff quotas. Within quota, imports could be allocated as before and allowed to be duty free. But above quota, imports would be permitted subject to the payment of some duty. The reform process for these items would then consist of reducing the quota, or imposing tariffs on within-quota imports, at the same time as the quota tariff was subject to the standard reform process.

Export incentives

A major drawback of the existing policy regime is usually its inherent anti-export bias. While some exporters may be receiving assistance in the form of duty rebates (designed to provide them with imported inputs at world prices) or direct export subsidies (intended to partially offset the overvaluation of the domestic currency), typically not all exporters are covered and the level of assistance is insufficient to fully offset the anti-export bias. To be successful, trade liberalization will require a movement of resources into the exportable industries. Should exporters receive additional assistance as part of the liberalization process and, if so, when and what form should this assistance take?

Several points are relevant to this issue. First, the importance of resource movements into exportables should be kept in mind by governments when deciding on their stabilization packages. A devaluation which removes the currency overvaluation is still likely to leave an (albeit smaller) anti-export bias. Therefore the complete removal of export incentives at the time of devaluation may be inappropriate.

Second, doubt is often expressed as to the ability of the exportable industries (particularly 'traditional' exports) to expand in the short run, and therefore their ability to absorb the resources released by the importable industries which are likely to contract quite quickly once protection is removed. This appears to be a particular concern in Africa, and pessimism in this area has reduced enthusiasm for, and commitment to, reform. Michaely (1986) suggests that, in view of this, it might be advisable to begin a programme of export promotion prior to initiating the tariff reform, so that the exportable industries (at least, 'non-traditional' exports) are expanding just at the time the import-competing sector is contracting. The steps required for successful 'export promotion' should not be interpreted too narrowly. In Africa, inadequate investments in port, transport and telecommunications facilities and limited information on export markets may impede the response of both existing and potential exporters. Domestic policies regulating labour markets and private investment may hinder or prevent factor reallocations. Primary sector exports have often been hampered by low administered prices and inefficient government marketing monopolies, and important reforms in some African countries (Ghana, Madagascar, Mali, Nigeria, Sénégal and Tanzania) have been to abolish public sector marketing boards or to remove their monopsony purchasing powers.

Third, in terms of developing political support for reform, it is often important to establish some gainers quickly. For this reason it may be tempting to provide temporary assistance to exporters during the adjustment phase, and Rodrik (1989, p. 15) argues that preference should be given to the building up of exports rather than import liberalization in the early stages of reform. But the administrative and other costs of introducing new policies that would ultimately be abandoned once the liberalization phase is complete must not be overlooked. Further, once the beneficiaries of these incentives become identified it is only to be expected that they will lobby for their continuance. While support for reform is important, there are disadvantages in creating a new interest group opposed to full liberalization. Any new incentives should therefore be of a kind that will automatically phase out as import liberalization proceeds (for example, duty rebates).

Finally, the actual choice of incentives, if any are to be offered, will be constrained by international agreements on export promotion. Although developing countries are given special treatment, direct export subsidies may prompt countervailing duties by governments in importing countries.

The evidence on the issue of export promotion is mixed. The results surveyed in Michaely *et al.* (1991, p. 194) show a strong correlation between trade liberalization and rapid export growth, and no sluggishness in the response of exports following liberalization. This should not be interpreted as supporting a vigorous programme of export promotion, however. Michaely *et al.* attribute the growth in exports primarily to the relaxation of import restrictions and the fall in the real exchange rate. They find no statistically meaningful correlation between export growth and the presence or absence of export incentives. The general conclusion appears to favour giving exporters access to inputs at world prices, and against general export subsidies (Thomas and Nash, 1991). What is likely to be more important is providing an adequate export infrastructure and ensuring that domestic regulations do not hamper the expansion of exports.

Foreign investment

A second issue in liberalizing the capital account is raised by the possibility of inflows or outflows of foreign direct investment. The

Table 2.1 Trade reform and foreign investment policies

	Initial status of foreign investment	
Trade reform	*Restricted*	*Unrestricted*
Proportional tariff reductions	'Loosen' towards second best restrictions	Leave unrestricted
QR liberalization	Remove restrictions	Leave unrestricted

resource flows that accompany such investment can assist with the adjustment process. But should they be allowed to proceed before trade has been fully liberalized, knowing, that to some extent, they will be responding to distorted prices? Conversely, how far should trade reform proceed while restrictions remain on the movements of capital? Again, the relevant points can be made quite simply. Table 2.1 shows the appropriate foreign investment policies to accompany given programmes of trade reform. These policies depend on whether foreign investment was restricted or unrestricted prior to reform. If the existing trade restrictions are QRs only, then these have no second-best implications for restrictions on international resource flows and so the optimal policy is to leave foreign investment unrestricted or to remove any existing restrictions, *ceteris paribus*.[4]

If the existing trade restrictions are tariffs only, and these are to be liberalized by proportional tariff cuts, then the appropriate foreign investment policy depends on the initial situation. The product market distortions generated by the tariffs imply that domestic factor returns are not equal to their marginal products evaluated at shadow (world) prices. The foreign investment level generated by any incipient difference between domestic and foreign returns will then be non-optimal. Some interventions on foreign investment are, therefore, appropriate as long as tariffs remain. If foreign investment restrictions already exist, the appropriate response then is to loose them towards the appropriate levels (assuming that an increase in restrictions is undesirable in the context of a 'liberalization').

If foreign investment was unrestricted initially, then investment levels have already adjusted to equate domestic and international returns. One can then show that a proportional tariff cut will increase welfare, both through its direct effects in goods markets and through the indirect effects of the international resource flows it induces.[5] In which case, foreign investment might as well be left unrestricted during the tariff reform process.

Foreign investment restrictions would not need to be retained if investors used shadow prices, rather than actual prices, in evaluating their investment projects (Edwards and van Wijnbergen, 1989). This provides another argument for pre-announcing the final target of a trade liberalization. Investors are then more likely to use target rather than current prices in allocating their resources – provided the liberalization is credible. Governments should not be complacent over their credibility, however, because, as Michaely *et al.* (1991, p. 255) observe:

> Experiences surveyed do not lend much conviction to this argument. Preannounced, comprehensive schemes of removal of protection have been rare and full adherence to them even rarer; liberalization attempts are almost always as likely to be reversed as to survive.

So much for the implications of trade reform for foreign investment policy. The implications of investment restrictions for trade reform will by now be familiar. If the investment restrictions are QRs, they do not spill over into other goods markets, and trade reform can proceed independently of investment reform. But if international investment is taxed, this implies free trade in goods is not optimal, and trade and foreign investment reform should proceed in tandem (for example, equiproportionate reductions in all tariffs *and* international factor taxes) to ensure welfare gains.

Speed of liberalization

Once it has been decided that a particular market or collection of markets is to be liberalized, the appropriate sequence of liberalization has been determined, and the desirable long-term degree of liberalization has been identified, the appropriate speed for liberalization must be decided. Should all restrictions in a particular market be removed immediately? Or should liberalization occur gradually according to some pre-announced plan? Are there circumstances under which it is desirable to overshoot the proposed long-run target in the short term? The underlying problem here is designing a path of policy settings that will move the economy to its new long-run equilibrium in an optimal manner. In Africa, the chosen pace of reform has typically been very slow (Nash, 1990). Three major considerations are involved – the implications of speed for government revenue, adjustment costs and the credibility of the whole process. We consider each of these in turn.

Government revenue

For many African countries the revenue from the taxation of international trade is a significant proportion of total government revenue (Greenaway and Milner, 1991). Trade liberalization, which ultimately will involve deep cuts in both import and export taxes, can then be expected to have a negative impact on a government budget that is already unbalanced. Restructuring the tax system to give it a broader base will take time, and government revenue will need to be maintained in the interim. Reforms may be reversed if fiscal problems become unmanageable (for example, Zambia).

The implications this has for the speed of trade reform depends on the circumstances of the country involved. The early stages of trade reform may involve increases in revenue, as tariff exemptions are abolished, those tariffs above their revenue-maximizing levels are cut, and QRs are converted to tariffs. Working against this are the expenditures involved in any increase in export incentives, and potential revenue losses associated with any accompanying stabilization programme. Output, and therefore income and profit tax revenue, are likely to fall, and social welfare expenditures may increase. The balance between these effects will determine the extent to which trade reform needs be delayed until alternative sources of government revenue are functioning.

The revenue implications of trade policy reform is a relatively neglected topic in this area (Thomas and Nash, 1991). The evidence that does exist suggests that it is an important concern for governments[6] and that one cannot say in advance whether trade liberalization will lead to fiscal enhancement or depletion. Greenaway and Milner (1991) stress that trade taxes will continue to be important in low-income countries for administrative reasons, and therefore emphasize that attention be given to reducing tariff exemptions and extending tariff coverage to imports previously restricted by QRs during the early phases of the reform. Expenditure cuts tend to be concentrated on capital projects rather than recurrent expenditure, where wages dominate (Greenaway and Morrissey, 1992). Public funds may not then be available for the investments in 'export-orientated' infrastructure required for a smooth transition.

Adjustment costs

If factor and commodity prices adjust instantaneously, and resources move costlessly and instantaneously between activities, then the appropriate speed of liberalization is a trivial issue. Policy parameters should immediately be adjusted to their desired long-run levels. In practice, any change in policy is likely to generate adjustment costs, both in terms of output forgone while factors are 'idle' in the process of moving between sectors, and in the resources actually absorbed in this movement. These costs will depend on the extent of inter-industry versus intra-industry adjustment, and so on. While we know little about the likely scale of adjustment costs, it is reasonable to expect that they will be higher the more rapidly resources are required to move. In Africa, this adjustment may involve a reversal of the rural–urban migration prompted by the prior protection of urban-based import-substituting industries.

But the existence of adjustment costs increasing in the speed of adjustment does not in itself imply a case for gradualism. As Mussa (1986) has noted, as long as those private economic agents who collectively control the allocation of factors perceive private costs and benefits from factor movements which correspond to their true social costs and benefits, then the pace of adjustment they choose following a full-scale liberalization will be the socially correct one. A policy of gradualism in reform will then result in factor movements slower than socially optimal. Arguments for gradualism therefore rely on the presence of distortions which might cause private and social costs and benefits to differ, the existence of unemployment of some factors and possible concerns over the income distribution implications of 'rapid' liberalization.

The main arguments can be illustrated by considering several examples (see Mussa, 1986 for details). Factor income taxes create a divergence between pre- and post-tax returns, and reduce the private (post-tax) benefit from a factor relocation below its social (pre-tax) benefit. But note that this implies private adjustment will be too slow rather than too fast, from a social perspective, and is not therefore an argument for gradualism.

Capital market imperfections are quite common in developing countries, as a result of their underdeveloped capital markets and their past policies of interest-rate ceilings and credit rationing. If these imperfections are not to be eliminated early, trade policy reform might be desirable, although, again, in other circumstances, private adjustment could be too slow. Clearly, for private adjustment to be socially optimal, the private and social discount rates must coincide. If, as is often argued, the private discount rate tends to exceed the social, then the private benefits from adjustment would again appear to be below the social benefits, implying that private adjustment would be too slow. On the other hand, if domestic agents treat the world interest rate as exogenous when in fact it tends to increase with total domestic borrowing on international markets, then the private discount rate will be less than the social, and a case for gradualism can be made (although, obviously, the first-best policy is the appropriate tax on foreign borrowing).

Barriers to the entry of firms or the pricing of commodities and services away from social costs can also generate second-best circumstances where an immediate move to long-run trade reform is not socially optimal. Ideally, these distortions should be removed as part of the overall reform process. But if they remain, whether gradualism or overshooting is the appropriate response must be determined on a case-by-case basis.

Clearly, if domestic economic agents incorrectly anticipate that a permanent liberalization is only temporary they will not adjust at the socially desirable speed. Equally clearly, if they incorrectly anticipate an unsustainable liberalization will be permanent they will have undertaken more adjustment than turns out to be socially desirable (ex-post). Since expectations are endogenous, errors in expectations are not a fixed distortion to be worked around. This problem is intimately linked with the credibility of the reform programme discussed below.

In summary, the presence of distortions which may generate a difference between private and social costs and benefits of adjustment does suggest that an immediate shift to the long-run reformed level of trade barriers may not be optimal. There appears to be no necessary presumption that a gradual reform is to be preferred, however: overshooting may be the preferred response in many circumstance.

A case for gradualism might be made on income-distribution grounds. The main losers from trade reform are those factors specific to the activities that are no longer favoured, and for them the only possible adjustment is permanent unemployment or unreplaced depreciation. A gradual programme of liberalization will slow down the decline in the rents to these factors, and provided the reform is sufficiently rapid to deter the entry of new factors into these activities, adjustment will still occur – albeit at a pace slower than optimal on efficiency grounds. Given that these factors had sufficient influence to be favoured by the protection in the first place, one can imagine that governments might have difficulty in maintaining policies that reduce their rents too rapidly.

The speed of reform may also be constrained by the government's capacity to administer changes in policy. Some strengthening of the relevant government institutions may be required if institutional bottlenecks of this type are not to impede reform (as happened in the Côte d'Ivoire and Malawi).

Suppose a case for gradual reform is accepted. Does this alter the piecemeal trade reform recommendations derived above? Since industries are likely to adjust at different speeds, one can readily imagine there might be gains to tailoring tariff cuts to the adjustment speeds of different industries, at least in principle. The problem is that, in practice, such tailoring is inevitably a matter of guesswork. Much will be left to the (informed) discretion of those administering the scheme, creating opportunities for lobbying, rent-seeking and corruption. Distortions will inevitably be created, and the appearance of 'fairness' that a rules-based reform provides will be lost.

Finally, note that all these arguments for gradualism relate to adjustments in incomes and resource allocation. No argument has so far emerged for gradual adjustment in final consumption. Yet gradual tariff reform will maintain unnecessary consumption distortions. Consideration should therefore be given to a switch away from tariffs, wherever feasible, to some form of direct assistance to producers. Obviously, revenue and other considerations may preclude such a move, but it is important that the consumption costs of the trade regime are not overlooked.

Credibility

As should be apparent from the discussion so far, an important element in the success of any programme of trade liberalization is its credibility. The willingness of agents to bear adjustment costs depends on their views as to the permanence of the reforms. If the future is uncertain, the incentives to adjust are much weaker. Indeed, Rodrik (1989, p. 2) goes so far as to argue that:

> the predictability of the incentives created by a trade regime, or the lack thereof, is generally of much greater importance than the *structure* of these incentives. In other words, a distorted, but stable, set of incentives does much less damage to economic performance than an uncertain and unstable set of incentives generated by a process of trade reform lacking credibility.

Clearly, the degree of distortion relative to the degree of instability will be important. But consumers who perceive a supposedly permanent reform as being temporary will stock up on imported goods while their prices are relatively low, and investors will prefer to hold their wealth in liquid form, inside or outside the country, rather than to make irreversible investments in response to incentives they perceive as being reversible. Loss-making firms may go into debt in order to remain in operation while waiting for a reversal of policy (Edwards, 1990).

Credibility problems arise from several sources. Programmes of trade reform initiated in an unsettled macroeconomic environment (for example, while problems with persistent government budget deficits remain unsolved) are likely to be reversed and are therefore unlikely to be credible. The extent of the government's commitment to the reform may also be unclear. Is it just a temporary change to attract 'conditional' financing from international lenders in a crisis, or does it represent a permanent shift in policy? What is the extent of the political opposition to these reforms, and how likely are current policy-makers to be replaced by those with an opposing view? Part of the danger here is self-fulfilling expectations. If most private agents expect the reform programme to fail, and act accordingly, it is unlikely to succeed.

What can a government do in terms of timing and sequencing to enhance the credibility of policy reforms of this type? Basically, it should initiate them at times when they are most likely to succeed, in a way that signals commitment, and tie their own hands with respect to changing course. As long as macroeconomic instability persists, for example, perhaps only those trade reforms that contribute directly to stabilization and fiscal balance should be pursued. This would include the conversion of QRs to tariffs, which increases government revenue, but exclude tariff cuts, which do not. GATT membership and tariff bindings are a means of commitment to a more liberal trade regime.

The difficulty in signalling commitment is that the reform programme under consideration is usually not the first to be tried, but rather the latest in a series of partial successes and total failures. Trade policy reform does not have a particularly happy history in many African economies (Nash, 1990). The government then lacks a 'reputation' for credible reform. Indicating commitment in such circumstances may require quick and decisive action – a 'radical' reform. Rodrik argues that radical reform on too wide a front is unlikely to be credible, as it will arouse too much opposition and is therefore likely to be reversed. In his view, radical trade reform should not be attempted simultaneously with radical tax, labour market or financial market reform. Credibility is enhanced by reforms which are 'large in magnitude but narrow in scope' (Rodrik, 1989, p. 12). Unfortunately, narrow reforms give rise to the second-best problems discussed in the preceding sections.

Conclusions

As anticipated, our review of timing and sequencing issues led to few strong conclusions. Even so, theory and accumulated experience does allow us to make some broad recommendations. Rather than list these item by item, it may help to focus the discussion if these recommendations are presented in the form of a hypothetical programme of trade liberalization. We assume that this is a credible reform, involving both the current and capital accounts of the balance of payments. Such a programme could contain four phases:

Phase I (a) Macroeconomic stabilization; (b) Conversion of QRs to tariffs and removal of tariff exemptions; (c) Export incentives; and (d) New government revenue measures.

Comments Macroeconomic stability is likely to be important for the credibility of the reform, if nothing else. If macroeconomic stabilization is not required, then Phases I and II can be combined. Should difficulties arise in implementing I(b), the tariff – quota option could be considered. On second-best grounds these new tariffs should probably not be set outside the range of the existing tariffs. A programme of export incentives may already exist, but any new incentives that are offered should be of a kind that will automatically phase down with the subsequent tariff reform – duty rebate schemes, for example. In particular, direct export subsidies should not be offered, as these are subject to retaliation and create their own interest group. The new revenue measures should be those that will eventually replace trade taxes as a source of revenue.

Phase II (a) Initial tariff adjustments; and (b) Announcement of remaining tariff adjustments.

Comments These initial tariff cuts should be proportional or follow a 'concertina' formula, and should be deep enough to make the whole programme credible. The announcement of the remaining cuts can be detailed or may just indicate the ultimate objective in terms of a tariff structure and the target date of achieving it.

Phase III (a) Second round of tariff adjustments; and (b) Begin capital account liberalization.

Comments If we reach this phase then the trade reform appears to be sustainable and the risk of destabilizing capital movements from liberalizing the capital account should be more than offset by the gains from the resource flows.

Phase IV (a) Final tariff adjustments; and (b) Complete capital account liberalization.

Clearly, these are only broad guidelines,[7] which can be modified depending on the circumstances of the reforming economy. In particular, if adjustment appears to be proceeding more smoothly than anticipated, the overall pace of reform should be increased and the timing of the capital account liberalization can be advanced. What should be avoided are the reversals of policy that generate an inefficient resource allocation and are so often fatal to credibility.

Notes

1. Additional imports are possible for products restricted by tariffs but not for those restricted by quotas. To put it another way, shadow prices equal world prices for tariff restricted goods, but equal domestic prices for quota restricted goods.
2. This is an example of the 'anti-agnostic' proposition in Corden and Falvey (1985).
3. For a dissenting view see Lal (1987).
4. Under QRs, shadow commodity prices equal domestic commodity prices, and the marginal product of capital evaluated at shadow prices equals its domestic return. There may be other arguments against full freedom of foreign direct investment, of course.
5. The implication is that the international resource flows induced by the imposition of the tariffs in the first place were welfare-reducing.
6. Michaely *et al.* observe that most reforms are structured so that net government revenue does not fall (1991, p. 235).
7. A similar but more comprehensive proposal with detailed guidelines is given by World Bank (1991). See also Greenaway and Morrissey (1992).

References

Bhagwati, J. (1978) *Foreign Trade Regimes and Economic Development* (Cambridge: NBER).

Corden, W. M. and R. Falvey (1985) 'Quotas and the Second Best', *Economics Letters*, pp. 67–70.

Edwards, S. (1986) 'The Order of Liberalization of the Current and Capital Accounts of the Balance of Payments', ch. 7 in A. M. Choksi and D. Papageorgiou (eds), *Economic Liberalization in Developing Countries* (Oxford: Basil Blackwell).

Edwards, S. (1990) 'The Sequencing of Economic Reform: Analytical Issues and Lessons from Latin American Experiences', *The World Economy*, vol. 13, March, pp. 1–14.

Edwards, S. and S. van Wijnbergen (1986) 'The Welfare Effects of Trade and Capital Market Liberalization', *International Economic Review*, vol. 27, February, pp. 141–8.

Falvey, R. (1988) 'Tariffs, Quotas and Piecemeal Policy Reform', *Journal of International Economics*, August, pp. 177–83.

Greenaway, D. and C. Milner (1991) 'Fiscal Dependence on Trade Taxes and Trade Policy Reform', *The Journal of Development Studies*, vol. 27, April, pp. 95–132.

Greenaway, D. and O. Morrissey (1992) 'Structural Adjustment and Liberalization in Developing Countries: What Lessons Have We Learned?', mimeo, Department of Economics, University of Nottingham.

Krueger, A. (1978) *Liberalization Attempts and Consequences* (Cambridge: Ballinger).

Lal, D. (1987) 'The Political Economy of Economic Liberalization', *The World Bank Economic Review*, vol. 1, January, pp. 273–99.
Michaely, M. (1986) 'The Timing and Sequencing of a Trade Liberalization Policy', ch. 3 in A. M. Choksi and D. Papageorgiou (eds), *Economic Liberalization in Developing Countries* (Oxford: Basil Blackwell).
Michaely, M., D. Papageorgiou and A. M. Choksi (1991) *Liberalizing Foreign Trade: Lessons of Experience in the Developing World* (Oxford: Basil Blackwell).
Mussa, M. (1986) 'The Adjustment Process and the Timing of Trade Liberalization', ch. 4 in A. M. Choksi and D. Papageorgiou (eds), *Economic Liberalization in Developing Countries* (Oxford: Basil Blackwell).
Mussa, M. (1987) 'Macroeconomic Policy and Trade Liberalization: Some Guidelines', *World Bank Research Observer*, vol. 2, January, pp. 61–77.
Nash, J. (1990) 'An Overview of Trade Policy Reform with Implications for Sub-Saharan Africa', mimeo, Trade Policy Division, The World Bank.
Rodrik, D. (1989) 'Credibility of Trade Reform – a Policy Maker's Guide', *The World Economy*, vol. 12, pp. 1–16.
Thomas, V. and J. Nash (1991) 'Reform of Trade Policy: Recent Evidence from Theory and Practice', *The World Bank Research Observer*, vol. 6, July, pp. 219–40.
Whalley, J. (1989) *The Uruguay Round and Beyond* (London: Macmillan).
Wolf, M. (1986) 'Timing and Sequencing of Trade Liberalization in Developing Countries', *Asian Development Review*, vol. 4, pp. 1–24.
World Bank (1991) *World Development Report 1991*.

3

African Trade Liberalizations: Alternative Strategies for Sustainable Reform

Paul Collier and Jan Willem Gunning

Introduction[1]

Most African governments must, except for short periods of time, set macroeconomic policies which are *compatible*. That is, trade restrictions, the exchange rate, and budgetary-cum-monetary policy must be co-ordinated in such a way as to avoid depletion of foreign exchange reserves. Often, the potential for departure from compatibility is minimal: for example, for some years the Tanzanian economy was run with reserve cover of only a few days of imports.[2] Trade liberalization must therefore involve continuous co-ordination with other policies so as to maintain compatibility. One theoretical possibility is for a gradual creep towards liberalization with co-ordination achieved by ex-post 'fine tuning'. However, recent surveys of numerous non-African trade liberalizations (Papageorgiou *et al.*, 1991) conclude that large, abrupt liberalizations have proved to be more sustainable. Apart from economic considerations, it is quite possible that for political reasons gradual trade liberalization is not feasible in Africa: transient political windows of opportunity are either seized with an abrupt liberalization or missed altogether. Further, donors may insist on liberalization being abrupt. Such a liberalization starkly poses the co-ordination problem, and this chapter uses a simple computable general equilibrium (CGE) model to explore alternative compatible strategies in an Africa-type economy.

The essence of the compatibility problem can be seen by considering the consequence of a liberalization in which no other policies are changed. The reduction of tariffs, or more commonly the relaxation of quotas, will lower the domestic price of importable goods and thereby reduce the demand for money.[3] Being a stock effect, in the short term this will dominate any changes in the money supply brought about by the fiscal implications of liberalization, since these are flow effects. Hence there will be an excess supply of money and so a payments deficit. This chapter investigates three alternative strategies which prevent such an outcome, each maintaining compatibility. The first is to achieve an offsetting increase in the demand for money through devaluation. The second is to use programme aid to finance a deficit until the money supply is sufficiently depleted. These two extremes respectively characterize the post-1986 Nigerian trade liberalization and all trade liberalizations in the Franc Zone. Between these polar cases is the combination of aid and exchange-rate depreciation. In this chapter we rank the three strategies on various criteria. The first of these is welfare, which in the context of the model is the utility of the representative agent. Whatever the merits of welfare as a criterion it is not the one which governments use. We therefore supplement it with the impact on export performance, the price level and income of the worst-affected social group: namely, the owners of sector-specific capital in the import-substitute sector. We also consider the *coherence* of the path of resource reallocation, defining incoherence as a resource shift which is subsequently reversed. After this, we introduce expectations, comparing some of the consequences of credible and incredible liberalizations.

The co-ordination of trade liberalization with other macroeconomic policy changes has not been well managed in Africa. For example, the Kenyan government has twice embarked on liberalizations which were not adequately co-ordinated with exchange-rate-cum-aid policies, and as a result had to be aborted. Part of the explanation for this may be institutional. Africa's liberalizations have usually been at external behest. Anachronistically, negotiations on trade policy are the responsibility of the World Bank, while those on exchange rate policy are the responsibility of the IMF. Although in theory the two organizations co-ordinate their negotiations, in practice aid-for-trade deals are sometimes struck which are manifestly incompatible with contemporaneous aid-for-exchange-rate depreciation deals. Incompatible liberalization, being unsustainable because of limited reserves, will induce speculative purchases of imports while they are temporarily cheap. Additionally, the uncertainty surrounding future relative prices will lead to the deferral of fixed investment. These two effects interact: alone, speculative purchases of imports might be constrained by lack of finance, but in conjunction with investment deferral they can be achieved simply by portfolio switching. Speculative purchases of imports erode the reserves and are therefore a self-fulfilling response to incredibility. The deferral of investment undermines the effectiveness of trade reform by inhibiting

Table 3.1 Base year values

A Real variables: structure of production and demand

		q	c	i	g	x	m
1	Exportables	300	–	–	–	300	–
2	Importables (QRs)	200	250	–	–	–	50
3	Other importables	25	75	–	50	–	100
4	Non-tradables	300	225	–	75	–	–
5	Capital goods	–	–	275	–	–	275

B Nominal variables

Exchange rate (e)	1	Government expenditure	(E)	125
Domestic prices (p)		Government revenue	(R)	75
Exportables	1	Lagged money supply	(M_{-1})	1144
Importables (QRs)	2	Deficit as percentage of	M_{-1}	4.4
Other importables	1			
Non-tradables	1			
Capital goods	1			

the resource reallocation that is a principal objective of the liberalization. Thus, unless a liberalization policy is manifestly compatible, it contains the seeds of its own destruction. Compatibility is therefore a necessary, though by no means a sufficient, condition for a successful liberalization.

The CGE model uses the minimum specification and disaggregation for the problems posed. It has only four productive sectors: exportables (not consumed domestically); non-tradables; quota-protected importables; and other importables. Capital is sector-specific and labour is costlessly mobile. It is thus a standard, small, open-economy model, except that we introduce import quotas. In such a model the only mechanism of adjustment usually incorporated is the movement of labour between sectors. With labour instantly mobile and capital completely fixed, such a model is well suited for short-run comparative static questions, but ill-suited to the dynamics of adjustment. Since the latter is our primary focus, we augment the model by introducing limited capital mobility. There are various ways of doing this. For example, a 'moving sector' is sometimes added, allowing for costly relocation of existing capital goods. Here we introduce depreciation and replacement investment. The model has been calibrated so that in the base case there is no net investment: savings are just sufficient to cover replacement investment. The inclusion of savings and investment makes the model sufficiently complex to warrant a CGE formulation.

In the base run (Table 3.2), in which trade restrictions are maintained, there is a zero-growth steady state, with mild inflation of 4 per cent caused

Table 3.2 Base run (no trade reform)

	t = 0	*t* = 6	*Growth rate (%)*
GDP	825	825	0.0
Utility	100	100	0.0
Consumer prices	1	1.28	4.2
Exchange rate	1	0.78	–4.2
Money supply	1194	1530	4.2

Note: Production of importables is valued at world prices.

by a small budget deficit. This domestic inflation takes place against a background of world price stability, but it is precisely neutralized by exchange-rate depreciation. Trade restrictions, initially entirely in the form of quotas, are applied to consumer but not to capital goods, raising the domestic price of protected importables (p_2) to double the world price. With this as the counterfactual, the policy experiment is of an abrupt trade liberalization which abolishes the quotas and replaces them with a low, 10 per cent tariff, payments balance being preserved by aid or exchange rate depreciation. (An Appendix (see page 52) sets out the CGE model more fully.)

Compatibility maintained by exchange-rate depreciation

We begin with the simple analytics of trade liberalization when compatibility is maintained by devaluation. We address the impact effect: that is, the time period prior to an export supply response. Consider a model in which there is no domestic consumption of exportables, and no investment. The removal of import quotas directly lowers the price of importables. It will therefore worsen the balance of payments unless it is offset by exchange-rate depreciation, which raises the price of importables. As long as the depreciation is sufficient to restore the price of importables to its initial level, the demand for money, and therefore the balance of payments, is unaffected. Hence, in the context of liberalization, a devaluation is not inflationary. Its sole effect is to raise the price of exportables relative to both non-tradables and importables. This will lead to an export supply response that will raise real income. As these gains from trade liberalizations are gradually realized, the demand for money rises. In the absence of endogenous increases in the money supply this reduces the price level relative to its counterfactual. In turn, this appreciates the exchange rate at which current account balance is achieved. Hence, compatibility maintained solely by exchange-rate

Table 3.3 Compatibility maintained by devaluation (results in the first year of the reform; base run = 100)

Exchange rate	80.3
Consumer prices	82.2
Production of exportables	106.5
GDP	101.8
Capital goods imports	75.9
Consumption (Σc_i)	117.2

adjustment involves overshooting: the initial devaluation exceeds the long-run depreciation.

In view of these simple analytics, the CGE model delivers a surprising result (Table 3.3): the consumer price level initially falls by 18 per cent relative to the counterfactual and thereafter there is virtual price stability over the next decade. This is surprising, because the simple analytics considered above implied that there would be only a minimal initial impact on the price level. There are various factors contributing to the result. The first is that the trade liberalization produces a gain in real income and so increases the demand for money, lowering prices for a given money stock. However, this effect should initially be trivial: the welfare gains arising from the reallocation of consumer expenditure do not increase the demand for money, and those arising from the reallocation of production take time to accrue. This is borne out by the model: the lags in the reallocation of the capital stock sufficiently slow down the reorientation of production that the gains in real income are only gradually realized over the decade. They are responsible for a significant part of the sustained fall in the rate of inflation, but not for the initial fall in the price level: initially GDP rises in real terms, but by less than 2 per cent. Second, the introduction of the tariff increases government revenue a little and hence reduces the budget deficit. Again, cumulatively, this has a significant effect on money supply and inflation, but plays only a negligible part in the initial impact on the price level:[4] in the first year of the reform the increase in government revenue (relative to the counterfactual) amounts to only 2 per cent of the money supply. The mechanism doing the work in the model lies outside the scope of the simple analytics considered above, since it works via investment. Recall that in this economy imports of capital goods are assumed to be unrationed. That is, the extent of exchange rate overvaluation is sufficiently moderate that not all imports need to be rationed: this is a Kenya-type economy, where exports are sufficient to finance the demand for imported capital goods without rationing, rather than a pre-reform

Ghana-type economy, in which there is insufficient finance for any category of imports. The import restriction on consumer goods constitutes a subsidy on investment through its effect on the exchange rate. Its removal raises the domestic price of capital goods, reducing the volume of investment.[5] Even were there to be no initial increase in exports (in fact there is a 6 per cent increase in the first year), the decline in imports of capital goods implies an increase in imports of consumer goods. Thus, at constant prices (that is, in real terms) there is a fall in investment and an increase in consumption. An example of this effect occurred in the context of the Nigerian devaluation and liberalization of late 1986, a policy package which (unusually) did not include aid financing. From 1986 to 1987 aggregate expenditure remained constant, but there was an unprecedented drop in capital formation, which accommodated increased consumption.

Whether the switch from investment to consumption affects the price level depends on the specification of the demand for (base) money function. In particular, it matters whether the demand for money is sensitive to the composition of gross domestic expenditure. In the model, we assume that it is entirely driven by the transactions demand for consumer expenditure. The switch from expenditure on investment thus increases the demand for money in proportion to the increase in the real value of consumption. This is clearly an extreme specification. At the other extreme, the switch would have no effect on the demand for money. Our specification, though extreme, may be a reasonable approximation to the true demand for money function in much of Africa. The point here is not to defend the assumption but to highlight that because of the large change in the composition of expenditure from investment to consumption inherent in this trade liberalization, the form of the demand for money function is critical in determining the impact on the price level. If, as in the present model, the demand for real money balances increases, this is accommodated by depressing the price level.[6]

The model has demonstrated the sensitivity of the effect of a trade liberalization to 'structural features' of the economy. First, in this stylized African economy, unrestricted imports formed a markedly higher share of investment than of consumption, giving rise to a subsidy on investment, the removal of which switches expenditure from investment to consumption. Second, this increases the demand for money for a given total level of expenditure, paradoxically lowering the price level. Only in economies where both of these features hold will a trade liberalization have a substantial anti-inflationary effect. The first, and possibly the second, can be expected to vary substantially among Africa's economies.

Compatibility maintained by aid

Now consider a liberalization supported not by devaluation but by programme aid financing: the exchange-rate path is the same as in the base run. It is debatable whether aid to finance an African trade liberalization should properly be regarded as a loan, the cost of which is its ostensible repayment profile, or, at the other extreme, as a gift without cost. Most public debt to Africa is at heavily concessionary rates and, with long and variable lags, tends to get forgiven. It is, for example, inconceivable that extra borrowing by the government of Zambia should incur concomitant debt repayments: the country is so remarkably over-borrowed that marginal 'debts' are unreal. This might seem to imply that in the context of Africa programme aid for trade reform has little or no opportunity cost. However, if, as is likely, donors work to some long-term notion of aid levels which are in aggregate appropriate for each country (often arrived at on political or humanitarian rather than economic grounds), aid now for one purpose has a true opportunity cost in terms of a loss of aid later for another purpose. Because of these ambiguities it is not appropriate to impose some particular interest rate as the cost of aid. Rather, we investigate that rate which, were it to apply, would keep utility constant. If this rate is high it does not really matter if aid for liberalization has a dollar-for-dollar opportunity cost. If, on the other hand, the return is close to zero, the precise nature of the aggregate aid constraint becomes critical.

As discussed in the Introduction, a liberalization without an offsetting exchange rate change can be expected initially to worsen the balance of payments. However, the monetary approach to the balance of payments tells us that such a deterioration, if sufficiently aid-funded, will be temporary. The liberalization lowers the price level, reducing the demand for money. The resulting excess supply is then purchased by the government with the aid. Payments balance is restored at a lower money supply. In addition to this money supply reduction effect, aid for liberalization causes temporary Dutch disease. The two effects are illustrated in Figure 3.1, based on Neary and Purvis (1982). Prior to liberalization, the economy is in equilibrium at *A*, with prices of importables and non-tradables at P_m^0 and P_n^0. The liberalization lowers the price of importables to P_m^1. While agents spend the aid (that is, while they run down excess money balances) the relative price of non-tradables rises from *OA* to *OB* (loci of equilibrium in the non-tradable goods market). This may even involve a temporary rise in the nominal price of non-tradables. During this phase (at points such as *B*) there is a payments

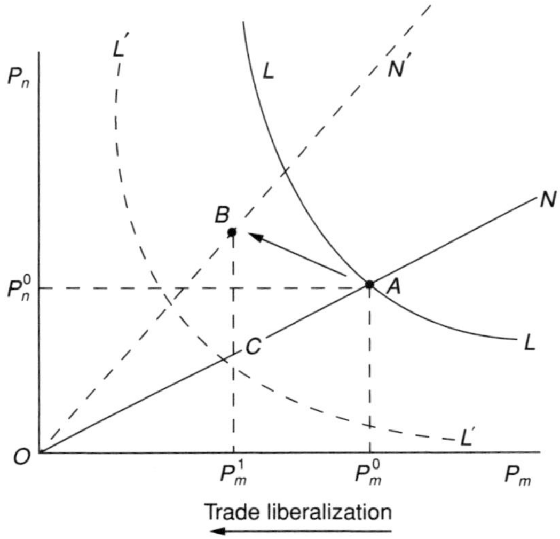

Figure 3.1 Liberalization achieved by temporary aid

deficit: the economy is below the monetary equilibrium locus, *LL*. This gradually reduces the money supply, shifting the locus to *L'L'*, at which stage the aid ceases, restoring the relative price of non-tradables to *OA* and the economy to a new equilibrium at *C*.

The temporary aid boom thus adds a second layer of relative price changes on to the permanent changes caused by liberalization. Further, because there is no exchange rate response to the liberalization, the implicit subsidy on capital goods is not removed (as in the exchange-rate-only liberalization), but rather temporarily extended to all imports. The extra aid produces a powerful monetary squeeze on the economy. First, it reduces the money supply sharply, the counterpart of the payments deficit. Second, in raising real consumption it raises the transactions demand for real balances. The price level must therefore fall substantially and fast.

In the model, the drastic fall in the domestic price of protected imports (from double the world price to only 10 per cent above it, now with no offsetting exchange-rate change) contributes to this fall (Table 3.4). However, the required change is so great that to maintain market-clearing there has to be a 7 per cent fall in the price of non-tradable goods and an 18 per cent fall in nominal wages in the first year. The exchange-rate-only strategy considered in the previous section avoided these extreme

Table 3.4 Compatibility maintained by aid (results in the first year of the reform, relative either to the base run or to the preceding years)

	Base run *100*	*Preceding year* *100*
Exchange rate	100	95
Domestic prices		
Exportables	100	105
Importables (QRs)	55	58
Other importables	100	104
Non-tradables	89	93
Nominal wage	79	82
Real wage	114	114
Real product wage of import substitute (w/p_2)	142	142
Production non-tradables	110	110

requirements: non-tradables prices rose by 2 per cent, and nominal wages, though still required to fall, needed only a 4 per cent adjustment. Since not even African economies have sufficient nominal wage flexibility to deliver 18 per cent wage reductions in a single year, the implication is that fully-aided abrupt liberalization would result in temporary unemployment. Rising unemployment in conjunction with a temporary consumer boom may not be an ideal environment for political sustainability. These distributional effects are compounded by a sharper collapse in the rate of return on capital in the import-substitute sector. Other than the unemployed, owners of this capital are the group worst affected by trade liberalization.

The temporary consumer boom produces standard Dutch-disease effects. There is a temporary increase in the output of the non-tradable sector. Equivalently, the rate of return on capital in the sector rises temporarily. In the present version of the model, investment responds only to previous-period rates of return (we relax this later). Hence, investment is lured into the non-tradable sector during the period of temporary aid (three years in the model). This is an incoherent resource reallocation, in that the long-term effects of the liberalization are to shift capital out of the non-tradable sector. The initial increase in the capital stock has to be more than fully reversed. The same incoherence is true of labour allocation: employment rises in the sector, and subsequently falls. By contrast to this delayed adjustment in the non-tradable sector, that in the import-substitute sector is accelerated compared with the exchange-rate-only strategy. The first-year fall in the domestic price of import-substitutes, already 28 per cent in the exchange-rate-only strategy, is now 42 per cent. Even with the full wage flexibility assumed in the model, the real product wage in the sector now overshoots in an extreme fashion. In the first year it jumps by 42 per cent, as against 33 per cent in the exchange-rate-only strategy. Under both strategies, after a decade, the real product wage is only 20 per cent higher than pre-liberalization. This degree of real product wage overshooting is liable to yield 'incoherence' in labour reallocation: that is, workers may initially be sacked from the sector and subsequently rehired. It should be noted that wage overshooting does not inevitably yield this result, since offsetting the decline in the product wage is the gradual exit of capital. However, this means that the exchange-rate-only strategy is less likely to generate employment overshooting than the aid-only strategy. Finally, turning to the export sector, the temporary Dutch disease naturally slows the expansion of the sector relative to the exchange-rate-only strategy: two years after the reform, export volume has expanded by only 9 per cent as opposed to 12 per cent. This undermines the very purpose of the liberalization.

If the aid is modelled as a free good it raises the present value of utility. If aid is costly, the critical interest rate at which utility is unaffected is 9.2 per cent p.a. This rate of return is far greater than the interest rate charged to Africa on public debt (essentially negative in real terms), but below both the economy's time preference rate (assumed in the model to be 10 per cent) and the rate of return on investment (assumed initially to be 20 per cent). In other words, sheer time preference tells us that it is always better to have aid now rather than later, but if the device for doing so is that the aid has to be used for financing a trade liberalization the country gets less out of this than were it simply to bring consumption forward. Hence, if the economy is well captured by the model (in particular, if prices and wages are fully flexible) and if the powerful redistributions do not trigger any uncertainty as to policy sustainability, aid-only trade liberalization is welfare-improving over exchange-rate-only liberalization only if there is no other option offered by the donor by which the aid can be costlessly brought forward (though not increased in totality). We have already suggested two reasons why the welfare effects might be less good than implied by the model: unemployment, and the policy consequences of powerful redistributions. There are three further caveats. First, the temporary revenue boom for the government might lead to long-term destabilization of the budget. Second, the temporary aid implies that imports are temporarily cheap, so that there is a positive return from holding them as assets. In the model this effect is weak: the nominal return on buying imports immediately post-reform and holding them for two years is only 10 per cent, a period over which non-tradables prices are stationary. Such a real rate of return is unlikely to trigger hoarding. However, the potential is clearly there for the rate of return to rise above that on investment, at which point hoarding would begin to crowd out real investment. Third, the amount of extra aid required for compatibility is quite large. In the model, the aid-for-liberalization programme costs 15 per cent of initial annual GDP, most of which is needed in the first year of reform, with the rest over the next two years. If the private sector doubts whether aid will be sufficient, it might doubt whether the liberalization will be sustained, inducing effects considered below. Overall, the aid-only strategy does not come out too well. It yields incoherence in resource reallocation, unemployment, and a temporary consumption boom. However, the aid avoids the need for a sharp devaluation (20 per cent in the exchange-rate-only case).

It does this by reducing the money supply. Obviously, in practice, the government is likely to use at least part of the aid to increase its own expenditure. This further weakens the case for the aid strategy, since aid is effective only to the extent it reduces the money supply.

Devaluation and aid combined

Aid-cum-devaluation is the standard liberalization package in Africa. However, it is appropriate in only three circumstances. First, there may be a binding exogenous political constraint upon the pace of exchange-rate depreciation. The existence of political constraints of this form in some African countries is not in doubt: for example, it has characterized Kenyan policy, where the maximum feasible rate of devaluation appears to have been around 1 per cent per month. The constraint to bind implies that it would be preferable to achieve the same liberalization without aid but, since this is not feasible, aid-cum-depreciation is a second-best strategy. Conversely, the binding constraint may be the maximum available amount of aid for liberalization. This implies that it would be preferable to achieve the liberalization without devaluation, but that since this is not feasible, aid-cum-devaluation is again a second-best strategy. Finally, there may be no binding constraint, but some combination of aid and devaluation is superior on some or all of our criteria to either used alone.

The sequence of adjustments using both instruments is illustrated in Figure 3.2. The impact effect of liberalization shifts the economy from *A* to *B*, moving the economy off the monetary equilibrium locus *LL* (now depicted in policy space). Thereafter there is a gradual adjustment to *C*,

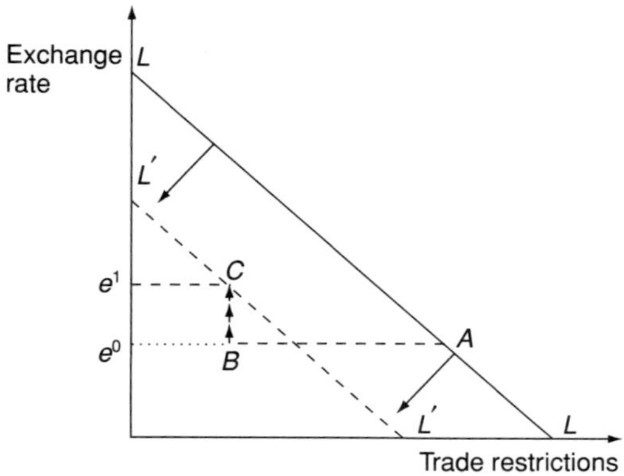

Figure 3.2 Liberalization achieved with aid-cum-devaluation

achieved partly by gradual devaluation from e^0 to e^1 and partly by the money supply reduction effect shifting the locus to *L′L′*.

We model this policy package by treating the binding constraint as the pace of exchange rate depreciation, assumed to be 1 per cent per month. This reduces and rephases the need for programme aid. The reduction is very marked, from 15 per cent to only 5 per cent of GDP. However, the rephasing is even more dramatic. As is to be expected, the gradual exchange rate change obviates the need for aid in later, relative to earlier, years of reform. In the model, all the aid is now required in the first year. These two characteristics: the reduced amount of aid but its increased bunching into year one, work against each other. In one respect this produces an outcome inferior to either the aid-only or the exchange-rate-only strategies. Because the aid only lasts for a year, the return on hoarding imports now rises to 11 per cent on goods bought in that year and sold the next. This is against a background rate of inflation in non-tradables of less than 3 per cent. A real return of 8 per cent is perhaps getting into the range at which hoarding might start to occur. In other respects the strategy produces an intermediate outcome, as might be expected. Resource incoherence is still present, but much weaker. Export growth is mid-way between the other policies. There is still a need for a large, abrupt fall in nominal wages, this time of 13 per cent, so rising unemployment is still to be expected.

To summarize, as compared with aid-only, the package substantially reduces the problem of 'incoherence', but does little to alleviate the problem of temporary unemployment. It accentuates the risk of import hoarding, but offsetting this by reducing the required aid so substantially it probably makes the programme more credible. Compared with the exchange-rate-only strategy, it seems to have little to offer unless exchange-rate depreciation is a genuine political constraint.

Some consequences of reform incredibility

So far we have assumed that private agents adopt the attitude 'sufficient unto the day': expectations have not entered into behaviour. In particular, investment has been determined purely by previous period rates of return. Recall that we have captured gradual adjustment of the capital stock in the model by assuming that the sector-specific capital stock depreciates and its replacement provides an opportunity for its relocation. Clearly, because in such a model capital once installed cannot be moved, expectations of relative price changes should play a role.

The expected path of relative prices is directly dependent on the degree of credibility of the liberalization programme. We compare three sets of expectations. The first, our specification in the above analysis in which only previous-period rates of return are considered, can be viewed as being appropriate in two types of circumstances. In some African conditions relative prices may have been so variable that they are viewed as an unforecastable random walk: although last year's returns are not expected to persist, they remain a better guide to the future than anything else. Alternatively, there may be no inter-sectoral financial markets so that investment, financed out of retained earnings, is inextricably linked to last-period returns, regardless of price expectations. The second set of expectations is of programme collapse. This is modelled as a generalized expectation of a reversion of rates of return to their pre-reform levels. The third, programme confidence, is modelled as a generalized expectation of the actual rates of return which prevail in the eighth year of a sustained, credible reform. Since, in the model, returns converge only very slowly, the results are not sensitive to more complex specifications of medium-run rational expectations of sectoral returns.

We allow for two related responses to the expectation of programme collapse. First, because programme collapse will alter the ranking of returns, we would expect investment to be reduced in the currently high return sector(s). Second, because programme collapse (and the consequent high returns in the protected sector) occur only in the future, there is a case for investment deferral, manifested as a switch into liquidity. We model the latter in only a limited way, introducing a possibility of reversible capital flight. As described in the Appendix, investment in a

Table 3.5 Incredible trade liberalization (compatibility maintained by exchange rate adjustment, programme collapse expected; results under expectation of programme maintenance = 100)

	$t = 2$	$t = 6$
Exports	94	91
Capital formation	98	93
Capital stock		
Exportables	93	89
Importables (QRs)	99	96

sector is now determined by comparison of the anticipated returns between sectors, as well as a comparison between the current and the anticipated return within the same sector. In the case where programme collapse is expected, the anticipated returns are those of the pre-liberalization period (that is, 20 per cent in each sector). This alone would, of course, lead to a replication of the actual investment allocation with the counterfactual, no-liberalization case. The cost would therefore be in a failure of the capital stock to be relocated to the export sector. This is, however, an implausible scenario, because agents are unlikely to hold point expectations of imminent collapse. We allow for this by a second-stage comparison of the anticipated return with the current return. If the current return is below the anticipated return, as it will be in the import-substitute sector prior to programme collapse, we assume that capital goods are imported but not yet installed. As a general specification of investment behaviour, this deferral rule is clearly inadequate. However, in the present context, deferral only occurs in the import-substitute sector, where current returns are more than halved by the liberalization. Thus the formula amounts to a 'wait and see' strategy for potential investment in that sector.

With three sets of expectations and three possible reform packages, the full depiction of outcomes would be lengthy. We concentrate upon the unaided, exchange-rate-only, liberalization package (Table 3.5). The different expectations have similar effects in the other two packages.

Moving from adaptive expectations to an expectation of programme maintenance produces some powerful effects. In particular, export response is much faster: after two years of reform, exports are 5 per cent higher than when investment is driven by previous-period returns. However, our primary comparison will be between an expectation of programme maintenance and an expectation of programme collapse. The effect of anticipated programme collapse combined with the opinion of capital flight is quite severe. There is a generalized investment collapse. It is to expected that investment in the export sector declines relative to the high level induced by an expectation of sustained liberalization. However, more remarkably, it is lower even than in the absence of liberalization: a liberalization that is incredible reduces export sector investment. This works through a double effect. First, as discussed above, liberalization accomodated by exchange rate adjustment removes an implicit capital subsidy, lowering aggregate investment for a given savings rate. Second, whereas when investment allocation is driven by expectations of programme maintenance this is more than offset by the increased share of the export sector, now there is no such effect, because investors do not believe the high returns will persist. The investment collapse in the export sector is not offset by greater investment in the import-substitute sector. The higher anticipated returns in this sector generate temporary capital flight rather than current investment.

The generalized investment collapse rebounds on the economy. Because resource reallocation is slowed, the equilibrium exchange rate depreciates faster: after six years of liberalization it is 8 per cent lower than when there is programme confidence. Similarly, the decline in the capital stock requires continuing nominal wage falls over the six years at an annual average rate of 2 per cent. By the sixth year, exports are 9 per cent lower than when there is programme confidence.

Conclusion

The fundamental rationale for liberalization is export promotion. In the simple exchange-rate-only model a higher export price is the only impact effect of liberalization. However, the CGE model has shown that, with this policy, investment suffers from the removal of an implicit subsidy on imported capital goods. We suggested that this may account for the investment slump in Nigeria between 1986 and 1987. More generally, it may at least in part explain the finding of Mosley *et al.* (1991) that Structural Adjustment Programmes tend to depress investment. Because of this effect on investment, the supply response to the price change may only be modest. In the aid-only case, this effect on investment does not operate, since the implicit subsidy on imported capital goods is not removed, but rather is extended to all imports. However, in this case, export supply response is held back for a different reason. The temporary influx of aid has a Dutch-disease spending effect, drawing both investment and labour into the production of non-tradables. In our simulation results these detrimental effects are not commensurate; two years after the liberalization, exports have increased by 12 per cent in the case of exchange-rate adjustment, as against 9 per cent with aid.

The discouraging effect on aggregate investment through the removal of the implicit subsidy on imported capital is in the longer run an unavoidable consequence of trade liberalization, whether or not there is temporary aid financing. We have also highlighted an avoidable discouraging effect, which arises if the liberalization is not fully credible. Savings are held in liquid form in anticipation of programme collapse. In our simulations this effect was so powerful that it caused investment to fall as a result of liberalization, even in the export sector. Although there can be many contributing factors to the incredibility of a liberalization programme, if the programme is incompatible (reserves being insufficient to sustain it), well-informed agents will anticipate collapse. As discussed above, some African liberalization attempts have failed to satisfy this necessary condition. However, compatibility is not sufficient for credibility; liberalization must be politically as well as economically sustainable. Aid-financed liberalizations may be politically incredible on a number of counts. The impact effect on unemployment and capital owners in the protected sector may constitute distributional consequences thought likely to be unacceptable to the government. The enormous foreign exchange requirement is liable to raise a question mark at the onset of the reform as to sustainability. Additionally, the very acceptance of aid may lead agents to mistrust the government's motives (see Rodrik, 1989; Collier and Gunning, 1992). If, for whatever reason, export supply response is weaker than expected, this may lead the government to question the wisdom of the reform package it has been sold by the donors.

The above analysis has two broad implications. First, abrupt trade liberalizations should probably only be attempted in conjunction with abrupt exchange-rate depreciations. Aid-only liberalizations, although technically feasible, produce perverse resource shifts and require massive rapid nominal wage flexibility to avoid unemployment. Although the return on aid so deployed is positive, it is (in our simulations) lower than society's rate of time preference and so the bringing forward of aid for any non-economic reason (for example, wildlife protection aid) would at least be equally beneficial. Second, liberalizations work much better if they are credible; if they are incredible they are in some key respects (notably, investment in the export sector) quite possibly worse than no reform. Hence, in those in which abrupt exchange rate adjustment is politically not feasible it is probably better to achieve liberalization only gradually. This conclusion is in stark contrast to that of Papageorgiou *et al.* (1991).

Appendix

The model

We use a general equilibrium with five goods: (i) exportables; (ii) importables subject to QRs; (iii) other importables (where imports are subject neither to tariffs nor to QRs); (iv) non-tradables; and (v) capital goods. There is no domestic demand for exportables and only the first four goods are produced domestically; capital goods are entirely imported. Production functions are CES functions in capital and labour. Capital is sector-specific while labour is mobile.

There are two agents: a representative private agent and the government. The private agent's income consists of the value of production (net of direct taxes at a fixed rate τ), the rents generated by QRs (y_r), and an exogenous transfer from the rest of the world ($\bar{y}$). Income is used for consumption (where the allocation between goods 2, 3 and 4 is given by a CES utility function), savings (at a fixed rate σ) and changes in money balances. Money is held only for transaction purposes and velocity (v) is constant so that money demand is proportional to the value of consumption. Only the government holds foreign assets; domestic currency is the private agent's only asset. The government receives direct taxes and aid. It spends on goods 3 and 4 and in each case its expenditure is proportional to total GDP ($\Sigma p_i q_i$). The budget deficit is equal to the increase in the money supply. The government sets the exchange rate (or chooses a combination of exchange rate adjustment and additional aid) such that money demand and supply are equal at an unchanged level of reserves.

World prices are given. Trade liberalization is modelled as the replacement of QRs by (low) tariffs: rents are eliminated and (3.10) is replaced by $p_2 = p_2^w\,(1 + t)\,/\,e$ where t is the tariff rate. When the exchange rate (e) is endogenous compatibility is maintained by a devaluation in response to the trade liberalization. Alternatively, the scope for exchange-rate adjustment is limited, and when this constraint is binding all further adjustment is through an endogenous increase in aid. Aid is then partly exogenous ($\bar{a}$) and partly endogenous ($\tilde{a}$).

The sectoral allocation of savings is determined by anticipated rates of return (r_i^*), a weighted average (with weights ω) of the current rate of return (r), the rate of return in case of programme collapse, that is, the pre-reform rate ($\bar{r}$), and the long-run rate of return ($\bar{\bar{r}}$). Whenever r_i^* exceeds the current rate r_i, that is, when the rate of return is seen as being temporarily low, there is no fixed investment in the sector. The capital stock then decreases with depreciation, and the savings which would otherwise have been used for gross investment in the sector ($\zeta_i i$) are used to add to the stock of uninstalled capital goods (k^s). Conversely, when the current rate of return is not seen as being temporarily low ($r_i \geq r_i^*$) then the sector's capital stock is increased, not only through the investment of current savings but also by the installation of previously imported capital goods.

Production

$$q_i = (a_i k_i^{-\rho_i} + b_i l_i^{-\rho_i})^{-1/\rho_i} \quad i = 1, .., 4 \tag{3.1}$$

$$q_i / l_i = (w / b_i p_i)^{1/(1+\rho_i)} \quad i = 1, .., 4 \tag{3.2}$$

$$\Sigma l_i = \bar{l} \tag{3.3}$$

Balance equations

$$q_1 = x \tag{3.4}$$
$$q_2 = c_2 - m_2 \tag{3.5}$$
$$q_3 = c_3 + g_3 - m_3 \tag{3.6}$$
$$q_4 = c_4 + g_4 \tag{3.7}$$
$$i = m_5 \tag{3.8}$$

Trade policy

$$p_i = p_i^w/e \quad i = 1, 3, 5 \tag{3.9}$$
$$m_2 \leq \overline{m}_2 \tag{3.10}$$
$$y_r = (p_2 - p_2^w/e)m_2 \tag{3.11}$$

Private sector

$$y = (1-\tau)\Sigma p_i q_i + y_r + \overline{y}/e \tag{3.12}$$
$$y = \Sigma p_i g c_i + s + (M - M_{t-1}) \tag{3.13}$$
$$s = \sigma y \tag{3.14}$$
$$Mv = \Sigma p_i c_i \tag{3.15}$$
$$u = (\gamma_2 c_2^{-\rho} + \gamma_3 c_3^{-\rho} + \gamma_4 c_4^{-\rho})^{-1/\rho} \tag{3.16}$$
$$c_2/c_4 = (p_4\gamma_2/p_2\gamma_4)^{1/(1+\rho)} \tag{3.17}$$
$$c_3/c_4 = (p_4\gamma_3/p_3\gamma_4)^{1/(1+p)} \tag{3.18}$$

Government

$$R = \tau\Sigma p_i q_i + (\overline{a} + \tilde{a})/e \tag{3.19}$$
$$p_i g_i = \mu_i \Sigma p_i q_i \tag{3.20}$$
$$E = p_3 g_3 + p_4 g_4 \tag{3.21}$$
$$M - M_{t-1} = E - R \tag{3.22}$$

Investment

$$r_i = (p_i q_i - w l_i)/(k_i p_5) \tag{3.23}$$
$$r_i^* = w_1 r_i + w_2 \overline{r}_i + w_3 \overline{\overline{r}}_i \tag{3.24}$$
$$\zeta_i = (r_i^*)^\alpha k_i / \Sigma (r_i^*)^\alpha k_i \quad i = 1, \ldots, 4 \tag{3.25}$$
$$i = s/p_5 \tag{3.26}$$
$$k_{i,t+1} = (1-\delta)k_i + \begin{cases} \zeta_i(i + \lambda k^s) & \text{if } r_i \geq r_i^* \\ 0 & \text{otherwise} \end{cases} \tag{3.27}$$
$$k_{t+1}^s = k^s - \lambda k^s \sum_{I_2} \zeta_t + i \sum_{I_2} \zeta_i \tag{3.28}$$

where I_1 denotes sectors with $r_i \geq r_i^*$ and I_2 other sectors.

Endogenous variables

$\tilde{a}$	additional aid
c	private consumption
e	exchange rate
E	government expenditure
ζ	sectoral allocation of investment
g	government consumption
i	real investment
k_{t+1}	next year's capital stock
k^s	uninstalled capital goods
l	employment
m	import
M	money supply
p	price
q	output
r	current rate of return
r^*	anticipated rate of return
$\bar{\bar{r}}$	long-run rate of return
R	government revenue
s	savings
u	utility
w	wage rate
x	export
y	private income
y_r	rents

Exogenous variables

$\bar{a}$	aid
$\bar{l}$	labour force
$\overline{m}$	quota
p^w	world price
$\bar{r}$	pre-reform rate of return
$\bar{y}$	transfer received from abroad

The model is one for a hypothetical African economy, therefore the simulation results serve as no more than an illustrative example. However, the chosen values for the base year and for the parameters describe an archetype with a number of features that appear realistic: imports are very much larger than exports, the non-tradable sector is relatively large, trade policy is highly restrictive (the domestic price of importables is twice the world price; this is very close to the situation in Kenya in 1988), capital goods are entirely imported, and government expenditure is largely on non-tradables.

Notes

1. The authors would like to thank David Greenaway, John Whalley and Howard White for comments. An earlier version of this chapter appeared in the *Economic Journal*, vol. 102, July 1992, pp. 925–39.
2. There are some important exceptions. Botswana, with nearly two years of imports cover, could run incompatible policies for several years. The Franc Zone, with an unlimited credit line from France conditional upon meeting budgetary rules, could run incompatible policies for even longer.
3. The exception is if the value of rents rises sufficiently to offset this effect. See Mussa (1976).
4. The weak fiscal improvement is clearly not a necessary result of trade reforms of this type. However, we do not pursue this further. Fiscal effects within this type of CGE model are the focus of Bevan (1992).
5. In the model, the savings rate is assumed to be fixed as a percentage of current price GDP. The volume of investment therefore reduces proportionately to the price increase. However, the qualitative result of a fall in imports of capital goods is general as long as capital goods imports are not rationed initially.

6. Other results of the model only become interesting when compared with other policy sequences and so will be deferred.

References

Bevan, D. L. (1992) 'Fiscal Implications of Trade Liberalisation', mimeo, Centre for the Study of African Economies, Oxford.

Collier, P. and Gunning, J. W. (1992) 'Trade and Development: Protection, Shocks and Liberalization, in D. Greenaway and A. Winters (eds) *Surveys of International Trade* (London: Macmillan).

Mosley, P., J. Harrigan and J. Toye (1991) *Aid and Power: The World Bank and Policy-Based Lending*, vols 1 and 2 (London: Routledge).

Mussa, M. (1976) Tariffs and the Balance of Payments, in J. A. Frenkel and H. G. Johnson, *The Monetary Approach to the Balance of Payments* (London, Allen & Unwin), pp. 187–221.

Neary, J. P. and D. D. Purvis (1982) 'Sectoral Shocks in a Dependent Economy: Long-run Adjustment and Short-run Accommodation', *Scandinavian Journal of Economics*, vol. 84, pp. 229–53.

Papageorgiou, D., M. Michaely and A. M. Choksi (eds) (1991) *Liberalizing Foreign Trade* (Oxford: Basil Blackwell).

Rodrik, D. (1989) 'Credibility of Trade Reform: A Policy Maker's Guide', *The World Economy*, vol. 12, pp. 1–16.

4

Donor Trade Benefits from Aid: Evidence from the EC and Sub-Saharan Africa

Oliver Morrissey

Introduction

The objective of overseas development assistance, or aid, is in principle to contribute to economic performance in recipient countries. That it has apparently failed to do so is cause for concern. While it has proved difficult to demonstrate that aid flows on aggregate have had a significant impact on economic growth rates in recipient countries (Mosley *et al.* 1987), it is nevertheless evident that aid constitutes a vital source of foreign exchange and capital inflows for developing countries, especially those in Sub-Saharan Africa (SSA). Inappropriate economic policies on the part of developing countries and their frequent inability to utilize aid properly is one factor explaining the (macroeconomic) ineffectiveness of aid. But donor policies have also undermined the potential effectiveness of aid. On one level this arises from the multitude of donors operating with individual recipients with limited administrative and economic capacity; this lack of co-ordination, often amounting to donor competition and conflict, undermines the ability of recipients to absorb aid (Morrissey, 1992a). On another level, recipient development is not the sole, and rarely even the predominant, motive guiding donor aid policy. Donors use aid to serve their own political and economic objectives (Morrissey *et al.*, 1992). This is especially evident where donors use aid to serve their trade objectives, whereby aid becomes an instrument of trade competition which conflicts with development objectives (Morrissey, 1993).

When donors use aid to support trade, most notably through tied aid as a means of export support, the implicit (if not explicit) assumption is that aid can *generate* trade (that is, exports). This chapter examines aid and trade flows between major European donors and a sample of SSA countries to assess the veracity of such an assumption. If aid does generate exports it should be possible to observe a significant relationship between the aid and the exports from a donor to recipients. This testable hypothesis forms the motivation for this chapter. The next selection addresses the aid–trade relationship. The first part briefly reviews the standard arguments, or explanations, for why donors tie a large volume of their aid, paying particular attention to the argument that tied aid generates exports (that is, aid is trade creating). The second part briefly examines the aid policies of the major European Community (EC) donors; throughout this chapter we focus on the bilateral aid of France, Germany, Italy, the Netherlands and the UK as being the major EC donors. Attention is paid to the issue of trade links as a factor explaining the allocation of aid by donors. Models of aid allocation have often posited, and found, that aid is more likely to be granted to developing countries with strong trade links to the donor: that is, aid follows trade. In so far as such models have failed to account for the reverse causality – of trade following aid – they may be subject to simultaneity bias.

The following section discusses the specification issues, paying attention to the problems of historic links and possible simultaneity between aid and exports, as indicated in the aid allocation literature, and to alternative estimation methods for pooled data. Next, we present the results for the relationship between aid and exports from the major EC donors to a sample of SSA countries.[1] We are interested in identifying the extent to which aid flows can explain trade flows. Put bluntly, to what extent is a donor likely to export more to those (SSA) countries to which it gives relatively more aid? We conclude by arguing for the existence of an aid–trade relationship, and suggests a number of directions for future research in this area.

The aid–trade relationship

Aid can engender trade dependency between donor and recipient in a number of ways. In general, if aid does generate some political goodwill, the recipient may feel better-disposed, if not obliged, to purchase goods from the donor. Furthermore, since so much aid finances projects that require the import of capital goods (which are more likely to be produced by donors than by the recipient or other developing countries), aid will, in general, tend to support donor exports. This also results if aid is deployed and utilized effectively so that it contributes to economic growth in recipient countries, leading to an expansion in world trade that benefits all exporters. The aid and trade link is made explicit when the aid is tied, so that the recipient must import from the donor. Such tying is, at the very least, an impediment to free trade which reduces competition in particular markets, thereby increasing the price to, and reducing the choice of, developing countries.

Aid as trade creation

The effect of tying depends on the form (see Jepma, 1989, for a detailed discussion), but we can content ourselves by distinguishing two types, formal and informal. *Formal tying* is where the granting of aid is contingent on purchasing goods from the donor, although normally about 30 per cent of the aid funds are allowable for local costs. A minimum of choice is left to the recipient under triple-tying, where the project, source country (donor) and contractor/supplier are all specified (Jepma, 1991, p. 5). Tying is *informal* when it results from some other donor policy, such as French reciprocal trade arrangements in Francophone Africa, or the West German policy of funding projects (untied) for which its industries had a competitive advantage (Bhagwati, 1967). Where aid is given to countries – such as ex-colonies – which have strong trading ties with the donor, or where the recipient is aware of the goodwill that would result if it purchased goods from the donor, the appearance is similar to informal tying but very difficult to distinguish from genuine political goodwill and competitive trading advantages. The simple point is that tied aid may be used as an instrument of export competition between donors (this argument is developed in Morrissey, 1993).

Since few developing countries have adequate capital industries, a large share of present aid finances capital exports from donors to recipients. Depending on their international competitiveness, donor industries will win a share of global orders which, in the absence of tying, should reflect their market shares (see Jepma, 1991, for the associated implications of EC-wide untying). In other words, tying is not essential to ensure donor benefits. One rationale for tying is that it may help a donor to derive benefits from increased trade that are more than proportional to its share of world export markets. Two issues are salient to this use of tied aid. First, it is necessary that tied aid be trade-creating: that is, there is no net benefit if the export orders would have been won in the absence of aid. Jepma (1989, p. 37) terms this 'fungibility' and concludes, from a survey of the evidence relating to the major donors, that some 30 to 50 per cent of tied aid is not trade-creating. Second, is the incidence of competitive tying between donors; although tying may not be trade-creating relative to a base year or trend, as other donors tie their aid, any individual donor must offer tied aid to protect its market share. While tying may not appear to increase market share, the absence of tying may lose market share. Once tying exists it is, therefore, self-perpetuating.

In their study of the impact of own-aid on the Netherlands economy, covering the period 1962–80, Jepma and Quist (1986) place considerable emphasis on substitution effects, which are the same as fungibility. Aid may not be trade-creating if recipients substitute the aid-financed exports for other exports they would have ordered from the donor. There may also be net trade-creation if the *radiation effects*, increased orders resulting from goodwill arising from granting aid, or the advertising effect of a successful project, outweigh the substitution effects, which will tend to be greater the larger the recipient economy. Thus, donors who concentrate their tied aid on the smallest, poorest recipients are the least likely to experience net trade creation. This is another reason why pressures for export-orientated aid focus on tied aid to the relatively rich recipients, for whom the radiation effect may be large.

Trade objectives and donor aid policies

The trade-creating argument for tied aid, which applies to all aid, implies that there will be a causal relationship between aid flows and exports from the donor to the recipients. Donors will tie aid because they use aid to meet their own commercial and political interests. This argument has attracted deserved prominence in the literature on the allocation of aid (for a comprehensive survey, see McGillivray and White, 1993). In general, any model that seeks to explain the pattern of donor aid allocation across recipients will include explanatory variables to represent the 'vested interests' of the donor in particular countries. We do not review this literature here but address it in the next section, because some aid allocation studies include donor exports as an independent variable: that is, they posit that exports are an indicator of trade links and hence of commercial interests. Consequently, aid is more likely to be allocated to countries to which the donor exports. This argument implies the reverse causality from that of our 'aid as trade creating' argument, a problem discussed in a later section.

Summary statistics on elements of the major EC donors' aid budgets in 1990 are given in Table 4.1. The potential of aid to support donor export competition will depend on the volume offered and the degree of tying. The five EC donors listed are, after the USA and Japan, the largest donors in volume terms (Canada offers similar volumes to the UK and the Netherlands). There was a tendency for the major donors to increase the degree of tying during the 1980s, reflecting the collapse of Middle East markets in the early 1980s and the related contraction in LDC markets

Table 4.1 Aid patterns for major EC donors, 1989–90

Donor	*Net aid*[1] *$m*	*World (%)*	*GNP (%)*	*Untied*[2] *(1989)*	*SSA share*[3]
France[4]	7614	13.6	0.78	40.2	51.0
Germany	5097	9.1	0.41	39.4	33.3
Italy	3191	5.7	0.36	5.8	49.0
Netherlands	2125	3.8	0.94	33.0	34.3
UK	2445	4.4	0.29	13.9	43.7
DAC[5]	47640	86.5	0.35	33.0	32.8

Notes: Aid refers to the DAC definition of official development assistance. Figures are annual averages for 1989–90 (except for untied proportion). World total is for donors – DAC, OPEC and others.

1. Volume of net aid in $m at 1989 prices and exchange rates.
2. Untied aid is the share of total aid 'fully and freely available for essentially world-wide procurement'; other aid is to some extent formally tied.
3. The share of net disbursements, including imputed multilateral flows, allocated to countries in Sub-Saharan Africa.
4. Figures include French transfers to DOM/TOM (if excluded, French aid as a percentage of GNP would be 0.55 in 1989–90, 9.5 per cent and total world aid).
5. 1990 figures include non-aid debt forgiveness, including some US military debt.

Source: Development Assistance Committee (DAC) of the OECD, *1991 Annual Report* (Paris, OCCD).

following the debt crisis. The share of total DAC aid defined as being formally tied increased from 30 per cent to 33 per cent between 1982 and 1989 (Morrissey, 1983, table 4.1). Within the EC and globally, Italy, France and the UK tend to make the greatest use of tied aid, whereas Germany and the Netherlands are less inclined to do so. EC donors grant at least a third of their aid to SSA countries, and about a half for France and Italy, which is above the DAC average (and is one reason for our focus on SSA).

The degree of tying of German aid remained among the lowest of the major donors in the 1980s (Morrissey, 1993). Although not formally permitted, aid is tied in practice in mixed (public and private) financing, but foreign suppliers or subcontractors will be used if they assist the overall financial competitiveness of the project (Gluch and Riedel, 1988, p. 138). The impact of own-aid on the British and German economies has been analyzed in some detail by May *et al.* (1989) and we can compare Germany and the UK in terms of the potential employment supported by tied aid. By 1984, given the variability of exchange rates, both countries supported some 35,000 employees per $1bn equivalent of aided exports. The macroeconomic effects are not great, and tying is not an effective means of employment creation, but this does not deny the significant benefits of tying to particular industries and individual companies (see also Morrissey *et al.*, 1992).

Italy adopted an export-orientated aid policy in the late 1970s when, in response to lobbying from major exporters, its parliament passed the Ossola law in 1977 guaranteeing the provision of matching financial support to exporters, later expanded. Italy has only had a significant (and commercial) foreign aid policy since that period. The government adopted a clear export-orientated aid policy supported by a massive increase in the volume of aid (it increased more than ten times in real terms in the 1980s). In the early 1980s up to 15 per cent of contract value was repatriated; the effect on Italian exports has been estimated as being positive with a two-year lag (Norsa, 1988, p. 91). The Italian example is evidence of how the aid budget can be used to promote exports, and how governments respond to business lobbying.

There is less evidence of a large response to the business lobby in respect of the UK aid budget. The real value of British aid fell significantly in the 1980s, by almost a third between 1979 and 1987, and the business lobby became increasingly vociferous in demanding more tied aid to match other donors. Although a few large firms gained from the mixed credits scheme, the business lobby had a limited influence on the Thatcher governments in respect of the aid budget. International and internal political interests, notably public expenditure restraint, were the major determinants of the budget, and business was unable to exert the influence required to elicit a real increase in tied aid (Morrissey *et al.*, 1992).

France, on the other hand, has a reputation for adopting a commercial aid strategy, offering considerable support to its exporters, which is not undeserved. This has been especially noticeable through using export subsidies to support construction firms. The major contribution of construction exports has been to help achieve balance-of-payments equilibrium, itself an underlying motive for export credit subsidies (Melitz and Messerlin, 1987). Studies of the allocation of French aid find the most significant determinant to be some measure of political interests or historic links; McGillivray and White (1993, p. 41) also found that France granted more aid to those countries from which it imported the most, which is a measure of trading links.

To summarize, Italy and France adopt the most clearly export-directed aid policies; their governments are responsive to business demands. The UK, Germany and the Netherlands are less responsive to business demands and have made less use of their aid budgets to promote exports (the latter two, in particular, have relatively low degrees of formal tying).

This conclusion is supported by the finding that if EC countries abandoned bilateral tying of aid and allowed procurement from all EC countries, Germany and the UK would be among the gainers while France and Italy would be prime losers. If EC-wide untying was a zero-sum game under existing trade patterns, the UK could expect to increase its exports to a sample of forty-one developing countries by 5 per cent, and Germany by over 4 per cent. Dutch exports could fall by 0.4 per cent, but France would lose 2.5 per cent of exports and Italy would lose over 18 per cent (Jepma, 1991, p. 50). The aid–trade link is perceived by donors.

Specification issues

There is a pronounced one-way trade relationship between Africa and the EC. In 1988–9, 53 per cent of Africa's exports went to the EC and 7 per cent to Africa, while 3 per cent of EC exports went to Africa. On the other hand, 49 per cent of Africa's imports were from the EC, and 5 per cent from Africa, whereas only 3 per cent of EC imports were from Africa. This relationship became even more one-sided in the 1980s: the trade dependency of Africa on the EC increased, but Africa's share of EC exports declined (Davenport, 1992). Attention here is on France, Germany, Italy, the Netherlands and the UK as being the largest EC aid donors by the late 1980s (accounting for almost 90 per cent of total aid from EC countries) and the largest exporters (accounting for almost three-quarters of EC exports in the late 1980s).[2] The aspect of the aid–trade relationship of interest is whether donors are more likely to export to those countries to whom they give more aid.

We are positing a general relationship of the form $X_{ij} = f(A_{ij}, M_j)$ where: X_{ij} are exports from donor i to recipient j; A_{ij} is aid from donor i to country j, and M_j is total imports of j, which is used as a measure of trade potential (other things remaining equal, i would export more to those countries that import more). Other explanatory variables could be included but, reflecting a desire to keep the specification as simple as possible, we have decided not to do so. The hypothesized link between X_{ij} and A_{ij} is twofold: direct, where the aid is formally tied; and general where the aid, in practice, helps finance recipient imports. The underlying assumption is that the LDCs face a trade gap but aid as 'external import financing' allows them to avoid import compression. The effects of aid on exports (via import capacity) are concurrent so there is no particular reason to use lagged values of A_{ij} (which implies that we have to be careful about possible simultaneity, as discussed below). It would be appropriate to deduct the direct effect (that is, subtract tied aid from X_{ij}), but the data do not identify tied aid at the individual recipient level. It is not obvious that one should deduct all aid ($X_{ij} - A_{ij}$), as the interaction of radiation and substitution effects weakens any direct correspondence between aid and exports. Thus, our specific intention is to estimate:

$$X_{ij} = \alpha_0 + \alpha_1 M_j + \alpha_2 A_{ij} + \varepsilon_1 \tag{4.1}$$

Equation (4.1) would be estimated separately for each donor, using pooled cross-section and time series data. The coefficients are assumed constant over time and across countries. The α_1 represents the 'normal', which we would like to interpret as competitive, import share of donor, *i*. While the import share is expected to vary between SSA countries, we implicitly hypothesized that such variations can be explained by aid flows, implying that α_1 be interpreted as a minimum import share. Our initial interest is to determine if α_2 is positive and significant.

There are two problems with (4.1) which are potentially very serious and related: are there missing variables, and is there a simultaneity problem? It may be believed that countries will trade most with those countries with which they have existing trading or historic links. To model this, one may wish to include a lagged dependent variable or a dummy for historic links. The former approach would not be in keeping with (4.1), given the inclusion of M_j to incorporate trade potential, but the latter deserves consideration. It may well be the case that exports are related to historic links (so that α_1 is greater, for example, in former colonies), but should also be the case that aid is related to historic links (so that A_{ij} is greater, for example in former colonies). It is not clear how an historic dummy should be incorporated into (4.1).

Including an historic dummy (H_j) introduces simultaneity, which may already have existed. Models of the aid allocation process are of the general form $A_{ij} = f(.)$. A political/strategic dummy or H_j is usually a significant determinant of aid allocation (see McGillivray and White, 1993), but we are especially concerned with those cases where $f(.)$ includes X_{ij}. The conventional hypothesis is that the coefficient on X_{ij} is positive here, as donors give more aid to their trading partners (or those who have traditionally been trading partners, in which case the variable may be lagged). Grilli and Reiss (1992) found lagged X_{ij} positive and significant in regressions for the determinants of total EC bilateral aid allocation to thirty seven ACP countries (where X_{ij} is total EC exports to the country). Gulhati and Nallari (1988) included X_{ij} (apparently unlagged) in cross-section regressions to explain bilateral allocations from a number of donors to eighteen African countries: the coefficient was positive (except for Sweden and the UK), but only reached significance for Italy and Japan.

They also used $X_{ij} - A_{ij}$ in time-series regressions for the aid of some donors to each of five recipients; again, the coefficient was generally positive, but only significant for aid to Kenya.

McGillivray and Oczkowski (1992) include donor exports but argue that the coefficient should be negative if donors adopt a more aggressive policy of export promotion in new markets. As it happened, the coefficient on the X_{ij} was generally insignificant and negative, although it was positive in the two regressions for which it was significant. The arguments we introduced earlier would all point to a positive coefficient, which is consistent with the evidence: donors are not as aggressive as McGillivray and Oczkowski (1992) suggest, and where they are aggressive it tends to be in a protectionist way. It is also worth noting that the export variable is lagged in the models of aid allocation – present aid may depend on past trade.

These considerations suggest that a simultaneous equation system may be the most appropriate. We leave this as a possibility for future research. As aid flows can be zero, or so minimal as effectively to be zero, models of aid allocation should utilize limited dependent variable techniques, as employed by McGillivray and Oczkowski (1992); this would be extremely complex in a simultaneous system. Any two-way causality between A_{ij} and X_{ij} could be accommodated by using lagged aid in (4.1). Incorporating H_j would remain a problem, so we propose to estimate:

$$\Delta X_{ij} = \beta_0 + \beta_1 \Delta M_j + \beta_2 \Delta A_{ij} + \varepsilon_2 \tag{4.2}$$

where

Δ indicates change in the variable (year-on-year difference); and
ε_2 a stochastic error term, with standard properties.

This should be a better test of the relationship between exports and aid than (4.1) and it is reasonable to assume that historic links need not be included as explanatory variables in (4.2); such links affect (starting) levels but need not affect year-on-year changes. There is no obvious simultaneity between changes in exports and in aid: if 'marginal' aid directly finances incremental trade, the coefficient β_2 would be unity; a value of β_2 greater than unity is consistent with trade creation, while $\beta_2 < 1$ suggests substitution effects, or more generally a weak aid–trade link. It is reasonable to point out that (4.2), being in differences, is in a sense a test of the continuity or permanence of the aid–trade link: a definite link may have been established at some starting point but is likely to be eroded slowly, if at all. Hence, finding a significant β_2 is strongly suggestive of the existence of a link.

A final piece of analysis we can consider, following the work on assessing the relationship between export growth and economic growth (for example, Greenaway and Sapsford, 1993), is to test the correlations between export growth and aid growth over the relevant period. We estimate aid and export growth rates using the semi-log method for each donor separately, then we identify the correlation between aid and export growth rates across the sample. A significant result would not demonstrate causality but would support the hypothesis that aid and trade are related. The results of applying this approach to our sample are given in Table 4.2.[3]

Table 4.2 Aid and trade growth rates: EC–SSA, 1969–87

Donor	*SRC*	*Cons*	*Coeff.*	R^2	*dm*	*da*
France						
N = 28	0.52	0.07	0.25	0.27	0.09	0.10
	(0.005)	(5.83)	(3.28)		(60.6)	(125.2)
N = 16	0.58	0.03	0.56	0.25	0.1	0.13
	(0.018)	(4.65)	(2.44)		(49.2)	(37.8)
Germany						
N = 28	0.16	0.88	0.07	0.01	0.09	0.14
	(0.402)	(4.36)	(0.58)		(50.9)	(54.8)
Italy						
N = 28	0.15	0.09	0.07	0.0	0.11	0.27
	(0.46)	(3.65)	(0.91)		(65.0)	(65.9)
N = 10	0.27	0.07	0.06	0.0	0.09	0.23
	(0.45)	(1.07)	(0.21)		(81.8)	(38.8)
Netherlands						
N = 28	0.25	0.08	0.15	0.01	0.1	0.15
	(0.20)	(4.72)	(1.11)		(57.3)	(77.3)
N = 20	0.30	0.07	0.13	0.01	0.1	0.17
	(0.20)	(2.91)	(1.09)		(63.5)	(66.0)
UK						
N = 28	–0.01	0.07	–0.02	0.0	0.07	0.09
	(0.96)	(4.94)	(–0.15)		(71.2)	(90.0)
N = 22	0.17	0.06	0.06	0.0	0.06	0.10
	(0.45)	(3.58)	(0.48)		(77.2)	(89.8)

Notes: Growth rates are estimated as $\ln x_t = a + bT$, where T is a time trend and x is the variable, thus b is estimated growth rate (*dm* for imports and *da* for aid). Table reports statistical results, with significance in parentheses, as indicated below. Full sample is 28 SSA countries for each donor estimated over 19 years; sub-samples are number of countries for which the estimation period had non-zero (aid) values for 14 or more years.
SRC = Spearman Rank Correlation (significance level is probability of given correlation being observed if the series were independent).
Cons. Coeff. estimated from *dm* = Cons + Coeff*da* (t-stats in parentheses); R^2 is adjusted.
dm = mean value of import growth rate (coefficient of variation in parenthesis).
da = mean value of aid growth (coefficient of variation in parenthesis).

Although significant results are found for France alone, itself an interesting result, the patterns identified in Table 4.2 are relevant (and are consistent with donor policy differences discussed above).

Aid and export growth rates appear to be significantly correlated for France and this is most evident for the full sample (N = 28 SSA countries over nineteen years). The subsample (N = 16) refers to those countries to which France was a donor for at least fourteen years: while the significance levels are lower than for the full sample, the relationship still holds and the coefficient on aid growth is larger. Furthermore, none of the twelve countries omitted from the full sample (that is, countries for which France was a donor for less than fourteen years in the period) were ex-colonies of France, and all such ex-colonies are in the subsample and received aid throughout the period. It is thus relevant to note that the mean growth rates (*dm* and *da*) were higher, with much lower variance, for the subsample. The data suggest that France exports more to those countries to which it grants more aid, that this relationship is significant over time, and that the relationship is most pronounced with ex-colonies in SSA.

There is no evidence of a significant correlation between aid and export growth rates for any of the other donors, but there are some interesting differences. Germany is notable as having been a donor to all the countries for virtually the entire period (or at least for no less than fourteen years in any case, hence the subsample is the sample), and has the lowest variance of mean growth rates. The Netherlands is close to having a significant correlation, and the subsample is not much different from the full sample. Italy is notable in having by far the smallest subsample (only ten SSA countries received Italian aid for at least fourteen years; most only became recipients from the late 1970s), and is the only donor exhibiting lower mean growth rates for the subsample as against the sample. This is consistent with Italy expanding its role as a donor after 1977, and the growth in aid flows being greater for more recent than for long-standing recipients; export growth was also greater for recent recipients, suggesting the existence of an aid–trade relationship. The UK evidence is interesting for a number of reasons: it is the only donor for whom the correlation may be negative, and recorded the lowest mean aid and trade growth rates. Ten of the SSA countries are Commonwealth members, all of which are in the subsample, but they tended to experience lower aid growth rates (negative in two cases) than did non-Commonwealth countries in the subsample. The UK appears to be a case where the aid–trade link did not exist and/or the donor did not exploit the potential of the link.

The observations from Table 4.2 are consistent with other 'descriptions' of aid and trade links between the EC and SSA (Morrissey, 1992b). France grants the most aid and sells the most imports (in total, the ratio is \$3.7 m of imports for each \$1m of aid), and its major aid and trade partners are in Francophone Africa: seven of the ten countries that imported the most from France were also among the ten countries to which France granted the most aid. Although the UK granted the least aid of the five by 1987, it ranked second in terms of total imports, with a ratio of \$8.7m of imports for each \$1m of aid. Eight of the ten countries importing the most from the UK were also among the ten that received the most aid, and all but Ethiopia had strong ex-colonial links. Italy had become the second largest donor by 1987, but ranked fourth in terms of imports, with a ratio of \$1.6m of imports for each \$1m of aid. Seven of the ten countries importing the most from Italy were also among the ten that received the most aid. For most of the period 1969–87 France had the largest share of aid and exports of the EC donors to SSA; Germany and the Netherlands had relatively stable shares; Italy held a fairly stable share of exports but this did rise slightly in the 1980s, when its aid share rose dramatically; the UK is notable as being the only one of these five donors which recorded trend declines in both aid and export shares. Trade and aid links between SSA and the EC are significant, especially from the perspective of SSA recipients. These observations suggest that the nature of the relationship differs between donors: strongest for France, recent for Italy and perhaps negative for the UK; stable patterns seem to emerge for Germany and the Netherlands. The relationship for each donor is explored in more detail in the next section.

Results

This section provides the results for our analysis of aid and trade flows from five major EC donors to a sample of twenty-eight SSA states over the period 1969–87; tied aid is not distinguished because of lack of data and also the fact that aid need not be formally tied to support trade relations. Following the discussion of the previous section, we are estimating an equation expressed in differences (simple year-on-year changes). The equation to be estimated for each donor separately utilizes pooled cross-section ($N = 28$) and time-series ($T = 18$) data, and is of the general form:

$$\mathbf{y} = \mathbf{X}\beta + \varepsilon \qquad (4.3)$$

where

$\mathbf{y}$ = a NT by 1 column vector of the dependent variable;
$\mathbf{X}$ = a NT by K matrix of K explanatory variables (including constant term);

β = a K by 1 column vector of coefficients; and
ε = a NT by 1 column vector of error terms.

We first estimate this model by simple OLS (adjusted for heteroskedasticity). Doing so, however, assumes that the coefficients are constant over time and across countries. These assumptions may not hold. In particular, we wish to allow for the likelihood that coefficients vary across the countries because of the omission of historic links from the equation. To account for this we can estimate a fixed-effects, or covariance, model. This introduces a dummy variable for each country (the effect is fixed because any inference is conditional on the sample selected). The disadvantage is a reduction in degrees of freedom, but this is more than offset by the advantage of allowing for the cross-sectional characteristic; even if the cross-sectional characteristic is correlated with the explanatory variables, as would be the case for historic links and aid, the fixed-effects model does not exhibit specification error (Kmenta, 1990, p. 634). An appropriate estimation form is the least squares dummy variables model (Kmenta, 1990, p. 631).

$$\mathbf{y} = \mathbf{X}\beta + \mathbf{Z}\lambda + \varepsilon \tag{4.4}$$

where

$\mathbf{y}$ = a *N.T* by 1 column vector of the dependent variable;
$\mathbf{X}$ = a *N.T* by *K*-1 matrix of *K* explanatory variables (no constant term);
β = a *K*-1 by 1 column vector of coefficients;
$\mathbf{Z}$ = a *N.T* by *N* matrix of binary (dummy) variables;
λ = *a N* by 1 column vector of coefficients for the binary variables; and
ε = a *N.T* by 1 column vector of error terms.

Equations of form (4.4) are frequently used for pooled regressions, but assume that the disturbance term (ε) is non-auto-regressive and homoskedastic. We present results with corrections for heteroskedasticity and our final estimation method accounts for autoregression. The generalized linear regression form of this model can be estimated as a cross-sectionally heteroskedastic and timewise autoregressive model (Kmenta, 1990, pp. 618–22), which is relatively straightforward on SHAZAM (White, 1993, pp. 241–6). The special features of this model, estimated in the form (4.3), are:

$$E(\varepsilon_{it}^2) = \sigma_i^2 \quad \text{heteroskedasticity;} \tag{4.5i}$$

$$E(\varepsilon_{it}\varepsilon_{jt}) = 0 \quad (i \neq j) \quad \text{cross-section independence;} \tag{4.5ii}$$

$$\varepsilon_{it} = \rho_i \varepsilon_{i,t-1} + \upsilon_{it} \quad \text{autoregression;} \tag{4.5iii}$$

where

$$
\begin{aligned}
\upsilon_{it} &\sim N(0, \sigma^2_{\upsilon i}) \\
\varepsilon_{i1} &\sim N(0, \sigma^2_{\upsilon i}/(1-\rho_i^2) \\
E(\varepsilon_{i,t-1}\upsilon_{it}) &= 0 \quad \text{for all } i, j
\end{aligned}
$$

We limit attention to estimation of the static forms given in the equations (4.3), (4.4) and (4.5) The Kmenta model, as given by Equations (4.5) allows the ρ_i to vary by country; the estimated static model corrects for autoregression in the time-series, generating a consistent estimator of the covariance matrix, and for heteroskedasticity in the cross-section. The procedure generates a transformed model with error terms that are asymptotically non-autoregressive and homoskedastic, which is then estimated by OLS to provide unbiased consistent estimates of the regression coefficients. The results for each donor are presented in Tables 4.3 to 4.7.

Table 4.3 Aid and trade estimates, France

	Δa	Δm	*Cons.*	R^2	*F-test*
1 OLS					
	0.654	0.091	2.455	0.591	246.90
	(3.62)	(26.57)	(1.19)		
	[1.84]*	[14.07]**	[1.03]		
2 Fixed effects model					
	0.592	0.091	0.577	24.21	
	(3.16)	(26.0)			
	[1.43]	[13.25]**			
3 Kmenta model					
	0.376	0.070	0.398	0.372	98.71
	(4.99)**	(15.11)**	(0.98)		

Notes: Results estimated in the general form $\Delta x_t = a + b\Delta a_t + c\Delta m_t$, where variables are year-on-year change in donor exports to the SSA country (Δx), donor aid (Δa) and total recipient imports (Δm). Figures in parentheses are t-statistics. All OLS and fixed effects equations were tested for heteroskedasticity (using the Breusch–Pagan–Godfrey and Engle's ARCH tests) and re-estimated using the White correction: heteroskedasticity-corrected t-statistics are in square brackets. Reported R^2 is adjusted except in the case of the Kmenta model, where the goodness-of-fit statistic reported is the Buse raw-moment R^2 (White, 1993). Reported F-stats are for the coefficients being significantly different from zero (sample size is N = 504). The fixed effects model also includes 28 country dummies and estimates their coefficients; these are not reported here and only Cameroon (positive) and Ethiopia (negative) were significant at the 10% level in a two-tailed test in the heteroskedasticity-corrected estimation.
* = significant at the 10% level in a two-tailed test.
** = significant at the 5% level in a two-tailed test.

Table 4.4 Aid and trade estimates, Germany

	Δa	Δm	*Cons.*	R^2	*F-test*
1 OLS					
	–0.306	0.105	–0.117	0.741	481.24
	(–1.50)	(37.89)	(–0.07)		
	[–1.68]*	[6.90]**	[–0.07]		
2 Fixed effects model					
	–0.310	0.212	0.728	45.86	
	(–1.47)	(36.86)			
	[–1.72]*	[6.71]**			
3 Kmenta model					
	0.037	0.067	0.182	0.422	121.92
	(0.65)	(17.52)**	(0.75)		

Notes: Results estimated in the general form $\Delta x_t = a + b\Delta a_t + c\Delta m_t$, where variables are year-on-year change in donor exports to the SSA country (Δx), donor aid (Δa) and total recipient imports (Δm). Figures in parentheses are t-statistics. All OLS and fixed effects equations were tested for heteroskedasticity (using the Breusch–Pagan-Godfrey and Engle's ARCH tests) and re-estimated using the White correction: heteroskedasticity-corrected t-statistics are in square brackets. Reported R^2 is adjusted except in the case of the Kmenta model, where the goodness-of-fit statistic reported is the Buse raw-moment R^2 (White, 1993). Reported F-stats are for the coefficients being significantly different from zero (sample size is N = 504). The fixed effects model also includes 28 country dummies and estimates their coefficients; these are not reported here and none were significant at the 10% level.
* = significant at the 10% level in a two-tailed test.
** = significant at the 5% level in a two-tailed test.

The tables are self-explanatory, but some general comments are in order. Being the most general approach, the Kmenta model results are 'favoured' but do not explicitly incorporate country dummies. The simple OLS results are the least 'favoured' but are useful for comparison with other results, especially those of the Fixed Effects model. We would wish to observe a significant coefficient on the aid variable in both the Fixed Effects and Kmenta models before claiming to have detected a significant relationship, as only in such a case can we claim that the result persists when we allow for country dummies, autoregression and heteroskedasticity. On this criterion, the link is only found to be significant in the case of the UK (Table 4.7). Further examination of the results permits tentative comments on the nature of the relationship for each donor.

The OLS pooled regression for France suggests that both aid and total imports are significant determinants of French exports to a recipient. Once fixed effects are allowed for, the coefficient on aid is insignificant but still positive, suggesting that a strong relationship is only present with some countries in the sample. The results for the Kmenta approach

Table 4.5 Aid and trade estimates, Italy

	Δa	Δm	*Cons.*	R^2	*F-test*
1 OLS					
	–0.001	0.041	0.960	0.072	13.89
	(–0.005)	(6.42)	(0.25)		
	[–0.01]	[1.17]	[0.19]		
2 Fixed effects model					
	–0.019	0.041	0.021	1.33	
	(–0.07)	(6.22)			
	[–0.271]	[1.12]			
3 Kmenta model					
	0.067	0.032	0.250	0.295	69.80
	(2.06)**	(13.36)**	(1.33)		

Notes: Results estimated in the general form $\Delta x_t = a + b\Delta a_t + c\Delta m_t$, where variables are year-on-year change in donor exports to the SSA country (Δx), donor aid (Δa) and total recipient imports (Δm). Figures in parentheses are t-statistics. All OLS and fixed effects equations were tested for heteroskedasticity (using the Breusch–Pagan-Godfrey and Engle's ARCH tests) and re-estimated using the White correction: heteroskedasticity-corrected t-statistics are in square brackets. Reported R^2 is adjusted except in the case of the Kmenta model, where the goodness-of-fit statistic reported is the Buse raw-moment R^2 (White, 1993). Reported F-stats are for the coefficients being significantly different from zero (sample size is N = 504). The fixed effects model also includes 28 country dummies and estimates their coefficients; these are not reported here and none were significant.

* = significant at the 10% level in a two-tailed test.

** = significant at the 5% level in a two-tailed test.

suggest that the aid–trade link is stable. The results for Germany are weak: where aid is significant the coefficient is negative, and it is not significant in the Kmenta model. Germany export patterns appear to be determined by recipient import volumes, implying that it is Germany's trading strength that is the important factor, and not aid. Significant results for Italy are only found with the Kmenta model. This is not surprising, as Italy only became a major donor late in the period, but there is an indication that the relationship may have become significant. The results for the Netherlands are also weak, but there is an indication of a positive relationship. In the case of the UK, as indicated above, the results consistently favour a significant positive relationship between aid and trade. The declining trend of British exports to SSA countries, as identified when discussing Table 4.2 above, appears to be secular, given the constant term estimated for the Kmenta model.

Overall, the results suggest that total recipient imports are the principal determinant of donor exports to an SSA country. This is to be expected, and the absence of a significant constant term in all cases except the UK is

Table 4.6 Aid and trade estimates, the Netherlands

	Δa	Δm	*Cons.*	R^2	*F-test*
1 OLS					
	0.109	0.033	0.320	0.296	71.66
	(0.38)	(14.6)	(0.24)		
	[0.54]	[1.89*	[0.32]		
2 Fixed effects model					
	0.113	0.032		0.258	6.85
	(0.38)	(14.15)			
	[0.62]	[1.93]*			
3 Kmenta model					
	0.120	0.123	0.141	0.302	72.12
	(2.45)**	(13.21)**	(1.23)		

Notes: Results estimated in the general form $\Delta x_t = a + b\Delta a_t + c\Delta m_t$, where variables are year-on-year change in donor exports to the SSA country (ΔX), donor aid (Δa) and total recipient imports (Δm). Figures in parentheses are t-statistics. All OLS and fixed effects equations were tested for heteroskedasticity (using the Breusch–Pagan–Godfrey and Engle's ARCH tests) and re-estimated using the White correction: heteroskedasticity-corrected t-statistics are in square brackets. Reported R^2 is adjusted except in the case of the Kmenta model where the goodness-of-fit statistic reported is the Buse raw-moment R^2 (White, 1993). Reported F-stats are for the coefficients being significantly different from zero (sample size is N = 504). The fixed effects model also includes 28 country dummies and estimates their coefficients; these are not reported here and none were significant.
* = significant at the 10% level in a two-tailed test.
** = significant at the 5% level in a two-tailed test.

consistent with EC exporters maintaining their market share. Nevertheless, in most cases the coefficient on aid was found to be significant and positive. There is some evidence that this link is most evident in respect of donors (the UK and France) with historic links to sample countries. The results for the UK suggest that even donors who are losing market share can stem this loss through the use of aid.

Conclusion

The approaches pursued in this chapter do no more than test for a (positive) relationship between aid and exports; the results do not allow us to infer causality. If adequately long time-series data were collected, it would be possible to conduct Granger causality tests. Here, we cannot strictly answer the question. 'Is aid trade creating' but we can assess the aid–trade relationship for five donors and twenty-eight SSA recipients. We made use of pooled data to supply extra information and to compensate for the relatively small cross-section and time-series samples, and

Table 4.7 Aid and trade estimates, the UK

	Δa	Δm	*Cons.*	R^2	*F-test*
1 OLS					
	0.745	0.170	−3.257	0.751	507.05
	(1.52)	(38.91)	(−1.25)		
	[2.09]**	[8.39]**	[−1.24]		
2 Fixed effects model					
	0.742	0.170		0.738	48.276
	(1.47)	(37.89)			
	[2.12]**	[8.39]**			
3 Kmenta model					
	0.508	0.084	−0.754	0.355	91.78
	(4.66)**	(15.62)**	(−2.23)**		

Notes: Results estimated in the general form $\Delta x_t = a + b\Delta a_t + c\Delta m_t$, where variables are year-on-year change in donor exports to the SSA country (Δx), donor aid (Δa) and total recipient imports (Δm). Figures in parentheses are t-statistics. All OLS and fixed effects equations were tested for heteroskedasticity (using the Breusch–Pagan–Godfrey and Engle's ARCH tests) and re-estimated using the White correction: heteroskedasticity-corrected t-statistics are in square brackets. Reported R^2 is adjusted except in the case of the Kmenta model where the goodness-of-fit statistic reported is the Buse raw-moment R^2 (White, 1993). Reported F-stats are for the coefficients being significantly different from zero (sample size is N = 504). The fixed effects model also includes 28 country dummies and estimates their coefficients; these are not reported here although a number were significant (with negative coefficients) at the 5% level in the heteroskedasticity-corrected estimation: Burundi, Cameroon, Chad, Ethiopia, Mauritius and Rwanda.
* = significant at the 10% level in a two-tailed test.
** = significant at the 5% level in a two-tailed test.

maintained a simple specification to focus attention on the direct relationship under consideration. We also employed a number of estimation techniques to help evaluate the stability of the results. Overall, we can conclude that there is a positive link between aid and exports, and that this relationship merits further analysis.

Donor governments, and commercial export lobbies within donor economies, frequently justify tied aid by arguing that it is trade-creating. We have assessed this argument and found evidence of a significant positive link between aid and exports, although we cannot infer that aid is trade-creating. The aid–trade link appears to be strong for some donors, notably France and the UK, but is much weaker for others. In many cases it will be former-colonial ties that lead to high shares of both aid and trade. The aid–trade link, in particular the direction of causality, is important for understanding the motivations behind donor aid policy; it is also an important factor in evaluating aid policy. The link can also be of considerable importance to aid recipients – a strong link can undermine the effectiveness of aid. It does seem likely that a significant part of many SSA countries' imports are linked to donors. This need not be a problem, but can mean that the countries are paying relatively more for imports than they would otherwise need to.

The analysis in this chapter suggests a number of possibilities for future research. Most obviously, more sophisticated econometric techniques could be applied to the pooled data used, in particular to account for lagged effects, historic links and a dynamic specification. Also, data could be collected for other donors and other groups of recipients. As economic performance and import growth in SSA has been poor, especially in the 1980s, it can be argued that one would not observe the trade-creating effects of aid for such a sample. It would be interesting to apply the approach to aid recipients in Asia and Latin America, but one should be aware of the need to distinguish trade expansion resulting from economic growth from potential trade-creation attributed to aid. Second, our results have implications for models of aid allocation which, to date, have not incorporated explicitly the two-way causality between aid and trade. Finally, the most conclusive analysis would be of individual recipients over long time periods, but this awaits the availability of adequate data sets.

Notes

1. The sample comprises twenty-eight SSA countries for which data were available on aid and exports from each of the five EC countries over the full period 1969 to 1987, the longest period for which we could obtain all the relevant data. I am grateful to Jonathon Perraton for collecting much of the data on which the analysis is based.
2. These five EC countries accounted for between 27 and 40 per cent of total net aid flows to our sample of SSA countries over the period 1969–87, and accounted for between 41 and 51 per cent of merchandise imports by the sample countries over the same period.
3. All data are in current $US. Aid data are from the OECD, *Geographical Distribution of Financial Flows to Developing Countries*. Data on imports by each SSA country fro each EC donor (representing the X_{ij}) are from IMF *Direction of Trade Statistics Yearbooks*; and data on total merchandise imports by SSA countries are from IMF, *International Financial Statistics Yearbooks*.

References

Bhagwati, J. (1967) 'The Tying of Aid', reprinted in J. Bhagwati and R. Eckhaus (1970) *Foreign Aid*, (Harmondsworth: Penguin), pp. 235–93.

Davenport, M. (1992) 'Africa and the Unimportance of Being Preferred', *Journal of Common Market Studies*, vol. 30, no. 2, pp. 233–51.

Gluch, E. and J. Riedel (1988) 'The Federal Republic of Germany', in Strassmann and Wells (eds), pp. 120–40.
Greenaway, D. and D. Sapsford (1993) 'Exports, Growth and Liberalization: An Evaluation'. *Journal of Policy Modelling*, vol. 16, pp. 165–186.
Grilli, E. and M. Reiss (1992) 'EC Aid to Associated Countries: Distribution and Determinants', *Weltwirtschaftliches Archiv*, vol. 128, no. 2, pp. 202–20.
Gulhati, R. and R. Nallari (1988) 'Reform of Foreign Aid Policies: The Issue of Inter-Country Allocation in Africa', *World Development*, vol. 16, pp. 1167–84.
Jepma, C. (1989) *The Tying of Aid*, International Foundation for Development Economics and Dept of Economics, University of Groningen.
Jepma, C. (1991) *EC-Wide Untying*, International Foundation for Development Economics and Dept of Economics, University of Groningen.
Jepma, C. and M. Quist (1986) 'The Direct Impact of Foreign Aid on Trade: The Case of the Netherlands', *EADI Bulletin*, vol. 1, pp. 29–45.
Kmenta, J. (1990) *Elements of Econometrics* (New York: Macmillan).
McGillivray, M. and E. Oczkowski (1992) 'A Two-part Sample Selection Model of British Bilateral Foreign Aid Allocation', *Applied Economics*, vol. 24, pp. 1311–19.
McGillivray, M. and H. White (1993) 'Explanatory Studies of Aid Allocation among Developing Countries', ISS Working Paper No. 148, The Hague.
May R., D. Schumacher and M. Malek (1989) *Overseas Aid: The Impact on Britain and Germany* (Brighton: Wheatsheaf).
Melitz, J. and P. Messerlin (1987) 'Export Credit Subsidies', *Economic Policy*, vol. 4, pp. 149–75.
Morrissey, O. (1992a) 'Bilateral Aid to Africa and Structural Adjustment Loans: Conflict or Consistency', in C. Milner and A. Rayner (eds), *Policy Adjustment in Africa* (London: Macmillan), pp. 133–47.
Morrissey, O. (1992b) 'EC Aid and Trade Relations with Africa: A Preliminary Analysis', CREDIT Research Paper No. 92/1, University of Nottingham.
Morrissey, O. (1993) 'The Mixing of Aid and Trade Policies', *The World Economy*, vol. 16, no. 1, pp. 69–84.
Morrissey, O., B. Smith and E. Horesh (1992) *British Aid and International Trade* (Buckingham: Open University Press).
Mosley, P., J. Hudson and S. Horrell (1987) 'Aid, the Public Sector and the Market in Less Developed Countries', *Economic Journal*, vol. 97, pp. 616–41.
Norsa, A. (1988) 'Italy', in Strassmann and Wells (eds), pp. 86–103.
Strassmann, W. and J. Wells (1988) *The Global Construction Industry* (London: Unwin and Hyman).
White, K. (1993) *SHAZAM Econometrics Computer Program: User's Reference Manual Version 7.0* (London: McGraw-Hill).

5
The Credibility Problem and the Speed of Trade Liberalization: Modelling the Costs of Speculative Behaviour with an Application to Kenya

Ritva Reinikka

Introduction

The failure of import-substitution to sustain growth has made unilateral (as opposed to reciprocal bargaining) trade liberalization commonplace in developing countries. A reduction in import restrictions is a standard condition for external financial assistance, often less willingly implemented by the recipients. The basic premise of this chapter is that the long-term benefits arising from a removal of permanent protection of import-competing industries[1] outweigh the costs associated with liberalization.[2] The analysis will focus on the side-effects should the liberalization lack credibility. These side-effects inflict additional adjustment costs and, more importantly, may endanger the survival of the liberalization process itself. We shall examine whether the adverse side-effects can be mitigated by gradualism: that is, a slower pace of implementation of the reform. Furthermore, we shall model different types of welfare cost that can arise from an undesired response by private agents who are uncertain about the permanence of the reform. As there are few empirical studies concerning the credibility problem in trade liberalization,[3] and none of them examines the issue in African economies, we shall also analyze the extent to which speculation, induced by a lack of credibility, took place when import controls were relaxed in Kenya, making the reforms fragile and resulting in their abandonment.[4]

The rest of the chapter is organized as follows. The next section contains a discussion on the implications of the credibility problem on the speed of liberalization, and the following section will develop three simple models to capture the consumption and production costs created by incredibility. New features relative to the existing literature on the consumption costs (for example, Calvo 1987, 1988) are an explicit inclusion of uncertainty into the model and that of unavailability of consumer credits to finance speculative action. Stocks of importables, if accumulated, must be financed by consuming less of the exportable good. The latter adaptation makes the model more suitable for the analysis of African economies with rationed credit markets. On the production side, we shall first examine how reallocation of capital is affected by uncertainty. Thereafter, we shall look at how uncertainty about the future returns to capital affects the investors' decisions when foreign savings are not available but they have an option of acquiring other assets, such as inventories of importables, until uncertainty concerning returns from physical investment has been resolved. In order to determine the social cost incurred because of non-optimal consumption and output decisions, the case where private agents anticipate a policy reversal will be compared with its perfect-credibility counterfactual.

Then, in the next section, we shall analyze speculative behaviour in conjunction with Kenyan liberalization episodes since the mid-1970s. Four episodes are distinguished on the basis of changes in trade policy instruments. We shall also calculate two quantitative trade policy indices, the implicit tariff and the ratio of total private consumption to consumption of imports, in order to determine whether or not the four episodes surface at the aggregate level – that is, whether the trade regime became any more liberal after a series of relaxations and subsequent tightening of import controls. Changes in external reserves will be used to determine credibility of the episodes.

Two hypotheses will be tested with Kenyan data. First, we shall examine how uncertainty concerning the permanence of a more liberal trade policy affects the size of inventories of importable goods held by private agents. The null hypothesis is that inventories of imported consumer durables and storable intermediate goods go up shortly before private agents anticipate that the reform will be reversed. This is because the expected gain from holding stocks goes up when it is anticipated that the reform cannot be sustained and the price of importables will increase. For consumers, it does not matter whether the future price increase is caused by depreciation, or by a reimposition of previous trade restrictions. The price of importables is temporarily low, inducing inventory accumulation, or intertemporal substitution in consumption. For investors, future policy *does* matter, determining their preferred sector of investment. Our second hypothesis is that uncertainty about future policies makes investors wait and accumulate inventories of importables – in the absence of access to foreign savings – rather than invest in physical plant, or low-yielding domestic financial assets.

Gradualism versus big bang when reform is not credible

There are two necessary conditions for credibility in trade liberalization. First, the reform has to be compatible with macroeconomic policies, such as fiscal, monetary and exchange-rate policy. Second, it has to be perceived to be time-consistent by the private sector. The sufficient conditions are much more difficult to predict. Even if the necessary conditions are being met, there can be a continuum of other reasons that create a credibility problem, such as the number of years to the election, or an expected shift in the balance of political power.

Even if both the necessary and sufficient conditions for credibility are being met – that is, the reform is credible – there are certain cases where gradualism can be superior to an abrupt removal of trade restrictions. Employment and income distribution considerations, for example, may make the government favour gradualism. Unemployment obviously has an adverse effect on welfare, but its emergence and the associated short-term costs may also reduce the chance of the reform's survival. The extent to which unemployment goes up will be affected by characteristics of different sectors, mobility of factors and speed of the reform. If, for example, the import-substituting sector is very capital-intensive and the export sector labour-intensive, then employment is likely to be less severely affected, even if the reform is strong and fast. The notion of labour mobility can have different interpretations. On the one hand, immobility can refer to a low quit rate. Then unemployment may not rise very much, despite a reduced output price in the import-competing sector. Workers will accept lower wages if the propensity to hire in the exportable sector is smaller than the quit rate. On the other hand, immobility may refer to sector-specificity of the labour force. Then labour would neither be substituted for capital, nor hired by the other sectors, and the shed labour would remain unemployed. Finally, the government may be more sensitive to high peaks of unemployment than to its persistence at lower levels – that is, to the lost person-years – and would, therefore, favour gradualism. The welfare cost, however, comes from the loss of production, which depends on both the duration and level of unemployment.[5]

The main short-run impact of trade liberalization on income distribution arises from its effect on employment. In the absence of compensation mechanisms, the unemployed will suffer the largest income loss. In the case of macro incompatible reform, for example, a reduction in tariffs without depreciation, lay-offs can be expected due to a sudden fall in profitability of the import-substituting sector. The severity of unemployment depends on the ability of the export sector to expand and to absorb labour. If compatibility is maintained by depreciation, the import-competing sector will not reduce employment immediately. The export sector becomes more profitable and will instead bid labour away from the other sectors, making the labour relocation less painful. This is, of course, true in a highly aggregate model only. When protection is not uniform, the sub-sectors will be affected differently. Owners of other (sector-specific) factors in the manufacture of exportables and in agriculture will benefit from the dismantling of protection. If the export sector is labour intensive, the long-run effect is likely to be increased demand for labour, higher wages, and a higher share of labour, in GNP.[6]

In the second-best situations the policy-maker can mitigate the capital market distortion (created, for example, by financial repression) temporarily by adopting a gradual rather than an abrupt reform. The reason being that, once trade liberalization is perfectly credible, a temporary retention of the tariff induces more savings than would be the case in abrupt liberalization (Edwards and van Wijnbergen, 1986). The welfare gain results from the expected fall in the future price level, thus increasing current savings and relaxing the capital constraint. The question remains, however, whether a policy instrument other than trade reform would be more appropriate in bringing about the required change in the price level. Similarly, in the presence of a temporary labour market distortion, a temporary retention of the tariff mitigates the adverse effects of the distortion (Reinikka-Soininen, 1990).

Let us now examine whether the absence of credibility makes a gradual reform more desirable from the viewpoint of welfare than an instantaneous removal of implicit or explicit tariffs (see, for example, Froot, 1988). Assume that exchange-rate management is politically constrained, as in many African economies, so that the necessary conditions for credible trade reforms are not being met. A compensating devaluation is therefore prevented, and relaxation of quantitative import restrictions becomes incompatible. Abrupt liberalization reduces the domestic price of importables, and thereby the demand for money, more than does a gradual reform. An excess supply of money leads to a balance-of-payments deficit unless the money supply is reduced, or the demand for money is maintained by depreciation. In the absence of devaluation, a gradual reform may prolong the depletion time of reserves, but cannot prevent it from happening eventually. When a slow depreciation is politically feasible but a quantum devaluation is not, then gradualism is superior to abrupt liberalization.

In Africa, trade liberalization typically involves the removal of binding quotas and other quantitative restrictions, so that the corresponding implicit tariff levels may be unknown and far from being uniform. Hence, the private sector may first and foremost be sceptical about the government's ability to forecast what would be the appropriate amount of devaluation to sustain the reduction in protection. In this case, gradual liberalization may be superior to an abrupt one, even when combined with a relatively large initial devaluation. Gradual reductions in protection will enable the government to reach a new equilibrium without the uncertainty that depreciation might turn out to be too small relative to reduction in the implicit tariff. External aid could then be used to compensate those who lose through devaluation. Gradualism results in a temporary balance-of-payments surplus and guarantees that the reform cannot become incompatible.

When trade policy is used as the adjusting macroeconomic variable, the government will liberalize trade in the face of a positive external shock to the economy, and tighten trade policy when the shock is negative (Bevan *et al.*, 1990a). If private agents recognize that the shock is temporary, then they know that liberalization will be reversed when the export boom is over. The only uncertainty is the duration of the boom. Hence, in the case of endogenous trade policy, a slow pace in liberalization is as incredible to the public as the 'big bang'. As will be shown in the next section, the social cost of consumer speculation is, however, likely to be smaller under gradualism, whereas the supply response in favour of the export sector is unlikely to take place in either case.

A big bang which is made compatible by virtue of temporary foreign aid temporarily cheapens imports, giving rise to speculative private behaviour. Foreign aid can, in fact, play a dual role in trade liberalization. First, it may enhance the credibility of a large reform when, for political reasons, currency depreciation cannot be of equal magnitude. Nevertheless, consumers still have an incentive to accumulate stocks of importables. Investors instead, convinced that tariffs can be permanently kept at lower levels thanks to external aid which allows politically feasible gradual depreciation, will, as expected by the policy-maker, shift resources to the export sector. The only uncertainty that remains is whether consumer speculation will drain the reserves so as to erode credibility and adversely affect investors' confidence. Second, aid can be a source of time-inconsistency and actually make the private sector suspicious about the permanence of the reform (Rodrik, 1989b). Liberal trade policies are expected to last as long as aid flows in, but are anticipated to be reversed once aid has dried up, particularly if no major political changes accompany the reform. The political cost for the government of sustaining the reform after the aid flow has stopped is perceived as being too high. In this case, an aided trade liberalization is likely to be harmful, by giving rise to speculative behaviour by both consumers and investors.

We can identify other reasons than foreign aid for the time-consistency problem. One way of analyzing it is to distinguish different types of governments whose characteristics or actions give rise to incredibility. First, a truly liberalizing government may face a suspicious private sector which perceives a positive subjective probability of reform collapse because of past events (Calvo, 1987,1988; van Wijnbergen, 1985). If the welfare costs of speculation are higher than those created by the trade restrictions themselves, a strictly Pigovian government would adjust its optimal policy to account for the private sector's behaviour, and maintain tariffs to mitigate the adverse effect of incredibility. Second, time-inconsistency may arise in the presence of a redistributive government (Staiger and Tabellini, 1987). The public knows that the government, despite its policy announcement in favour of free trade, will subsequently have an incentive to impose a tariff and distribute the receipts to its favoured group. A gradual approach may in fact confirm the belief held by the private sector that the reform will be a temporary one, because the costs of a large liberalization – in the form of increased unemployment, for example – may be too high for the redistributive government to bear. Third, time-inconsistency can result from the conflicting goals of the public and the government. Because of its self-concerned spending, the government is unable to commit itself to future policies (Daveri, 1989). Radical fiscal changes will be needed to enhance credibility of the reform. Fourth, there may be uncertainty as to whether the new government in power is a true liberalizer or merely redistributive (Engel and Kletzer, 1987). In other words, the public is uncertain whether or not the time-consistency problem will arise. A large reform helps to signal to the public that the government is indeed a true liberalizer.

In the next section we shall model welfare costs which result from a lack of credibility as private agents anticipate that the reform will be reversed. The issue of speed of liberalization will be discussed further in conjunction with each model.

Modelling welfare costs created by incredibility

When assessing the welfare costs, incredibility in trade liberalization may be viewed as a distortion in the future product market. It is useful to distinguish consumption costs on the one hand and production costs on the other. In some cases the social cost is created by speculative action and in others by a lack of desirable action. The former type of costs in consumption can take the form of non-optimal intertemporal substitution in consumption, or accumulation of stocks of durable goods during the liberal period (Calvo, 1987, 1988). A representative household maximizes its consumption over time, either by choosing a higher level of consumption during the liberal period, or by choosing constant consumption and the optimal level of stocks. The stocks must be larger and the optimal depletion time longer when the differential between intertemporal prices is sizeable, or when the probability of collapse is high. A gradual reform obviously induces a smaller accumulation of stocks at a time compared to an abrupt removal of tariffs, but there may be several occasions when stocks of a smaller size are bought, adding to the total welfare costs.

One can think of at least one instance where inaction in consumption is a source of welfare cost. As the rationale for trade liberalization is to increase real income, the expected permanent income will go up, increasing the households' present consumption, provided consumers have access to credit to finance the increased consumption against their future income. But if private agents consider that the reform will be short-lived instead of permanent, then the welfare-improving consumption effect will not materialize. In other words, inaction on the part of consumers implies a welfare loss in the form of lower-than-optimal current consumption.

On the production side, uncertainty about the duration of trade reform leads to inaction and partly or fully prevents the desired reallocation of resources. Rodrik (1989a) applies Dixit's (1989) hysteresis model to the analysis of interaction of the credibility problem and adjustment costs created by exit and entry. Although the net return to capital in the export sector is higher than in the import-substituting sector, private agents must also be compensated for a possible policy reversal. Two equilibria are possible: a 'good' one with a high degree of credibility and investment, and a 'bad' one with a lack of credibility and low investment. Clearly signalling its intentions by a big bang reform, the government can induce private behaviour such that the economy will end up in the 'good' equilibrium. Hence, adjustment costs do not provide a case for a gradual reform.

Private agents may also postpone investment decisions and accumulate foreign currencies until uncertainty has been resolved (van Wijnbergen, 1985). When uncertainty prevails, it is better to remain liquid than to undertake a project that is only marginally attractive under certainty. Uninvested capital has an option value and it is not worth exercising the option until it is deeper in the money. In the absence of access to foreign savings, investors may prefer to hold domestic financial assets over physical investments. It is also possible that inventories dominate the domestic financial asset as the option-preserving asset for the investor (Collier and Gunning, 1992). The social return of holding inventories is zero, while the social opportunity cost in the form of tied-up foreign exchange can be very high indeed.

A model for consumption costs in the absence of credit

In this section a simple two-period framework will be set up to analyze the welfare costs to consumption of incredible trade liberalization. We shall abstract from static gains from trade and concentrate on assessing the adverse effects of speculative behaviour. More precisely, consumption costs are created by a deviation from the optimal consumption path, or by a deviation from the optimal purchases relative to consumption, that is, accumulation of stocks. As was discussed earlier, temporary cheapening of imports is possible when trade liberalization is either time-inconsistent, macro incompatible or made compatible by virtue of foreign aid.

Two models by Calvo (1987, 1988) are our starting point. The former model analyzes non-optimal intertemporal substitution resulting from an expected future change in the price level. The latter imposes constant consumption over time but allows for storability of importables. While relying on Calvo's basic intuitions regarding the sources of welfare costs when liberalizations are perceived by the private sector to be temporary, our model deviates in two major respects. First, uncertainty concerning sustainability of the reform will be introduced. In both of the original models the public is assumed to be perfectly certain that the reform will collapse at time *T*. Second, in many low-income countries, particularly in Africa, consumer credit is not readily available. Unrestricted access to the credit market with horizontal cost of borrowing may reflect the realities of Latin America, and perhaps even those of Franc Zone African economies, but is definitely less applicable to Eastern and Southern African countries, where such credit markets are absent. In sum, we would expect that inclusion of uncertainty and restricted consumer credit would make some of the unrealistic predictions of Calvo's models more plausible.

Let us assume a two-sector economy, where both exportable and importable goods are consumed. The government adopts a liberal import policy in period one, but private agents are uncertain about the permanence of the reform and believe that liberalization will be reversed with probability π in period two, so that the pre-liberalization tariff τ will be reimposed.[7] If the product of the tariff and the subjective probability of reversal is sufficiently high, consumers will buy stocks of the durable importable good during the liberal period. They do not have access to capital markets, however, which implies that the accumulation of stocks must be financed by consuming less of the exportable good during the first period.

The private sector is represented by a single household that has an additively separable utility function, u. The marginal cost of stock-holding is now not horizontal but increasing, since any new unit of stocks costs the consumer more in terms of forgone consumption of the exportable good. Purchases of the importable and exportable good are denoted by c_i and x_i $(i = 1, 2)$ respectively, y_i stands for income, and s for stocks. We can think of s as being an asset with zero rate of return but with a positive capital gain. For the exportable good, purchases equal consumption, whereas for the importable good, purchases and consumption differ in both periods. To find the optimal size of the stock we can formulate the following intertemporal utility maximization problem for the representative household:

$$\max_{c_1 x_1 c_2 x_1^s} \quad u_1(c_1 - s, x_1) + \beta u_2(c_2 + s, x_2) \tag{5.1}$$

$$s.t. \;\; c_1 + x_1 \leq y_1; \;\; p_2 c_2 + x_2 \leq \bar{y}_2; \;\; c_1, x_1, c_2, x_2 > 0; \;\; s > 0; \;\; 0 < \pi < 1.$$

The price of the exportable good is determined by the world market, and can be normalized to equal unity. The same applies to the importable good in period one, whereas in the second period its price p_2 is equal to $1 + \tau$ $(= p)$ with probability π, and to unity with probability $(1 - \pi)$. The domestic discount factor then becomes $\beta[\pi\,(1 + \tau) + (1 - \pi)] < \beta$, where β is the world discount factor. If we think beyond the two periods, it is easy to see that the domestic discount factor decreases over time, since the expected price of good c goes up. Because consumers substitute more and more intertemporally, we can conclude that the resulting welfare loss is a monotonically increasing function of the duration of uncertain liberalization. Period two income is given by:

$$\bar{y}_2 = y_2 + \pi \tau c_2^{\pi} \tag{5.2}$$

where c_2^{π} stands for the period two consumption in the case where the reform has been aborted. We assume, however, that private agents do not recognize this but treat the period two income $\overline{y}_2$ as being exogenously given when they choose their optimal consumption. In other words, income is exogenous to the demand system, while it would be endogenous in the general equilibrium which includes the production side.

We can solve the problem by using dynamic programming. This yields us the optimal stocks as a function of income y, the discount factor β, tariffs τ and the probability of collapse π:

$$s = s(y_1, \overline{y}_2, \beta, \tau, \pi) \qquad (5.3)$$

Let us assume an additively separable utility function of simple iso-elastic form:

$$\max_{c_1 x_1 c_2 x_2^s} [(c_1 - s)x_1]^{1-\alpha}/(1-\alpha) + \beta[(c_2 + s)x_2]^{1-\alpha}/(1-\alpha) \qquad (5.4)$$

For the second period, the household solves the following problem:

$$\max_{c_2 x_2} [(c_2 + s)x_2]^{1-\alpha}/(1-\alpha) \qquad s.t.\ \ \overline{y}_2 \geq p_2 c_2 + x_2 \qquad (5.5)$$

The optimal purchases of the two goods are:

$$x_2 = \overline{y}_2/2 + p_2 s/2 \qquad c_2 = \overline{y}_2/2p_2 - s/2 \qquad (5.6)$$

We are able to compute the value of the objective function as a function of s for each of the two possible prices of importable goods. When the trade reform persist ($p_2 = 1$), the optimal value is $\beta(\overline{y}_2/2 + s/2)^{2(1-\alpha)}/(1-\alpha)$, while if it is aborted ($p_2 = 1 + \tau = p$) the optimal value is $\beta p^{1-\alpha}(\overline{y}_2/2p + s/2)^{2(1-\alpha)}/(1-\alpha)$.

For period one, the representative household solves the problem:

$$\max_{c_1 x_1} [(c_1 - s)x_1]^{1-\alpha}/(1-\alpha) \qquad s.t.\ \ c_1 + x_1 \leq y_1 \qquad (5.7)$$

This gives us the optimal purchases:

$$x_1 = y_1/2 - s/2 \qquad c_1 = y_1/2 + s/2 \qquad (5.8)$$

The optimal stock of durables can then be derived by solving (5.9). Note that consumers are assumed to discount future consumption at the world rate – that is, they would rather stock than substitute intertemporally.

$$\max_s\ (y_1 - s)^{2(1-\alpha)} + \pi\beta p^{1-\alpha}(\overline{y}_2/p + s)^{2(1-\alpha)} + (1-\pi)\beta(\overline{y}_2 + s)^{2(1-\alpha)} \qquad (5.9)$$

The equation we obtain from the optimal stock cannot, however, be solved explicitly:

$$\pi\beta p^{1-\alpha}(y_2/p+s)^{1-2\alpha}+(1-\pi)\beta(y_2+s)^{1-2\alpha}-(y_1-s)^{1-2\alpha}=0 \qquad (5.10)$$

How can we interpret this result? There are several forces at work when a decision concerning the optimal stock is taken, and the size of the stock results from interaction of these forces. First, the presence of the discount rate β (< 1) implies, in general, a preference for consuming now rather than later. The optimal stock would then be negative, but we have eliminated that possibility, so that s is either positive, or equal to zero ($s > 0$), depending on the combination of parameter values. Simulation of Equation (5.10) shows that the higher is β, the larger is the stock s. Second, the consumer is willing to transfer income from periods of high income to those when income is lower (consumption smoothing). In order for there to be a positive stock, income in period one must exceed the present value of period two income. Third, the importable good is expected to be more expensive in the second period, which gives rise to storage. By simulating Equation (5.10) we can see that s is an increasing function of p, τ and π. Finally, the higher the elasticity of marginal utility α, *ceteris paribus*, the smaller the stock s.

Let us illustrate the magnitude of welfare costs with an example. Assuming that the elasticity of marginal utility α is 0.75, the world discount factor β is 0.95, a collapse is perceived to be equally as likely as the persistence of the reform ($\pi = 0.5$), the implicit tariff is 100 per cent[8] ($\tau = 1$, or $p = 2$), and $y_1 = 100$, we can derive the optimal stock from Equation (5.10). Assuming, further, that the representative household expects its period two income to be 110 units because of the anticipated transfer from tariff revenue, inventories of imported durables at the end of period one will be 16.2 units (or 16.2 per cent of GNP), and consumption in period one would be 41.9 units of each good.

In period two, when private agents realize that the reform will not be reversed (and income is 100 units as there are no transfers), purchases of imports will be 41.9 units while their consumption is 58.1. As to the exportable good, 58.1 units will be purchased and consumed. In the absence of a credibility problem, there would be no accumulation of inventories, and income would be evenly spent on both goods, that is 50:50 in each period. Comparison of the results under perfect and imperfect credibility is summarized in Table 5.1.

We can now calculate the welfare loss by inserting the optimal consumptions into the utility function. The social cost of inventory

Table 5.1 Comparison of results under perfect and imperfect credibility

	Certainty	*Uncertainty*	
c_1	50	58.1	(purchases)
c_1^{-s}	50	41.9	(consumption)
x_1	50	41.9	
c_2	50	41.9	(purchases)
c_2^{-s}	50	58.1	(consumption)
x_2	50	58.1	
s	–	16.2	

Notes: $\tau = 1$; $\alpha = 0.75$; $\beta = 0.95$; $\pi = 0.5$; $y_1 = 100$; $\bar{y}_2 = 110$.

accumulation is found to be fairly low: that is, 0.5 per cent of the total attainable utility under credibility. Instead of limiting our analysis to just one example, more simulations could be carried out to see how the consumption costs are affected by different π's as well as by different values of the other parameters. None the less, our simple example conveys the basic idea of how consumer behaviour changes in the presence of uncertainty and storability of imports.

It is useful to compare the predictions of the above model with those of the perfect capital market and one consumer good version. Depending on the level of tariff, the probability of collapse and the interest rate, the optimal stock in the latter case would either be zero or the entire period two consumption. In the model without a credit market, however, the interest rate becomes endogenous, and we are able to derive an interior solution to the stock-holding problem within the second period. The predictions for the level of stocks relative to GNP and the welfare cost also become more realistic. Despite the fact that our model is very simple, consumption in period two comes from both stocks and purchases. Incredibility increases purchases of the importable good in period one and reduces them in period two, but will not drive them to zero. At the aggregate level, some agents in the economy typically have access to capital and some do not. The latter group will have to make purchases in both periods, while the former can accumulate stocks during the liberal period. The main idea behind Calvo's model (1988) is to show how considerable openness in capital markets can be harmful when trade liberalization lacks credibility. Our model is more applicable to Sub-Saharan Africa, where consumer credit is restricted but private agents still accumulate speculative inventories of durables during a more liberal trade regime.

A model for uncertainty and reallocation of capital

When examining the social cost created by uncertainty about the persistence of the trade policy reform for factor reallocation, we shall make use of Rodrik's (1989a) intuition that the reform must be large enough not only to make the returns in the two sectors comparable but also to compensate for the adjustment costs as well as for the possibility that the capital has to be shifted back in case of reversal. Similarly, if labour movements are costly, its relocation is curtailed by uncertainty. Our model differs from Rodrik's in two respects: the entire supply side is modelled explicitly, and the magnitude of production loss caused by the perceived subjective probability of reform default is determined by using a perfect-credibility counterfactual.

Consider a two-sector model for a small open economy which produces an importable good c and an exportable good x, the former being protected by tariffs τ. Good x is the numeraire, and the world prices of both goods are normalized to equal unity. Other factors than capital are constant and kept in the background. Hence the fixed capital stock K stands for all factors that can be moved at a cost across the sectors. Production can be modelled by means of a revenue function $R(P, M)$, where P is the price vector, M is the amount of capital allocated in the export sector and $(K - M)$ is that in the protected sector. F and G are standard Cobb–Douglas production functions for exports and imports, respectively:

$$R(P, M) = F(M) + G(K - M) \tag{5.11}$$

where $F(M) = F_0 M^{\delta}$ and $G(K - M) = G_0(K - M)^{\gamma}$. We are interested in the total cost of inaction caused by lack of credibility, and shall, therefore, examine the effects on total allocations between the two sectors. Trade liberalization is assumed to reduce the output price of the import-substituting sector from $p_c = 1 + \tau$ to $p_c = 1$. Entrepreneurs, however, are uncertain whether the change will be permanent, or whether the policy might be sustained and protection will be brought back. The representative capital owner has to decide whether or not to shift capital to the export sector.

The value of capital when none of it is shifted to the export sector in response to the reform can be expressed:

$$V_o = \left[R(1, \overline{M}) + \pi(V_o^R - V_o)\right]/\rho \tag{5.12}$$

where $\overline{M}$ is the initial allocation of capital, $(V_o^R - V_o)$ stands for the capital gain in case of policy reversal and ρ is the interest rate. Solving for V_o and substituting $V_o^R = R(1 + \tau, \overline{M})/\rho$ into Equation (5.12), we obtain:

$$V_o = (\rho + \pi)^{-1}\left[R(1, \overline{M}) + \pi R(1 + r, \overline{M})/\rho\right] \tag{5.13}$$

The value of shifting part of the capital to the export sector can be expressed:

$$V_1 = \left[R(1, \overline{M}_n) - \pi(V_1 - V_1^R)\right]/\rho \tag{5.14}$$

Where M_n is the new capital allocation after the reform and $(V_1 - V_1^R)$ denotes the capital loss in case of reversal to those who have responded to the reform. When the possible reversal is large so that a shift back is expected, the value of the capital stock is:

$$V_1^L = (\rho + \pi)^{-1}\left[R(1, M_n) + \pi R(1 + \tau, \overline{M})/\rho - \pi\theta(M_n - \overline{M})\right] \tag{5.15}$$

where θ denotes the cost of moving a unit of capital back to the protected sector. Note that there will be no shift back if the reform persists. We assume that in case of shifting back all capital will return to its original sector.

To make it worthwhile for capital to relocate, the net value of real assets in the export sector must exceed that in the import-substituting sector:

$$V_1^L - \epsilon(M_n - \overline{M}) \geq V_o \tag{5.16}$$

where ϵ denotes the adjustment cost of a unit of capital moved from the protected to the export sector. By substituting Equations (5.13) and (5.15) into Equation (5.16) we obtain:

$$R(1, M_n) \geq R(1, \overline{M}) + [\rho\epsilon + \pi(\epsilon + \theta)]\,(M_n - \overline{M}) \tag{5.17}$$

According to the above inequality, the revenue created by the new allocation of capital must exceed the sum of the revenue created by capital remaining in the import-substituting sector, adjustment costs and compensation for a possible reversal.

Let us further illustrate this result by a simple example, assuming that $\delta = 1/2$ and $\gamma = 1/2$:

$$F(M) = 2M^{1/2}; \quad G(M) = 2(K - M)^{1/2} \tag{5.18}$$

If we assume that τ is equal to unity (that is, the (uniform) implicit tariff rate is 100 per cent), then the initial (optimal) allocation of capital between the two sectors is 1/5K in the export sector and 4/5K in the import-substituting industries. In case of a perfectly credible abrupt trade liberalization without adjustment costs, the optimal allocation of capital would be 1/2K in both sectors. Let us further assume that the fixed capital stock is 100. Then the initial allocation is 20 units (or per cent) in the export sector and 80 units in the import-substituting sector, and the optimal allocation in the absence of adjustment costs and uncertainty could be 50 units in both sectors.

It is straightforward to calculate what the optimal allocation in the presence of adjustment costs but without uncertainty would be. The net present value of profits can be written:

$$\Pi(M^*) = 2(M^*)^{1/2}/\rho + 2(K - M^*)^{1/2}/\rho - \epsilon(M^* - \overline{M}) \qquad (5.19)$$

Suppose the real interest rate is 2.5 per cent, and the sunk cost associated with a move of one unit of capital to the production of exportables is 15 per cent of the cost of installed capital ($\epsilon = 0.15$). Then profits will be maximized when 28.7 units of capital are moved to the export sector, or the amount of capital in the export sector M^* is 48.7 units and that in the import–substituting sector ($K - M^*$) is 51.3 units. In other words, the presence of adjustment cost ($\epsilon = 0.15$) prevents only 1.3 units of capital from being reallocated in response to the reform. This is 4.3 per cent of the total amount of capital that would have been shifted without mobility being costly. The higher the adjustment cost, however, the smaller is the amount of capital shifted because of the reform.

By maximizing Equation (5.20) with respect to M_n we obtain the entrepreneur's optimal response to the reform in the presence of uncertainty concerning sustainability of the reform:

$$\max_{M_n} \; 2M_n^{1/2} + 2(K - M_n)^{1/2} - [\rho\epsilon + \pi(\epsilon + \theta)](M_n - \overline{M}) \qquad (5.20)$$

Let us assume the same entry cost as before, an exit cost of 10 per cent of the value of installed capital ($\theta = 0.1$) when the move is reversed, and a low probability of collapse, such as 10 per cent ($\pi = 0.1$). Then 20.1 units of capital will be shifted to production of exportables. If π is 20 per cent, only 12.5 units will be shifted. An increase in the likelihood of default will eventually prevent all relocation of capital. When π is 0.5, for example, or collapse is considered to be as likely as success, no capital at all will be shifted away from the formerly protected sector. Note that sufficiently high adjustment costs will prevent relocation of capital also at lower probabilities than $\pi = 0.5$.

Summarizing, the higher the probability of collapse, the less will capital reallocate in response to the reform. This implies that, at higher probabilities, a large reform – that is, abrupt rather than gradual – is required to induce investors to respond to it. If capital is sector-specific so that adjustment costs are relatively high, even low probabilities become prohibitive. Because of incredibility, relocation of capital in favour of the export sector is not sufficient from the social viewpoint. The total loss of production over time can be calculated as the difference between the net present value of output under perfect credibility and that under uncertainty:

	$\tau = 0.1$	$\tau = 0.2$	$\tau = 0.5$
Loss of output	0.4%	1.4%	4.7%

The largest possible welfare cost (4.7 per cent) in terms of lost output is somewhat higher than the average empirical calculations of costs of protection relative to GNP. Note that it is not directly comparable to the consumption cost derived earlier, the latter being expressed in terms of utility units.

A model for deferral of investment with stock accumulation

In some cases, such as during temporary export booms, deferring investment by means of foreign savings is likely to be beneficial, both from the private and the social points of view. Unlike an increase in permanent income, transient income is saved to a large extent which temporarily loosens financial constraints in a controlled economy. An investment boom results, causing a fall in the rates of return and pushing up the cost of capital goods, particularly if the private sector is not allowed to hold foreign assets (Bevan *et al.*, 1990b). Deferral combined with access to foreign savings would then even out the investment boom for a longer period of time, preventing a large fall in the rental to capital.

Our last model will address a situation where deferral of investment is detrimental from the social point of view, there being no positive external shock and investment boom in the economy. We shall restrict the analysis to depreciation investment, following a trade reform which is perceived to lack credibility. A representative investor is assumed not to have access to foreign savings but can invest either in physical plant in the export- or import-competing sector, in a low-yield but riskless domestic financial asset, or accumulate inventories of importable goods as foreign exchange is available for imports.[9] Inventories are preferred if their expected return exceeds the domestic interest rate, or the expected return to physical capital, adjusted by a risk premium if the investor is risk-averse.

Van Wijnbergen (1985) derives an option value to foreign exchange when investment in physical capital is irreversible and risk-neutral entrepreneurs are uncertain whether or not the liberal trade policy will last. Unlike van Wijnbergen, we assume that the supply of foreign savings is restricted, but foreign currency can be obtained for imports. This is a more relevant assumption for Sub-Saharan Africa where capital controls are usually retain in trade liberalizations but foreign exchange rationing is relaxed for imports. When the real interest rate on domestic financial assets is low (or negative), investors prefer to accumulate stocks of importables as a means of deferring investment. At the beginning of period one the government announces and implements a (large) reduction in protection of the import-substituting sector. However, private agents suspect that the reform may be reversed by the beginning of period two with the subjective probability π. We assume that investment takes effect immediately and is productive for two periods, and ignore any salvage value. The values of the different assets can then be expressed:

$$V_{IS} = r + \beta\pi r^* + \beta(1-\pi)r \tag{5.21}$$

$$V_{EP} = r^* + \beta\pi\tau + \beta(1-\pi)r^* \tag{5.22}$$

$$V_S = \beta\pi\tau + \beta r^*; \quad \beta < 1; \quad 0 < \pi < 1 \tag{5.23}$$

where r^* (r) is both the rate of return in the export sector if the reform persists (fails) and that in the import-substituting sector if the reform fails (persists), $r^* > r$. Stocks are a risky asset. The expected capital gain is denoted by $\pi\tau$. It is obtained in the beginning of period two if the reform fails, and investment in physical capital is then made in the sector that turns out to be favoured by the government policy in the beginning of period two. β (<1) is the discount factor.

It is easy to see from Equation (5.21)–(5.23) that, with all probabilities π, it is more profitable to invest in the export sector rather than in import-substitution. At probabilities lower than the critical level $\pi_c = r^*/\beta(r^* + \tau - r)$, there will be no deferral of investment, and investment in physical capital in the export sector will be chosen as anticipated by the liberalizing government. At π_c, however, the investor becomes indifferent between deferral and the export sector, and when the probability of collapse is higher than π_c, all investment will be deferred until uncertainty has been resolved. If the reform persists in period two, funds released from stocks will be invested in the export sector, whereas in the case of reversal, in the import-substituting sector. Assume, for example, that $\beta = 0.9091$, $r^* = 0.18$, $r = 0$ and $\tau = 1$, or the implicit tariff rate is 100 per cent. Then the critical probability to induce accumulation of stocks is as low as 17 per cent. At low probabilities ($\pi < \pi_c$) the welfare cost would be zero, since the private investor acts according to the policy-maker's (truly liberalizing) intentions. At π_c the cost jumps up, since all depreciation investment is deferred by accumulating stocks which yield a zero social return. The social cost of holding stocks in period one instead of investing in the export sector is then δKr^*, where δ denotes depreciation and K is the capital stock.

Gradual liberalization is likely to make inventories less attractive assets, so that the critical value of π_c is higher, and the range of probabilities, where investment in the export sector is chosen, expands. In this case, a gradual reform would be superior to an abrupt one. There is, however, another consideration against the slow speed of reform. If protection is only slightly reduced, the return to investment in the export sector may not increase enough to make the sector worthwhile investing in at all.

Summarizing, consumption costs are an increasing function of the subjective probability of collapse π with a jump. The rate of increase, however, does not remain the same throughout the interval $0 \leq \pi \leq 1$. Of the two components, sub-optimal intertemporal substitution is monotonically increasing in π, whereas at low probabilities, speculative holding of stocks is likely to be zero. When π reaches a critical level π_c^1 there is a jump when a stock is purchased, given the levels of tariff and interest rate. Hence, below π_c^1 there are no costs related to inventories (but there is sub-optimal intertemporal substitution) and above it the cost of holding stocks increases monotonically.

On the production side, when π increases, the anticipated return to capital in the export sector relative to the formerly protected sector becomes less attractive. The incentive to relocate resources diminishes, increasing the welfare cost monotonically in π up to another critical value π_c^2 at which the welfare cost reaches its maximum level, and thereafter no factor reallocation takes place. As to deferral of investment, at low probabilities, given the level of tariffs, the social cost would be zero, since the private investor is likely to act according to the policy-maker's intentions and to invest in exportables. At a third critical value of the subjective probability π_c^3 the cost jumps up, since all investment is deferred by accumulating stocks which yield a zero social return. When we combine the two types of social cost, a non-monotonic pattern with kinks emerges.

Government policies which aim at getting π smaller are sensitive to the ex-ante probability. Upon introduction of a reform it may be more important for the government to try and get π's down in the short term rather than worry about more distant expectations. For example, facing high immediate probabilities, the government may itself shift capital to the export sector through parastatals, or temporarily tighten the credit policy by targeting the manufacturing and commercial sectors to curtail stock accumulation.

Trade reforms and credibility in Kenya

Despite their pervasiveness, administrative controls are a relatively recent phenomenon in Kenyan trade policy. Although import licensing was first introduced in the late 1950s, and at independence the government adopted a deliberate industrial strategy based on import-substitution – a recommendation by the World Bank at the time – licensing was not then used extensively. The first balance of payments crisis in 1971 brought a clear change. It led to introduction of a number of fairly indiscriminate import quotas and foreign exchange controls, while tariffs remained subject to common external tariff policy of the East African Community. Trade policy became an endogenous instrument of macroeconomic management. Subsequent efforts in the 1970s toward relaxation of quantitative restrictions and a uniform tariff protection were undermined by the oil shock in 1974 and the simultaneous decline in the agricultural export prices, relative to the prices of imported manufactured goods. Only the coffee boom during the latter half of the 1970s make a temporary relaxation of trade restrictions possible.

All private-sector imports to Kenya require a license to receive a foreign-exchange allocation. Until 1982, imports were licensed in an *ad hoc* manner but since then have been administered according to schedules which establish explicit priorities for importables. Capital goods, raw materials and intermediate inputs are of the highest priority, with fairly easy access to licenses. Some items of relatively high priority, such as food, oil, fertilizer and so on, require technical approval from a relevant government ministry or agency but are otherwise licensed quite freely. Import–competing and consumer goods receive only a small residual allocation.

Trade policy indices

It is far from straightforward to define what constitutes a liberalization episode. A trade reform is typically a complex exercise, involving removal of, or reduction in, quantitative import restrictions, which are temporarily replaced by a tariff surcharge, a unification and subsequent reduction of tariffs, and an introduction of export incentives to make interventions in foreign trade more neutral to various sectors of the economy (Thomas and Nash, 1991). A comparative study of nineteen countries by the World Bank (Michaely *et al.*, 1991), for example, claims that it includes all liberalization episodes of a minimum duration of two years, undertaken by developing countries from the Second World War until 1984. The study, however, failed to identify an unambiguous measure or criteria common to all countries to determine when a liberalization episode began, or when an episode can be considered to have been reversed. An annual liberalization index was calculated, based partly on quantitative criteria, such as effective rate of protection, actual tariff rates, real exchange rate and so on, and partly on the judgement by the individual researcher in charge of each country study. As we show below for Kenya, different criteria, let alone judgement, yield different lengths for the same episodes. Whatever criteria may have been used in the World Bank study, the resulting geographical distribution covers countries in Latin America, Asia, the Pacific and the Mediterranean but excludes Sub-Saharan Africa.

Despite the fact that changes are made in trade policy instruments, they do not necessarily surface at the aggregate level because they may be in the opposite direction, or influenced by other policies, such as price controls, or by variations in world market prices. Bevan *et al.*, (1990b) suggest two unambiguous quantitative indices of trade policy to capture the change at the aggregate level: (i) the domestic prices of importables relative to their world price (that is the implicit tariff), or the combined effect of explicit tariffs and tariff equivalents of QRs; and (ii) the ratio of total private consumption to household consumption of imports.

Figure 5.1 depicts the two indices for Kenya. For the first index, domestic ex-factory manufacturing prices are derived by using the value of manufacturing output data and the manufacturing quantity index. The cif prices of equivalent import categories from the Customs and Excise

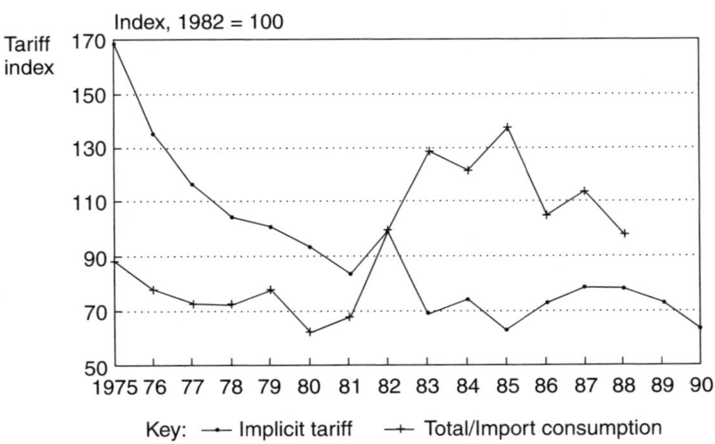

Source: Statistical Abstracts.

Figure 5.1 Trade policy indices

data are weighted by their respective shares in domestic manufacturing.[10] While food processing is an important industrial sector in Kenya, it is excluded from the implicit tariff index because its domestic ex-factory price is affected by price controls and import price by maize imports, which fluctuate from year to year. For the second index, the total private consumption is obtained from the national accounts and deflated by the lower income consumer price index (Nairobi), while the consumption of imports by households is derived from the end-use analysis of imports for home use, deflated by the non-oil import price index. The two indices are expected to be correlated for the constant exchange rate periods, such as 1975–80, when the Kenyan shilling was tied to the SDR. Since 1981 the shilling has been devalued, often concomitantly with trade liberalization, so that one can expect the latter ratio to indicate a somewhat tighter trade policy than the former.

As anticipated, the two indices exhibit a fairly similar pattern in the latter part of the 1970s, both indicating import liberalization during the coffee boom as a result of endogenous trade policy.[11] Since 1982 the indices have taken very different paths, however, as consumer imports became disproportionately discriminated against intermediate and capital goods in allocation of import licences. Hence, according to the import consumption index, trade policy was tightened in the 1980s, with the exception of a temporary relaxation of controls in 1980 and 1986 (a mini coffee boom). The index also shows liberalization in 1988, but in the absence of data it is not possible to say much about the permanence of that reform. The implicit tariff index shows a declining trend instead (that is, liberalization of trade policy) during the entire period 1975–90. Only in 1982 and 1987–8 was this trend temporarily reversed.

Because of data limitation, we are able to derive the implicit tariff and the import consumption index at annual level only. Therefore the two indices are not sufficient guides when we wish to investigate speculative behaviour in response to changes in trade policy. For example, if more than one policy change takes place during a year, they may even one another out in the annual index but still induce speculative behaviour. Hence, it is more useful to analyze discrete changes in trade policy, such as shifts in import-licensing practices or tariffs, in order to find out the extent of speculation in response to an expected policy change. Yet the quantitative indices are important as only they can tell us whether or not trade policy at the aggregate level became any more liberal after a series of relaxations and subsequent tightening of QRs over time.

Looking at policy changes, we can conclude that imports were endogenously liberalized during the coffee boom in 1976–8, when there was a temporary windfall in foreign exchange earnings. In late 1978, however, when export receipts fell substantially, tighter controls were reintroduced. Contrary to the previous practice of using trade policy as the adjusting macroeconomic variable, an exogenous trade liberalization was carried out in 1980 in order to correct the serious macroeconomic imbalance. This reform supported by temporary external aid as part of a stabilization package, included removal of import bans and non-objection certificates required from domestic producers, and a promise to shift 20 per cent of the items in the more restrictive categories to less restrictive ones each year.

Despite a complex system of QRs, the majority of imported items was not included in any of the schedules in 1980. The authorities were therefore unable to control the amount of composition of imports, following the relaxation of restrictions. In the absence of compensating devaluation, a foreign-exchange crisis ensued, and the reform was reversed before the end of the year. Failure to liberalize the existing regime led to a major reform of the import schedules, which was completed by 1982. All the items were included in the schedules, and intermediate and capital goods were prioritized with a relatively free access to foreign exchange. Import-competing and consumer goods were subject instead to stricter quotas. Another liberalization programme of the Kenyan economy was announced in 1986 (Republic of Kenya, 1986). Supported by the World Bank, the first phase of trade liberalization was implemented in 1988–9, followed by another two-year phase in 1990–1. Streamlining of the import licensing system was again abandoned shortly after the reform was launched. Emphasis has instead shifted to export expansion and diversification through improved incentives to exporters, including a more flexible exchange-rate policy and a tariff reform (Republic of Kenya, 1991a, 1991b).

As justified above, for the purpose of studying the effects of the credibility problem in trade liberalization on private behaviour, we define four episodes, based on a narrative of policy changes rather than on the two quantitative indices. The episodes are: (i) endogenous import liberalization during the coffee boom in 1976–8; (ii) exogenous import liberalization in 1980; (iii) systematic licensing introduced in 1982; and (iv) relaxation of import controls and subsequent emphasis on export promotion since 1988. The first two episodes are also captured by both quantitative indices, except for the implicit tariff, which fails to show the tightening of policy in 1979. The introduction of comprehensive schedules in 1982 is reflected as a reversal of earlier liberalization in both indices. The mini coffee boom in 1986 shows as a relaxation only in the

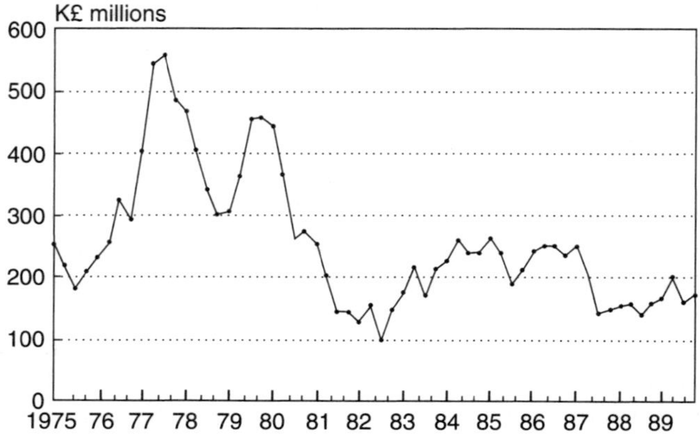

Source: Central Bank of Kenya and Statistical Abstracts, various issues.
Figure 5.2 External reserves deflated by import price index, 1976–89 (1982/IV–100)

import consumption index. The latter index also captures in 1988 reform, but the downward turn in the implicit tariff surfaces only in 1989.

Credibility of the reforms

The position of external reserves is an important indicator of the sustainability of a trade reform. Figure 5.2 depicts external reserves at the Central Bank of Kenya in 1976–89, deflated by the import price index (1982 = 100). As the latter is based on cif prices of imports in Kenyan shillings, it captures changes both in the world price of imports and in the exchange rate. It can be seen that in 1978 external reserves fell sharply, indicating that the coffee boom was coming to an end, and that the private sector correctly anticipated a reversal of liberalization and took advantage of the last opportunity of an easier access to licences. Considerable tightening of import controls in 1979 improved the reserve position.

Another fall occurred following the 1980 exogenous liberalization which, in the absence of exchange-rate adjustment, was incompatible and hence not credible. Despite external aid, a balance of payments crisis ensued. A two-month halt in the issuance of licences stopped the decline in reserves only temporarily. They continued to fall in 1981–2. The latter fall may reflect the fact that import schedules were reformed gradually so that import-competing and consumer goods were the last schedule to be revised. Hence, there was a short period when access to inputs was freer, but the licensing of import-competing and consumer goods had not yet been tightened. By 1983, however, the schedules were established and succeeded in stabilizing the reserve position quite well. In 1987, after the mini coffee boom and following the announcement of a new structural adjustment and liberalization programme, there was another fall in reserves. Since then, they have remained quite stable but at a very low level.

Despite the fact that the authorities have been able to prevent the external reserves from complete depletion by more systematic control over issuance of import licences, the liberalization episode, which began effectively in 1988, like its predecessors, also suffered from incompatibility. Tariff reductions and the removal of a number of QRs were initially carried out without sufficient devaluation and ahead of a package of aid and sales tax increases. Even if exchange-rate management has become more flexible, the speed of exchange rate adjustment still remains fairly low and import liberalization has been adjusted to the gradual pace of depreciation.

Summarizing, the coffee boom liberalization in 1976–8 and the exogenous trade policy experiment in 1980 were clearly not credible to the public. In the first case, relaxation of QRs was a direct consequence of endogenous trade policy as was its reversal when the windfall was over. The second reform was carried out, despite adverse terms of trade, and was not accompanied by compensating devaluation. Support from international financial institutions did not suffice to restore compatibility, and hence credibility of the reform. The two more recent reforms, revision of import schedules since 1982, and that initiated in 1988, have avoided any uniform relaxation of import restriction on final goods competing with domestic production. The revised schedules, which liberalized importation of inputs but simultaneously became stricter on consumer goods, seem to have suffered only from an initial lack of credibility, partly thanks to supportive exchange rate adjustments. Although not discernible as a fall in external reserves, the import reform during the latest episode was incompatible with macroeconomic policies which led to its reversal. Therefore, imports other than inputs and capital goods continue to remain under close administrative control, and the issuance of licences depends on the availability of foreign exchange at the time of application.

The next section will examine whether or not private agents accumulate stocks of importables in anticipation of a reversal of the reforms. Changes in stocks in bonded warehouses, and actual imports and stocks held by manufacturing firms and commerce will be studied.

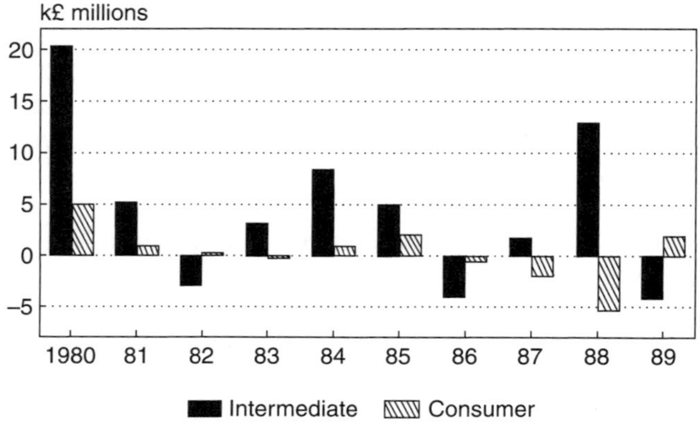

Source: Department of Customs and Excise 1988 and 1989, half-year data.
Figure 5.3 Annual change in bonded warehouses, 1982 prices

Stocks in bonded warehouses

There are currently 118 common bonded warehouses in operation in Kenya, a mixture of private and government-run. Until recently, importers were able to store their imports in these warehouses for at least two years before declaring them through customs. In an effort to curtail speculation, the length of time imported goods can be kept in bond has been limited to a maximum of one year. Figure 5.3 depicts the annual change (removals and re-exports deducted from entries) in the total value of durable consumer imports[12] and imported non-food, non-oil intermediate goods[13] held in the bonded warehouses. Unpublished data have been made available by the Department of Customs and Excise from 1980 to mid-1989, with the exception of the first half of 1983. When storing goods in bonded warehouses, importers face the risk of tariff increases, and that of devaluation, as tariff charges when declaring the goods through customs are based on the current tariff rate and the current value of the shilling.

The two series are deflated by the appropriate decomposed import prices indices.[14] Unlike the situation with consumer goods, there seems to have been an increase in the level of bonded stock of intermediate goods in the 1980s. As the data before 1980 are not available we do not know whether bonded imports increased towards the end of the coffee boom, as can be expected from rational private agents. The peak year of bond accumulation for both intermediate and consumer durables coincides with the incredible 1980 reform. Figures 5.4 and 5.5, which depict the monthly

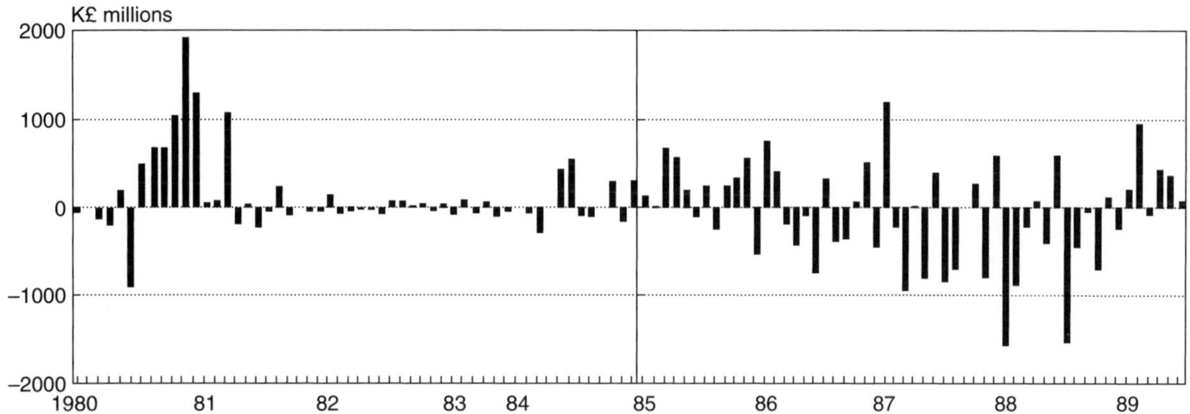

Source: Department of Customs and Excise 1983 and 1989, half-year data.
Figure 5.4 Net change in bonded consumer durables, 1982 prices

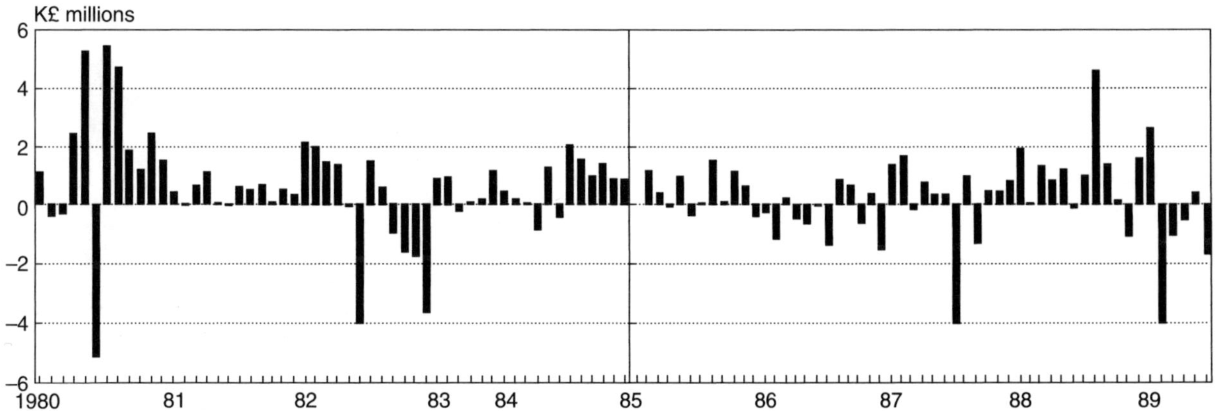

Source: Department of Customs and Excise 1983 and 1989, half-year data.
Figure 5.5 Net change in bonded intermediate goods, 1982 prices

changes, show that accumulation took place during the latter part of the year, accelerating towards its end. In other words, private agents correctly perceived the incompatibility of the reform and, by accumulation of bonded imports, prompted its reversal.

The reform of import schedules in 1982 meant tightened control for consumer durables, whereas intermediate goods were given priority access to licences and foreign exchange. As can be expected, there was no change in bonded consumer goods, but a small increase in intermediates during the first half of 1982 (Figures 5.4 and 5.5). The latter is likely to be caused by the initial lack of credibility in the new schedules, which was also observed in the external reserves (Figure 5.2). Finally, another major peak in bonded intermediate imports occurred in 1988 when the latest reform was initiated. Manufacturing firms seem to have anticipated the quick return of QRs. Instead, consumer goods were decumulated, which may reflect the expected increase in their tariffs.

Excess importation of durable goods

In addition to bonded imports, private agents can accumulate actual imports in order to take advantage of temporarily lower prices. Actual imports for home use are those declared through customs, either upon arrival in Kenya, or from bonded warehouses. In other words, imports entered in bond are not included in home consumption, but removals from bond are. From the importer's point of view, actual imports involve a higher cost of holding speculative inventories, as tariffs also have to be paid for before stocking, whereas the risk of adverse changes in tariff rates or the exchange rate are eliminated.

Unfortunately, import data is available only on an annual basis, so we cannot determine, for example, whether there was a peak in imports shortly after October 1980 (allowing some time for shipment) when foreign reserves fell considerably, and the reform came to a virtual halt and was subsequently abandoned. It is only possible to assess whether or not annual imports were significantly higher during 1980 compared to other years before and after the reform. Figure 5.6 depicts imports of consumer durables for home use at constant prices from 1975 to 1989. Actual imports of consumer durables increased throughout the coffee boom, but experienced their highest peak in 1978. This is a clear indication that consumers and traders anticipated the imminent reversal of the reform correctly and therefore accumulated stocks of durable goods.

Figure 5.7 depicts the total value of non-food intermediate goods as well their non-fuel and fuel components at 1982 prices imported for home consumption. Although imports of intermediates increased in 1978, their

Source: Customs and Excise Statistical Abstracts.
Figure 5.6 Imports of consumer durables, 1982 prices

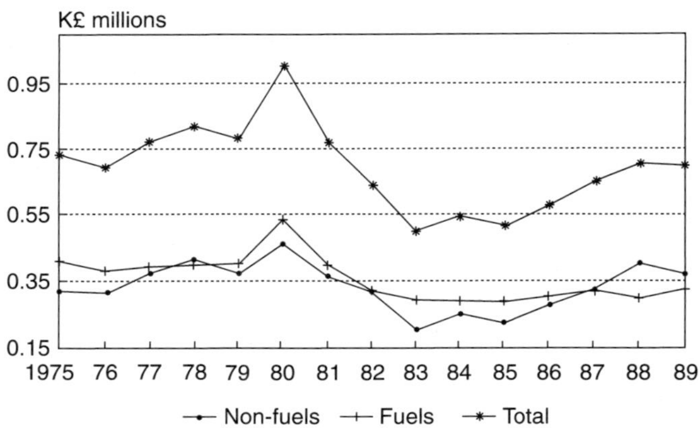

Source : Statistical Abstracts.
Figure 5.7 Imports of non-food intermediate goods, 1982 prices

highest peak occurred in 1980. As income and demand were falling, the import boom most certainly resulted from the expected reversal of the incompatible liberalization episode. We cannot observe from import statistics any speculative action in 1982. Both consumer and intermediate imports were in decline because of economic recession (and possible decumulation of previously-acquired stocks). In 1988 there was a small jump in the value of non-fuel intermediate imports, which may have been caused by speculative accumulation of stocks.

Finally, by looking at the changes in stocks held by firms, we can determine whether or not increased imports really ended up in storage. Data on inventories can be obtained from the Kenya Business Expectations Enquiry (BEE) maintained since 1973 by the Central Bureau of Statistics. From the viewpoint of inventories, the two most important sectors are manufacturing and commerce (retail), which hold 90 per cent of the total reported stocks. The stocks reported by the BBE include finished goods, work-in-progress, materials, fuels, components, spare parts etc.

Manufacturers do not hold stocks entirely as an alternative asset to physical plant or financial assets, but also for other reasons, such as production smoothing or avoidance of stock-outs. In order to extract the import component, which may be subject to speculation, it is useful to divide the total stocks into work-in-progress and finished goods, on the one hand, and materials, fuels, components, spares and so on, on the other. Materials dominate total manufacturing stocks, being on average three times the value of finished goods and work-in-progress. From the viewpoint of accumulating inventories of imports, the stocks of materials are obviously more interesting, bearing in mind the high import dependence and import-substituting nature of the Kenyan manufacturing sector.

Figure 5.8 depicts the value of materials, fuels, components, spare parts and so on held by manufacturing firms in 1978–90 at constant prices.

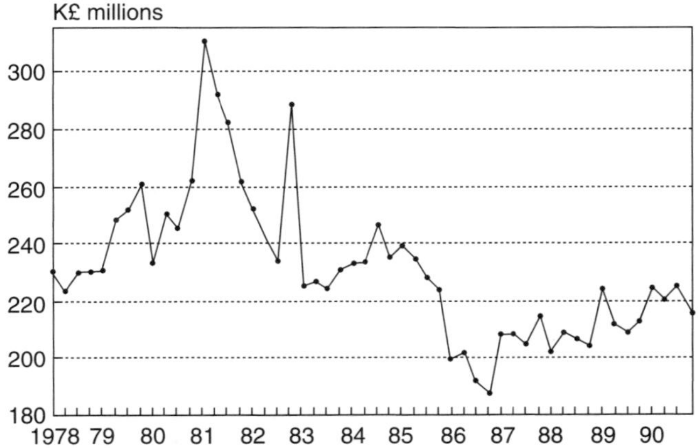

Source: Central Bureau of Statistics.

Figure 5.8 Manufacturing value of material stocks, 1982 prices

Stocks are deflated by the manufacturing input deflator. Two pronounced peaks appear, one in the first quarter of 1981 and the other during the last quarter of 1982. The former must reflect the surge in import orders in the last quarter of 1980. As we saw earlier, external reserves fell to an all-time low in 1982, indicating an initial lack of credibility in the new import schedules. However, this cannot be detected from actual imports of intermediates (which were the only liberalized goods), and only modestly in bonded intermediates, as the economy was simultaneously hit by recession, causing a fall in imports. Manufacturing stocks instead show a high peak in 1982 which may indicate the accumulation of speculative stocks otherwise hidden by the recessionary fall in other statistics. After 1982 the level and volatility of material stocks in manufacturing was reduced, reflecting the more systematic nature of licensing and preference given to imported inputs. On the one hand, manufacturers were assured that foreign exchange for the required inputs would be made available. On the other, the authorities responsible for issuing licences were now more in control and could prevent speculative peaks more effectively. A small peak can also be detected in the stock of manufacturing materials in the first quarter of 1989 but it is much smaller than those in the early part of the decade.

Figure 5.9 depicts quarterly data on total commercial stocks in 1975–90 at constant prices. As most of the stored goods, both imported and domestic, are for household consumption (industries import and stock their own input requirements), the series are deflated by the weighted

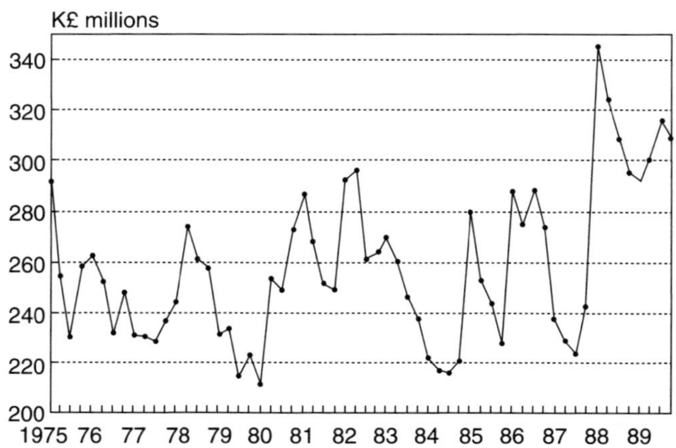

Source: Central Bureau of Statistics.
Figure 5.9 Commerce, value of total stocks, 1982 prices

average of clothing, footwear and household operations in the consumer price index for low-income group (Nairobi).

The trend in commercial stocks is positive but variations around the trend are highly volatile. Accumulation of inventories are followed repeatedly by decumulation. As can be expected, the positive trend seems to coincide with the tightening of import restrictions on consumer goods. A more restricted access to import licences calls for larger stocks in order to avoid stock-outs. The largest single accumulation took place during the first quarter of 1988, when controls on consumer goods were somewhat relaxed after a long restricted period. The two peaks in the actual imports of consumer durables in 1978 and 1980 (Figure 5.6) are also reflected in commercial stocks during the same year.

Was inventory accumulation financed by deferral of investment?

In order to determine whether investment in physical plant was deferred because of uncertainty concerning the future trade policy, we shall study the gross fixed capital formation in the manufacturing sector (Figure 5.10). There are two sources, based on different methods of data collection. The Kenya Business Expectations Enquiry (BEE) collects information on annual investment in fixed assets at factor cost during the last quarter of each year. In the national accounts, estimates of private-sector capital formation are undertaken, by and large, on a commodity flow basis. Statistics from the end-use analysis of imports and on completed buildings are the main sources of information, supplemented by data collected in agricultural and industrial surveys. Public-sector data are obtained directly from their accounting records. The manufacturing

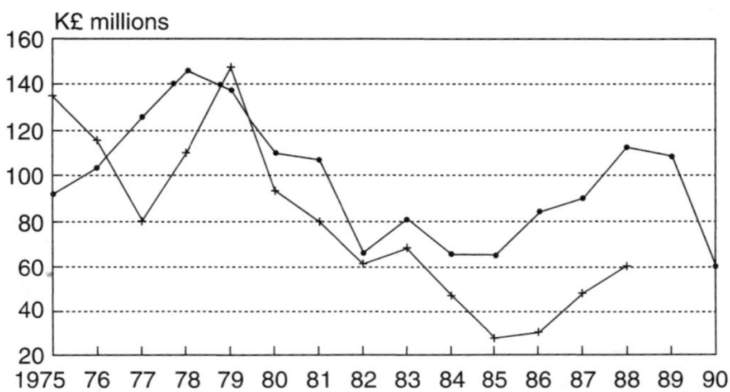

Source: Central Bureau of Statistics and Statistical Abstracts.
Figure 5.10 Manufacturing, capital formation, 1982 prices

gross fixed capital formation deflator, derived from the national accounts, is used to transform both series into constant prices. Note that the BEE seems to give consistently lower levels of investment than do the national accounts.

The BEE data shows that a surge in demand attributable to the coffee boom – in the absence of a sufficient relaxation of import controls – encouraged investment in manufacturing in 1978–9. Thereafter, it fell fairly sharply in 1980–2, there was a modest recovery in 1983, but this was followed by another slump in 1984–6. During the following three years investment went up but, as the national accounts data indicate, there was a steep decline in investment in 1990.

With annual data but without information about lags, it is not possible to determine whether or not investment was deferred in 1978 because of uncertainty about trade policy. As trade policy was correctly perceived to be exogenous, we might in fact want to infer that private agents were fairly confident that the import-substitution policy would continue after the boom, and that the decline in investment was caused solely by the economic downturn. If we assume a lag of one or two years between the investment decision and its implementation, we cannot reject the null that investment was deferred during the period of uncertainty about trade policy in 1988–9. It is, however, difficult to say anything about the magnitude of deferral without other sources of information. In 1990, the national accounts (provisional) investment figure dropped to its lowest level ever during the period under study. This may well be an indication that investors, suspicious about the permanence of an export orientation in trade policy, were waiting before investing in physical plant.

Summary and conclusions

In the absence of credibility, a gradual reform is likely to be associated with a lower social cost created by private action, such as stock accumulation. From the production point of view, gradualism – which is equivalent to a small reform, at least when it is initiated – leads to inaction: that is, to insufficient reallocation of factors to the export sector. Similarly, in new investment, returns to capital in the exportables sector are likely to remain too low to attract investors. They prefer either the import-substituting sector or deferral until uncertainty has been resolved. Hence a more instantaneous (strong and fast) reform is needed from the production point of view to overcome the credibility problem but, failing this, it has the negative side-effect of creating an incentive for consumers and enterpreneurs to accumulate inventories.

Another benefit from a sizeable reform is the signalling effect on the subjective probability of default. A large reform may be able to convince the private sector that the government is indeed willing to incur the political cost of implementing the reform so that the initial subjective probability of default decreases. As a matter of fact, when the government, whose intentions are not fully known to the public, announces the adoption of a gradual reform, the announcement itself will not convey any new information to private agents. A redistributive government would obviously like to reap the benefits of a more efficient economy, brought about by a shift of resources to the export sector, but without incurring the cost of changing the relative price. Such a government has an incentive to announce a gradual reform (if believed) and, subsequently, to deviate from it when the desired shift of resources has taken place. But rational agents recognize the time-consistency problem and do not want to be fooled. Hence, a genuinely liberalizing government may find it difficult to use the gradual strategy in the absence of credibility, even if it otherwise would be a sensible policy.

Summarizing, the trade-off is between socially-costly hoarding of imports and the beneficial shift of resources to the export sector. If the capital stock in place is sector-specific, for example, then the adverse consequences of incredible liberalization, whether gradual or abrupt, may dominate. Hence, it is important for the liberalizing government to assess the possible consequences of incredibility in advance. If its adverse effects are likely to endanger the whole reform, the government has either to find measures to enhance the credibility of its policies which counter the expected speculative action by using some other policy instruments (such as appropriately targeted temporary credit restrictions, by revising regulations and charges applied to import trade), or even to postpone the implementation of the reforms.

In empirical work it is essential to define an unambiguous indicator of trade policy, such as the implicit tariff, or the ratio of total private consumption to that of imported goods. Changes in trade policy instruments do not necessarily surface at aggregate level, and a quantitative index is required to determine whether or not relaxations and subsequent tightening have made the trade regime more liberal. However, in our study of speculative behaviour we used changes in policy instruments as criteria to determine distinct episodes, since annual indices may conceal changes in the opposite direction during a year, and speculation induced by them.

The data analysis confirms our first hypothesis, that private agents in Kenya were correctly able to detect episodes that were not sustainable, particularly in 1978 and 1980, inducing an accumulation of stocks of importables shortly before the reform was reversed. To a lesser extent, hoarding of stocks also took place in 1982 and 1988. If we assume a lag of one or two years between the investment decision and its implementation, we cannot reject our second null that investment was deferred during the period of uncertainty about trade policy. The most recent episode is a particular case in point. It is, however, difficult to say anything about the magnitude of deferral without more detailed information on investment.

The social cost of speculation is created when foreign exchange is tied up in stocks, investment is deferred, or protection persists. Even if we have not attempted to estimate the real magnitude of social costs it is obvious from the data that speculative stocks accumulation was indeed substantial, particularly in 1978 and 1980. In 1980, the private response to the reform undoubtedly forced the government to abandon it. Other studies, such as Michaely *et al.* (1991), have shown that past failures lead to a higher subjective probability of reversal being perceived by the private sector. Therefore, the cost of the next attempt at liberalization is likely to increase, even if the reform can be maintained. The World Bank advice for economies suffering from past failures is to reform with a big bang in order to achieve a more efficient allocation of resources. After studying the Kenyan episodes, we have to conclude that a big bang, when the necessary and sufficient conditions for credibility are not being met, involves a risk of adverse private response which may lead to a swift policy reversal.

Notes

1. Imposition of quantitative restrictions on imports may also be used as a means to ration scarce foreign exchange rather than as a deliberate industrial policy.
2. For a discussion of the disadvantages of economic liberalization, see Banuri (1991).
3. Gelbard (1990) on Argentina, and Hausmann (1991) on Venezuela are exceptions.
4. Other aspects of Kenyan trade liberalizations are analyzed by Ikiara (1987), Bevan *et al.* (1991) and N'geno (1991).
5. The empirical findings of a World Bank study (Michaely *et al.*, 1991) covering nineteen countries and thirty-six liberalization episodes suggest that (i) liberalizations have not generally done much harm to employment; (ii) an emergence of unemployment during the liberalization episode, for whatever reason, has not been significant in determining the fate of the reform; and (iii) much adjustment of employment seems to take place within individual sectors.
6. The empirical study by the World Bank (Michaely *et al.*, 1991) looked at the distributional effects by income level, the share of wages in national income,

and the relative change of low versus high wages. Since adverse effects on employment were absent, the main source of potential deterioration of income distribution was eliminated. The number of liberalization episodes when a deterioration seems to have occurred equals the number of improvements. In the rest of the sample, there is either a mixed outcome or insufficient evidence to draw any conclusions. The study claims that only in one country out of nineteen was the reform aborted because of unemployment and adverse distributional effects.

7. The subjective probability behaves in different ways. First, it can remain constant so that the pattern perceived by private agents at the initiation of the reform remains the same. Second, it may be revised over time. Revision can be thought of as a learning process. Signals that private agents extract to revise their expectations can come from various sources, such as data on foreign reserves, external balance, imports, stocks, unemployment, or from private investment response. It would be useful to endogenize the subjective probability in modelling but we shall not do so because we have adopted the simple two-period framework. Revisions are also likely to pose analytical difficulties for modelling.
8. For example, in Kenya, the average implicit tariff is estimated at 112 per cent (Bevan *et al.*, 1991).
9. In Zambia, for example, the foreign exchange auction, initiated in October 1985 and combined with trade liberalization, became incredible to the private sector around mid-1986, inducing accumulation of inventories which considerably exceeded gross fixed capital formation in 1986. The manufacturing sector was able to increasing borrowing to finance these purchases. As a result, they bid more and more for foreign exchange so that the kwacha kept falling in value until the auction-cum-liberalization had to be reversed in 1987 (Bates and Collier, 1991).
10. If the systematic bias in the import price index found by Maxwell Stamp Associates (1989) remains constant over time, then it does not distort the implicit tariff index.
11. Bevan *et al.* (1990b) calculated the same trade policy indices for 1975–80. There is, however, an error in their implicit tariff index calculation for 1979. As a result, their index shows tightening of trade policy when there was, in fact, a fall in the implicit tariff from the previous year.
12. Consumer durables include passenger motor cars (51), other non-industrial transport equipment (522), consumer durables (61) and consumer semi-durables (62) as defined by the Broad Economic Categories, BEC (United Nations, 1989).
13. Includes primary industrial supplies (21), processed industrial supplies (22), parts and accessories of capital goods (42) and transport equipment (53) as defined by the Broad Economic Categories, BEC (United Nations, 1989).
14. As to consumer goods, passenger motor cars (51), other non-industrial transport equipment (522) and consumer durables (61) are deflated by the import index for machinery and transport equipment. Consumer semi-durables (62) are deflated by the import index for miscellaneous manufactures. Intermediate imports are deflated as follows: primary industrial supplies (21) by the import price index for crude materials, inedible; processed industrial supplies (22) by the weighted average of the import price index for animal and

vegetable oils and fats, chemicals and manufactured goods; and parts and accessories for capital goods (42) and transport equipment (53) by the import price index for machinery and transport equipment.

References

Banuri, T. (ed.) (1991) *Economic Liberalization: No Panacea* (Oxford: Clarendon Press).

Bates, R. H. and P. Collier (1991) *The Politics and Economics of Policy Reform in Zambia*, Department of Political Science, Duke University and Centre for the Study of African Economies, University of Oxford.

Bevan, D., P. Collier and J. W. Gunning (1990a) *Trade and Exchange Rate Policies and the Effects of Terms of Trade Changes* (Centre for the Study of African Economies, University of Oxford).

Bevan, D., P. Collier and J. W. Gunning, with A. Bigsten and P. Horsnell (1990b) *Controlled Open Economies. A Neo-Classical Approach to Structuralism* (Oxford: Clarendon Press).

Bevan, D., P. Collier and J. W. Gunning (1991) *The Macroeconomics of Kenyan Trade Liberalization*, Centre for the Study of African Economies, University of Oxford.

Calvo, G. A. (1987) 'On the Costs of Temporary Policy', *Journal of Development Economics* vol. 27, pp. 245–62.

Calvo, G. A. (1988) *Costly Trade Liberalizations. Durable Goods and Capital Mobility*, Staff Papers, International Monetary Fund, vol. 35, no. 3, pp. 461–73.

Central Bank of Kenya, *Quarterly Economic Review*, various issues.

Collier, P. and J. W. Gunning (1992) 'Trade and Development: A Survey', in D. Greenaway and A. Winters (eds), *Surveys of International Trade Theory* (Oxford, Blackwell).

Daveri, F. (1989) *Trade Liberalization in a Low-Income Economy: Time Inconsistency and Fiscal Policy*, Discussion Paper No. 8905, Universita Degli Studi di Brescia.

Dixit, A. (1989) 'Intersectoral Capital Reallocation under Price Uncertainty', *Journal of International Economics*, vol. 26, pp. 309–25.

Edwards, S. and S. van Wijnbergen (1986) 'The Welfare Effects of Trade and Capital Liberalization', *International Economic Review*, vol. 27, no. 1, pp. 141–8.

Engel, C. and K. Kletzer (1987) *Trade Policy under Endogenous Credibility*, National Bureau of Economic Research, Working Paper No. 2449.

Froot, K. A. (1988) 'Credibility, Real Interest Rates and the Optimal Speed of Trade Liberalization', *Journal of International Economics*, vol. 25, pp. 71–93.

Gelbard, E. A. (1990) 'Changes in Industrial Structure and Performance under Trade Liberalization: The Case of Argentina', Unpublished Ph.D. thesis, University of Toronto.

Hausmann, R. (1991) 'Dealing with Negative Oil Shocks: The Venezuelan Experience in the Eighties', mimeo, Caracas: Instituto de Estudios Superiores de Administracion.

Ikiara, G. K. (1987) 'Kenya', in J. Whalley (ed.), *Dealing with the North. Developing Countries in the Global Trading System*, Ontario, Canada: CSIER Research Monograph.

Maxwell Stamp Associates (1989) *Study in Support of ISAC Trade Liberalization Programme Final Report* (London).

Michaely, M., D. Papageorgiou and A. M. Choksi (1991) *Liberalizing Foreign Trade.*

Lessons of Experience in the Developing World (Cambridge, Mass. and Oxford: Basil Blackwell).
N'Geno, N. K. (1991) 'Kenya's Export Performance', in J. H. Frimpong-Ansah, S. M. R. Kanbur and P. Svedberg (eds), *Trade and Development in Sub-Saharan Africa* (Manchester University Press).
Reinikka-Soininen, R. (1990) *Liberalization of Trade in Developing Countries: Effects on Employment and Welfare*, Helsinki School of Economics Publication, B-102.
Republic of Kenya, *Annual Trade Report*, various issues, Nairobi: Customs and Excise Department.
Republic of Kenya (1973–) *Business Expectations Enquiry*, Central Bureau of Statistics, Ministry of Planning and National Development, Nairobi.
Republic of Kenya (various dates) *Economic Survey*, Nairobi: Central Bureau of Statistics, Ministry of Planning and National Development.
Republic of Kenya (various dates) *Statistical Abstracts*, Nairobi: Central Bureau of Statistics, Ministry of Planning and National Development.
Republic of Kenya (1986) *Sessional Paper No. 1 of 1986 on Economic Management for Renewal Growth*, Nairobi: Government Printer.
Republic of Kenya (1991a) *Import Licensing Schedules*, Nairobi: Government Printer.
Republic of Kenya (1991b) *1991/92 Budget Speech*, June.
Rodrik, D. (1989a) *Policy Uncertainty and Private Investment in Developing Countries*, Working Paper No. 2999, National Bureau of Economic Research, June.
Rodrik, D. (1989b). 'Promises, Promises: Credible Policy Reform via Signalling', *Economic Journal*, vol. 99, September, pp. 756–72.
Staiger, R. W. and G. Tabellini (1987), 'Discretionary Trade Policy and Excessive Protection', *American Economic Review*, vol. 77, December, pp. 823–37.
Thomas, V. and J. Nash (1991) 'Reform of Trade Policy. Recent Evidence from Theory and Practice', *The World Bank Research Observer*, vol. 6, no. 2, July, pp. 219–40.
United Nations (1989) 'Classification by Broad Economic Categories, Defined in terms of SITC, Rev 3', *Statistical Papers*, Series M, no. 53, Rev. 3, New York: Department of International Economic and Social Affairs.
Van Wijnbergen, S. (1985) 'Trade Reform, Aggregate Investment and Capital Flight. On Credibility and Value of Information', *Economics Letters*, vol. 19, pp. 369–72.

Part II

Fiscal Reform Issues

6
The Design of Fiscal Reforms in Revenue-Constrained Developing Countries

Christopher Bliss

Sources and uses of public revenue in developing countries

While generalization is perilous, there are many (especially small) developing countries for which sales taxes and turnover taxes are fairly negligible as revenue sources and for which import duties and export taxes, particularly the former, are leading revenue sources. For evidence from the early 1980s, see Tanzi (1987), and Greenaway and Milner (1991). This observation is unsurprising when account is taken of the administrative constraints to which many developing countries are subject. Sales taxes can be difficult to collect, not to mention a complex tax such as VAT. Income tax is largely infeasible and often has to take a simple form, such as a payroll tax confined in practice to public and large company employment.

Some taxes that would be assumed to be eminently feasible in industrial economies may not generate as much revenue as might be supposed in a developing country. For instance, tax disks which the law may require heavy goods vehicles to carry may generate a flow of bribes to police and other officials if they are wise enough to set the bribe at a modest level, making it cheaper to pay bribes than to buy a disk. A cynic might say that the bribes are an unofficial source of revenue if their existence enables the state to get away with paying its officials absurdly low salaries. One would have to hope, if that argument is accepted, that the officials do something socially useful apart from stopping heavy goods vehicles.

Such considerations make it interesting to consider the design of public finance for a country severely constrained in its choice of what Musgrave called 'tax handles': that is, types of tax instrument it may practically employ. The existing literature, of which Newbery and Stern (1987) provide an excellent review, throws some light on this issue, but the problem is seldom treated explicitly. An exception would be by Drèze and Stern (1985), whose highly abstract and general treatment of cost–benefit analysis theory can be seen to incorporate principles of public finance which fully cover the restricted policy choices I have in mind. Because the approach of these authors is so general, however, it is not easy to extract conclusions for tax design in specific cases. This is no criticism of Drèze and Stern, of course, as the argument is addressed to cost–benefit analysis.

Generally speaking, theory has developed in the direction of sophisticated and complex tax systems. The next section discusses why this is so from the point of view of theory. Yet ideal tax systems would be difficult to implement in many developing countries. As I shall treat tariffs as a highly feasible revenue source, a position which has often been taken by commentators on developing-country finance, some words of caution are in order. True, the great advantage of tariffs from the point of view of administrative feasibility is that in many countries there are only a few ports through which traded goods can easily pass, so it only requires a few customs posts and some fairly uncorrupt officials to collect tariffs. Contrast this position with the difficulties confronting a VAT system, and the point will be clear.

While some indirect taxation may be acutely difficult to administer, tariffs should not be seen as being entirely free of problems. Smuggling is often a serious problem, and tariff evasion is not confined to smuggling. Under-invoicing is easily used to reduce the incidence of a tariff, but as most developing countries collect small shares of national income in all forms of taxation, we are never likely to be confronted by a complete revenue block because of tariff evasion. An ideal and detailed application of the theory would allow for under-invoicing, but this is perfectionism.

It has to be said, also, that while many tax handles may be outside the range of practicality, it is not plausible to single out tariffs as unique from the point of view of practical revenue raising. Many developing countries do raise substantial revenues from excise duties on, for example, liquor sales. If other developing countries are less successful in this regard, the lesson may be that they should try harder. In addition, note again that the pro-tariff case ignores problems of smuggling and under-invoicing, which are serious issues in many developing countries.

The particular contribution of my argument is to draw attention to another type of revenue source which is never classified as taxation, but which should at least be considered in close parallel with standard taxes: revenue from the sale of publicly-produced non-tradable goods. Electricity will serve as a good example. Other examples would be irrigation, publicly-monopolized transport services, publicly-provided education – especially secondary and higher education – and so on. It is only necessary to note that these activities can generate surpluses or run deficits to see that they, and their pricing, should be considered in tandem with taxation and tariffs. Purchases by the public sector should also be seen as a potential source of savings when the public sector is a monopsonist, or when it has made itself into a monopsonist by offering unusually favourable deals to its suppliers, as has often seemed to happen with public-sector employment.

Other writers have considered the pricing of publicly-provided services from the point of view of tax theory, notably Katz (1987). He, however, assumes that a given total subsidy has been allocated to these sales, and derives the optimal manner of pricing the services and allocating the subsidy. The level of subsidy, which might well be negative, should be derived from a more general framework. The precise designation of the relationship between standard taxation and public sales pricing and subsidy is a chief contribution of this chapter.

The pure theory of public finance and its application

The modern theory of public finance in developing countries begins with the paper by Diamond and Mirrlees (1971). These authors showed that public-sector efficiency remains desirable even when the lump-sum taxes, which theory shows to be ideal, are not available to the policy-maker. 'Desirable' in this connection means that any allocation for which the public sector is inefficient, in a sense which the paper makes precise, can be improved in the Pareto sense, provided only that the authorities make use of indirect taxes. This argument leads on to the proposal of ideal indirect taxation of the type first elucidated by Ramsey (1927).

The extension of this theory to the open economy is considered explicitly by Dasgupta and Stiglitz (1974). Moreover, many of the conclusions of the analysis extend to cases where tax instruments are restricted. Drèze and Stern (1985), explore the extension of cost–benefit analysis theory under much weaker assumptions. Obviously, if indirect taxes may not be levied, the Ramsey model of optimal indirect taxation cannot apply as such. There are two approaches to the problem of taxation feasibility. With one, that employed in this chapter, certain tax handles are simply treated as being unavailable and an optimal tax structure for the remaining taxes is derived. The alternative is illustrated by Newbery (1987), who considers evasion and the costs of collection in the context of general taxation theory. In principle, the second approach should be better, as it is strictly more general than the first. Infeasibility, after all, is only the limit of high collection cost. In practice, the greater generality of an approach based on collection costs and so on, has to be judged in terms of what the model can do. I offer no dogmatic opinion on this issue.

Several authors have noted that if a certain amount of public revenue is to be raised from import tariffs, whether for good reasons or bad, some tariff structures are better than others (see Corden, 1974). This consideration leads to the demonstration of an optimal structure of revenue-producing tariffs, and the principles for setting these tariffs are, not surprisingly, the same as the Ramsey optimal tax rules (on this theory, see Bliss, 1980). This is what might be called 'classical theory', because it only treats direct resource allocation costs. To be specific, it neglects rent-seeking. Note, however, that while rent-seeking theory was developed with tariff protection particularly in mind, it could apply generally to all tax systems.

What I shall call for convenience Ramsey tax theory leads to complex mathematical formulae for optimal taxes, the rate of taxation on a particular good depending on general cross-effects in demand, and also on income distribution considerations and on welfare weights. This can generate horrific problems for empirical application. Approximations, however, may work well in practice. The rules of thumb that emerge are well known. Other things being equal – the other things involve particularly income distribution considerations – indirect tax rates should be relatively high where demands/supplies are inelastic, and relatively low where demands/supplies are elastic. This accords with common sense, because inelasticity minimizes the distortion caused by the indirectness of sales taxation. Equally intuitively, a high tax rate on salt demanded with near-zero price elasticity does not commend itself, despite the fact that it causes minimal distortion, because it would be highly regressive and bear heavily on the poor.

The Ramsey taxation type of result is echoed when a similar constrained maximization technique is applied to different but parallel problems of tax design, including the choice of an optimal tariff structure. This is no surprise. Once again, tariffs, in this case, should be relatively high where demands/supplies are inelastic. Again, equally, this principle is moderated by considerations of income distribution. A high tariff is not necessarily recommended for an imported drug just because the demand for it is highly inelastic and a domestic supply absent, or again highly inelastic.

In order to highlight the new results of this chapter, I propose to concentrate on a highly stylized and special case. I would not defend this specification as even an approximate description of the exact state of affairs in any developing country. It is convenient, however, and generalizations are readily available when the number of tax handles is larger. What I assume explicitly is that there are only two sources of government revenue: tariff revenue and net profits from the trading of public enterprises. The mathematics of optimal prices, tariff levels and public production is developed in the Appendix. Here I present an informal statement of the problem. The reader needing more mathematical exactness is referred to the Appendix. I only present a one-consumer model, yet extension to many consumers is straightforward.

The objective function is the welfare of a representative consumer. This objective function, which is frequently employed in modern public finance models, has been criticized. The criticism would be especially pointed for developing countries, for which the character of the government often seems remote from the benign welfare maximization of utilitarian theory. Even so, such an argument must take care to avoid lapsing into simple mistakes. As the model will include arbitrary claims by the government on final resources, claims to which the maximization of welfare is subject, there is plenty of scope in the model for self-serving or megalomaniac government. Welfare maximization could even be interpreted as cost minimization on the part of a government keen to pursue its own objectives while satisfying a consumer welfare target. Perhaps more serious problems with the approach, which in this context is fairly standard, are the competitive nature of some assumptions and the neglect of public goods. Some of these shortcomings are not difficult to repair, but I do not pursue that issue.

To maximize welfare the government chooses prices. This should not be taken to suggest price regulation. Indeed, in the version of the model examined in detail, prices are competitively determined and leading constraints are respectively a balance of trade constraint, and market clearing constraints for non-tradable goods. In general, allowing the government to choose prices subject to budget constraints is equivalent to allowing it to choose taxes or tariffs. Which taxes are allowed is then determined by the way in which the choice of prices is specified.

This is a small country, so prices for tradables are constant and the government cannot influence them. Hence the government chooses three sets of prices. As usual, only relative prices count, but this causes no problem. These prices apply to tradable goods, general non-tradables, and non-tradables used or produced only by the public sector. In fact, the distinction between the two types of non-tradable goods is not particularly significant. It only implies a constraint that the net inputs or outputs for one of the second class of non-tradable goods shall be non-positive for the private sector. For the same reason, however, it is no trouble to distinguish the two types of good, and I happen to have done so.

The other variables chosen by the government are public-sector productions. As the government's final demands for all goods are constants, they can be folded into the public-sector production constraint, which then applies to public-sector transactions with the private sector net of the public sector's own final demands. The prices the government chooses are always those at which the private sector will trade. We may note the following points:

(i) By not requiring tradable prices to equal world relative prices, the model permits tariffs.
(ii) By requiring all private sector prices to be the same for consumers and producers, the model prohibits indirect taxes.
(iii) By folding public-sector final demands into the public-sector production constraint, a model prohibits lump-sum taxes.
(iv) By including public-sector final demands in total market demands which must clear markets, the model allows the marking-up of public-sector prices to generate revenue.

Interpreting the solution to the model

To understand the nature of the solution in detail, the reader will need to consult the Appendix. Here I explore some general features. First note that two distinct price systems emerge with the solution. First there are the prices which the private sector will face; and second, there are shadow prices for all goods considered in the model. These price systems are in general distinct and unequal. The public sector should maximize profit at shadow prices, and shadow prices for tradables are proportional to (that is, equal to in the relevant sense) international prices. Hence the general inequality of private-sector prices for tradables to world prices indicates the use of an optimal tariff structure. In maximizing profit, public-sector producers use world prices for tradables, just as in the open-economy version of the Diamond–Mirrlees result. Hence, public producers should neither be subject to tariffs, nor should they be credited with tariff-inflated prices for sales of protected goods.

Figure 6.1 illustrates the solution for a case where only two goods are distinguished: tradables (*T*) and non-tradables (*NT*). Goods produced by the public sector only are included in tradables. The private sector by itself

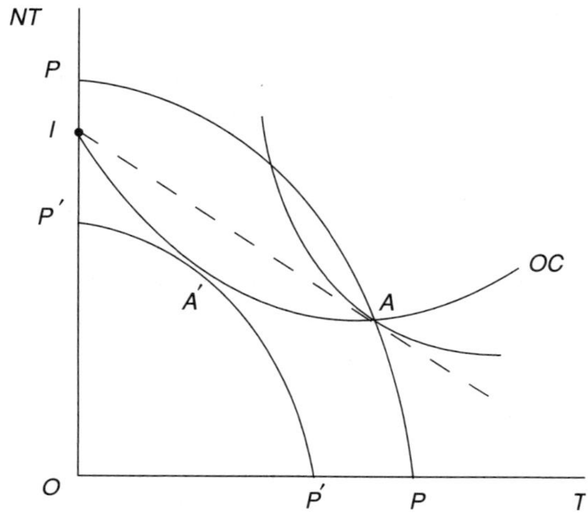

Figure 6.1 Public and private sector real exchange rates

starts at *I* and the offer curve through *I* is *OC*. *PP* is the original net trade possibility curve of the public sector. Its curvature reflects the fact that the transformation of non-tradables into tradables in the public sector is subject to diminishing returns. The final demands of the public sector have been subtracted from net trade. The optimum is at *A*, the furthest point out on the offer curve, hence the highest utility level, consistent with feasibility. The private-sector real exchange rate (relative price of tradables to non- tradables) is shown by the dotted line *IA*. The public-sector real exchange rate is given by the slope of the tangent to *PP* at *A* (not shown), which may be seen to be different from the private-sector real exchange rate.

This is the same as the Diamond–Mirrlees result, and a similar figure has been used to illustrate that theorem. The difference here lies in the nature of the offer curve. In Figure 6.1 it includes alterations in private-sector production consequent upon relative price changes. For this reason, and in general, there is no guarantee that consumer welfare will rise uniformly along the offer curve, as it must do with consumers only in the private sector. That could not imply that it would be optimal for the public sector to throw away output if we allow the assumption that an appropriate change to some price would improve consumer welfare, an assumption already made by Diamond and Mirrlees. The assumption is much weaker in the Diamond–Mirrlees case, of course, because producer prices can be held constant while consumer prices change.

The figure also illustrates what happens if public-sector final demands increase. This will shrink the possibility curve net of public-sector final demands and force *A* up along the offer curve to outcomes corresponding to lower consumer welfare. The limit is shown on the figure as the point *A*′. Here the public-sector possibility curve is tangential to the offer curve and a limit of public-sector extraction from the economy has been reached. As would be expected, the private real exchange rate is unfavourable, making tradables as expensive as possible. The reader may confirm that the angle between private- and public-sector prices is also a maximum at *A*′, which corresponds to the highest tariff on tradable imports.

Trade and public sector transactions

In this section I explore a particular implication of the model which throws light on the relationship between public-sector profits and tariff revenue. To illustrate general principles, consider an explicit example. A hypothetical developing country produces electricity in a publicly-owned generating company and also imports petroleum from the outside world at a price which, because this is a small country, is constant. The two energy sources are not perfect substitutes in demand, but we can imagine that their respective positions in the demand structure could be reversed. Equivalently, we can imagine that petroleum becomes domestically produced, with cost conditions identical to the cost conditions that used to apply to electricity. At the same time, domestic generation of electricity becomes impossible but a cross-border supply of electricity becomes available, at a price which, by chance, is equal to the old price of petroleum. Realism is not needed for this example to make its point.

In either of these cases, the previous optimal price structure, with the prices switched from one good to the other in one case, is unaffected. This is one case of a general theorem which is proved informally here.[1]

THEOREM 1 *The pricing rules for non-tradable goods are exactly the same as the pricing rules for tradable goods substituted by the public sector, where the latter are priced at marginal cost by the public sector.*

Proof Since tariffs or subsidies on tradable-goods trade can be imposed at will, the private sector cannot trade directly with the foreign sector. Therefore we can treat the substitution possibilities provided by international trade as part of the public sector's substitution possibilities. Suppose now that two goods have the same shadow price (we can choose units to make this the case) and are fully symmetrical in private net demands, but one is tradable, the other not, and they are priced differently from the private sector. When one price is lowered slightly and the other raised at the same rate, consumer welfare is unaffected, by symmetry. If both goods are priced optimally, the shadow costs to the public sector of accommodating all demand changes must differ in proportion to the price differences. Therefore a substitution concerning which the consumer is indifferent takes the public sector inside its possibility set, which we do not allow in an optimum. The proof is complete.

This result is so natural that one needs to stand back and note its radical implications, especially when they are compared with common practice in less-developed countries. Suppose a good is imported and tariff protection is justified, says the argument. Now domestic production becomes possible. Then the private sector should be 'protected' against competition from the public sector by price discrimination equally as fierce as the tariff protection which was in place previously.

The usual situation is similar but different in detail. Protection against imports is common and often strong. Equally, many public enterprises run at a loss and subsidize the private sector. Often the reason given for the latter situation is the promotion of domestic private production. Sometimes, but not always, inputs do not attract tariffs. Sometimes effective protection is encountered even when nominal protection is low. Non-economic objectives may be important here, and our analysis has neglected them. If public revenue is a central consideration, however, one must note that tariffs bring in revenue at the cost of distortion, while subsidy of public-sector sales costs revenue, again at the cost of distortion. That argues for lowering both distortions while holding public revenue constant, which is the essence of the theorem.

The argument points in the direction of lowering both protection and subsidies for public enterprises in a distorted economy. That has a familiar ring – it sounds like the standard structural adjustment package. There are differences, however. The level of public final demands is not being questioned here, it is treated as given. So the typical IMF-type criticism of so-called excessive expenditure on education, food handouts, or whatever, is not the present argument. We have only been concerned with the efficient means of attaining given levels of public net final demands in an economy with few tax handles.

Public-sector incentives and privatization

So far the emphasis has been on the nature of the optimum for the economy constrained by a lack of tax handles, and not on the detailed nature of the price system that supports that optimum. These points, however, are easily clarified. The private sector's optimization, given private-sector prices, was always assumed. From the optimization, shadow prices were derived and were shown to be proportional to public-sector marginal costs of production. Hence the public sector should maximize profit evaluated at shadow prices. It would be a mistake to require the public sector to maximize profitability at market (private-sector) prices.

This looks like a clear-cut decentralization rule. In an ideal case the public sector would consist of numerous similar enterprises or plants. Then performance could be evaluated using shadow prices, and managers could be rewarded or penalized according to their individual performances. This would provide managers with the right incentives to be efficient and to cut back on waste and the direct consumption of firm services, including idleness, nepotistic benefits, and so on. Unfortunately, this ideal is hard to realize, particularly when economies of scale imply that only one enterprise of a particular type is economic for the country concerned.

In fact, the efficiency of public enterprises may be poor, and privatization is often proposed as a solution to this difficulty. This is a large topic in its own right, but our model allows us to make some observations about privatization. In favour of privatization is the argument that, ideally, it creates competition and incentives for high performance, and even for a natural monopoly. Suppose, for example, that the ownership of the enterprise is auctioned. This might produce a bid close to the maximum present value of the enterprise if it is run efficiently. If a truly competitive auction can be organized, the successful bidder will pay something close to the maximized present value.

Note two problems, however: (i) if the enterprise is not price regulated, the bidder will evaluate the enterprise at *monopoly* prices for markets in which it is a large trader; and (ii) if the enterprise is not price regulated, the bidder will evaluate the enterprise at *market* prices for markets in which it is a small trader.

Neither of these actions replicates the ideal decentralization of the optimum, because in neither case are the prices used the shadow prices of the optimum programme. The logic of the argument is that a privatized enterprise should be taxed and subsidized so that it trades at shadow prices, and its would-be owners should bid for it in the knowledge that this will happen. This, however, drives a Trojan horse through the assumptions concerning tax feasibility, for such taxation would discriminate between production and consumption in the private sector, an approach that was explicitly excluded above.

Revenue maximization

One way of contrasting the monopoly behaviour of a privatized enterprise with the ideal pricing of an optimizing public enterprise is to state that the former manager maximizes profit, while the latter maximizes revenue subject to a welfare constraint. Revenue maximization is strictly ambiguous in a real model with variable relative prices. If we interpret it in terms of a public-sector objective function, however, revenue maximization is equivalent to the welfare maximization of the main model. This is shown in the Appendix. An individual enterprise, however, cannot be asked to maximize a global public-sector objective function. When the maximization is decentralized, the correct shadow prices for that purpose are the same as we have already encountered.

Conclusion

When public revenue is scarce, great attention needs to be paid to both its expenditure, avoiding wasteful or marginal uses, and its generation. For the latter purpose, tariffs are, in principle, a legitimate instrument. The tariff structure should be optimal, however, and optimality needs to respect both issues of distortion (elasticity of demand and supply) and income distribution. Tariffs, however, should never be considered in isolation. Even in the extreme case when no other tax instrument is available, the operating surpluses of public enterprises need to be considered, and the price structure must take these into account.

Incentives for the public sector are a difficult problem. In principle, performance should be evaluated at optimal shadow prices. Without relevant comparisons, however, it is not easy to evaluate performance at any prices. Privatization, via an auction, for example, looks like an answer to this difficulty. Enterprises transferred to the private sector, however, price too high, because they act as unconstrained revenue maximizers, and use the wrong prices – market or monopoly prices rather than shadow prices.

Appendix

The Appendix lays out the mathematical model which underlies some of the arguments of the chapter. For ease of exposition, we look at the 'one private consumer' case, although extension to a more general case is straightforward.

In the model, Roman lower-case letters are vectors, Greek or capitals are generally scalars. Subscripts denote differentiation. Where differentiation is concerned, the notation follows the natural course, and not the rule that vectors are denoted by lower-case Roman letters. Thus when differentiation of the scalar-valued function $\phi(\mathrm{x})$ creates a vector of partial derivatives, this is denoted $\phi_{\mathrm{x}}(\mathrm{x})$.

The notation of the model is:

p, q and r = prices for respectively traded, non-traded and public-sector goods for the private sector;
$\pi\,(p, q, r)$ = private sector profit function; and
$V\,(p, q, r; \pi)$ = the indirect utility of the private-sector consumer.

The consumer demand functions for tradables take into account the effect of price changes on profits. Thus the demand for tradables, denoted d^x, is:

$$d^x(p, q, r; \pi) = -\frac{V_p(p, q, r; \pi)}{V_\pi(p, q, r; \pi)}$$

Similarly, the demands for the two types of non-tradables, denoted d^y and d^z are:

$$d^y(p, q, r; \pi) = -\frac{V_q(p, q, r; \pi)}{V_\pi(p, q, r; \pi)}$$

$$d^z(p, q, r; \pi) = -\frac{V_r(p, q, r; \pi)}{V_\pi(p, q, r; \pi)}$$

Note that when we come to differentiate demand functions with respect to prices, the indirect effect of prices on demand through π will be included.

$(\bar{x}, \bar{y}, \bar{z})$ = the vector of the final net resource requirements of the public sector;
(x, y, z) = the vector of public sales to the private sector;
$f[x+\bar{x}, y+\bar{y}, z+\bar{z}]$ = the production function constraint of the public sector; and
p^0 = the constant vector of prices for tradable goods.

Now the model can be conveniently stated as:

$$\max \quad V(p, q, r; \pi) \tag{6.1}$$

subject to

$$p^0\left[\pi_p(p, q, r) - d^x(p, q, r; \pi) + x\right] \geq 0 \tag{6.2}$$

$$\pi_q(p, q, r) - d^y(p, q, r; \pi) + y \geq 0 \tag{6.3}$$

$$\pi_r(p, q, r) - d^z(p, q, r; \pi) + z \geq 0 \tag{6.4}$$

$$f\left[x+\bar{x}, y+\bar{y}, z+\bar{z}\right] \geq 0 \tag{6.5}$$

The Lagrangean;

$$\begin{aligned} V(p, q, r; \pi) + \lambda p^0[r_p(p, q, r) - d^x(p, q, r; \pi) + x] + \\ v[r_q(p, q, r) - d^y(p, q, r; \pi) + y] + w[\pi_q(p, q, r) - d^z(p, q, r; \pi) + z] + \\ \mu f\left[x+\bar{x}, y+\bar{y}, z+\bar{z}\right] \end{aligned} \tag{6.6}$$

The first-order conditions for an interior solution are:

$$\begin{bmatrix} V_p(p, q, r; l) \\ V_q(p, q, r; l) \\ V_r(p, q, r; l) \end{bmatrix} + \begin{bmatrix} \pi_{pp} - d_p^x & \pi_{qp} - d_p^y & \pi_{rp} - d_p^z \\ \pi_{pq} - d_q^x & \pi_{qq} - d_q^y & \pi_{rq} - d_q^z \\ \pi_{pr} - d_r^x & \pi_{qr} - d_r^y & \pi_{rr} - d_r^z \end{bmatrix} \begin{bmatrix} \lambda p^0 \\ v \\ w \end{bmatrix} = 0 \tag{6.7}$$

$$\begin{bmatrix} \lambda p^0 \\ v \\ w \end{bmatrix} + \mu \begin{bmatrix} f_x \\ f_y \\ f_z \end{bmatrix} = 0 \tag{6.8}$$

Dividing both sides of Equation (6.10) by – $V_i(p, q, r;\ \pi)$ and denoting by [X] the matrix

$$\begin{bmatrix} \pi_{pp} - d^x_p & \pi_{qp} - d^y_p & \pi_{rp} - d^z_p \\ \pi_{pq} - d^x_q & \pi_{qq} - d^y_q & \pi_{rq} - d^z_q \\ \pi_{pr} - d^x_r & \pi_{qr} - d^y_r & \pi_{rr} - d^z_r \end{bmatrix} \tag{6.9}$$

we obtain

$$\begin{bmatrix} d^x & & f_x \\ d^y & = \frac{\mu}{V_i}[X] & f_y \\ d^z & & f_z \end{bmatrix} \tag{6.10}$$

where:

$$\begin{bmatrix} d^x \\ d^y \\ d^z \end{bmatrix} = \begin{bmatrix} d^x(p, q, r;\ \pi) \\ d^y(p, q, r;\ \pi) \\ d^z(p, q, r;\ \pi) \end{bmatrix} \tag{6.11}$$

Or, given private demands, we may use (6.10) to obtain shadow prices as:

$$\begin{bmatrix} \lambda p^0 & & d^x \\ v & = \cdot \frac{V_i}{\mu} \cdot [X]^{-1} & d^y \\ w & & d^z \end{bmatrix} \tag{6.12}$$

These results may be compared with the equivalent pricing rules derived from 'revenue maximization'. This is defined by the following problem:

$$\max\ S(\overline{x}, \overline{y}, \overline{z}) \tag{6.13}$$

where $S(\,)$ is a public-sector utility function depending on resources commanded by the public sector. The maximization of (6.13) is subject to (6.2) to (6.5) as above, and:

$$V(p, q, r; \pi) \geq V^0 \tag{6.14}$$

With a Lagrangean:

$$\begin{aligned} S(\overline{x}, \overline{y}, \overline{z}) + \lambda p^0\left[r_p(p, q, r) - d^x(p, q, r; \pi) + x\right] + \\ v\left[r_q(p, q, r) - d^y(p, q, r; \pi) + y\right] + w\left[\pi_q(p, q, r) - d^z(p, q, r; \pi) + z\right] + \\ \mu f\left[x + \overline{x}, y + \overline{y}, z + \overline{z}\right] + v[V(p, q, r; \pi) - V^0] \end{aligned} \tag{6.15}$$

Now we obtain the same type of first-order conditions for an interior maximum, although note that the Lagrange multipliers, although denoted by the same symbols, do not take the same values. We also obtain:

$$\begin{bmatrix} S_x \\ S_y \\ S_z \end{bmatrix} = \mu \begin{bmatrix} f_x \\ f_y \\ f_z \end{bmatrix} \tag{6.16}$$

which says that the public sector substitutes in its 'consumption' at the same rates as it substitutes in production.

Note

1. The Appendix provides equations from which a formal proof is easily derived.

References

Bliss, C. (1980) 'Optimal Tariffs to Raise Revenue', in G. A. Hughes and G. M. Heal (eds), *Public Policy and the Tax System* (London: George Allen & Unwin).

Corden, W. M. (1974) *Trade Policy and Economic Welfare* (Oxford University Press).

Dasgupta, P. and J. E. Stiglitz (1974) 'Benefit–Cost Analysis and Trade Policies', *Journal of Political Economy*, vol. 82, pp. 1–33.

Diamond, P. A. and J. A. Mirrlees (1971) 'Optimal Taxation and Public Production. I. Production Efficiency; II. Tax Rules', *American Economic Review*, vol. 61, pp. 8–27, 261–78.

Drèze, J. and N. Stern (1985) 'The Theory of Cost–Benefit Analysis', in A. Auerbach and M. Feldstein (eds), *Handbook of Public Economics* (Amsterdam: North-Holland).

Greenaway, D. and C. Milner (1991) 'Fiscal Dependence on Trade Taxes and Trade Policy Reform', *Journal of Development Studies*, vol. 27, pp. 95–132.

Katz, M. (1987) 'Pricing Publicly Supplied Goods and Services', in Newbery and Stern (eds), *The Theory of Taxation for Developing Countries*.

Newbery, D. (1987) 'Taxation and Development', in Newbery and Stern (eds), *The Theory of Taxation for Developing Countries*.

Newbery, D. and N. Stern (eds) (1987) *The Theory of Taxation for Developing Countries* (Oxford University Press for the World Bank).

Ramsey, F. P. (1927) 'A Contribution to the Theory of Taxation', *Economic Journal*, vol. 37, pp. 47–61.

Tanzi, V. (1987) 'Quantitative Characteristics of the Tax Systems of Developing Countries', in Newbery and Stern (eds), *The Theory of Taxation for Developing Countries*.

7

Tax Revenue Instability in Sub-Saharan Africa: Causes and Consequences

Michael Bleaney, Norman Gemmell and David Greenaway

Introduction and overview

The motivation for the present study lies in the accumulating evidence that variations in the resources available to governments of less developed countries (LDCs) often exert a destabilizing influence on fiscal policy. This evidence emerges from the history of international debt in the 1970s and 1980s and from the experience of countries that have enjoyed commodity export booms.

A number of countries which were financing sizeable budget deficits by foreign borrowing in the late 1970s had great difficulty in adjusting to the sudden cessation of this source of finance after the Mexican default of 1982. Corden (1990) has referred to the 'euphoria' which gripped many countries in the 1970s with the explosion of opportunities for foreign borrowing, inducing governments to increase expenditure rapidly in response to the sudden relaxation of constraints on development ambitions.[1] The resulting budget deficits often proved difficult to close when foreign finance was withdrawn, with a consequent monetization of the deficit and an acceleration of inflation. This outcome might have been avoided had non-inflationary domestic sources of finance been available, but in most LDCs domestic bond markets are severely underdeveloped. One consequence of this was the divergent inflationary experience of the developing world and the OECD countries during the 1980s. Whereas the developed countries successfully dis-inflated, the number of developing countries with acute inflationary problems increased.[2]

Detailed studies of countries that have experienced commodity export booms tend to reinforce these conclusions about the behaviour of government expenditure (Bevan *et al.*, 1987; Cuddington, 1989). At the end of a review of a number of such experiences Cuddington (1989, p. 161) writes,

> During booms the ratios of both government spending and revenue to GDP typically rise, with the expenditure to GDP ratio growing faster than the revenue to GDP ratio . . . Therefore, booms are accompanied (with a slight tag) by a rise in the fiscal deficit – just the opposite or what would be expected based on the permanent income consumption strategy . . . As the boom subsides, government revenue collapses, but spending remains at pre-boom levels (or even increases), setting in motion long-term fiscal problems.

What is implied here is an asymmetry in the behaviour of government expenditure. If tax revenue increases or there are increased opportunities for borrowing against future tax revenue, government expenditure tends to increase rapidly. However, if the opposite happens, reductions in government expenditure are often difficult to achieve. In terms of the budget deficit, the same idea could be expressed roughly as follows: it is easier to increase the deficit than to reduce it, either because political resistance often renders expenditure increases or tax cuts difficult to reverse, or because politicians are prey to over-optimism, overestimating the probability that a shock is permanent rather than temporary when the shock is a favourable one, and underestimating the same probability when it is unfavourable.

Whatever the explanation, if there are exogenous forces causing significant variations in tax revenue, any such asymmetry carries the danger that this variability will have a destabilizing effect on fiscal policy. To evaluate the evidence of this for a cross-section of LDCs and for Sub-Saharan African countries in particular, is one of the objects of this chapter. However, we are not just interested in the consequences of tax revenue instability. The phenomenon itself has been little studied, and there is therefore an urgent need to document it, and to understand how it relates to the structure of taxation and to the characteristics of the economy.

There are some good *a priori* reasons for expecting real tax revenues to be less stable in LDCs than in developed market economies (DMEs). Such reasons would include the observation that LDCs appear to be more vulnerable to internal and external shocks than do DMEs, because of the greater importance of the agricultural sector and their dependence on exports of primary products whose prices are volatile. In addition, the structure of taxation in LDCs, which is biased towards taxes on international transactions, may therefore render tax revenue more sensitive to shocks, especially external shocks, than it might otherwise be. Given the known characteristics of Sub-Saharan African (SSA) countries these factors are likely to operate with even greater force there. In order to maximize the size of the sample, the present study is, however, not confined to SSA, though we do seek to highlight African experience in particular.

We should emphasize at the outset the almost complete absence of previous work on the issue. This necessarily constrains our approach to aggregate analysis directed at identifying the general characteristics of the phenomenon of revenue instability, rather than testing country-specific hypotheses. Our approach is as follows. In the next section we discuss measurement problems and present the raw data on the instability of tax revenue in a variety of countries. Among other things, we demonstrate that the problem *is* particularly acute in Sub-Saharan Africa. The focus in the following section is on the sources of revenue instability – what factors are likely to induce variability in tax revenues as a share of GDP? Two types of factor are considered: the structure of taxation, and the more fundamental characteristics of the economy which may in part explain the structure of taxation. Finally, we combine these to present our preferred model of the determinants of tax revenue instability. In considering consequences, we will argue that there are grounds for believing that real tax revenues are causally linked to inflationary pressures and debt problems. Thus, in the penultimate section our analysis switches to the consequences of revenue instability, and finally, in the last section we evaluate some of the policy implications of all of this – in particular, what it implies for commitments to conditionality, fiscal reforms and macro stabilization.

Revenue instability: some stylized facts

Several important issues of measurement arise at the start of the empirical analysis. One is that of choosing an appropriate deflator of nominal tax revenues. The most widely available price index, a consumer price index, is not always an accurate guide to economy-wide inflation because it is particularly sensitive to price controls on such commodities as rents and utilities. For this reason a wholesale price index or GDP deflator is preferable, but is not always available. The simplest solution, which we adopt here, is to work with the tax ratio: tax revenue as a proportion of GDP. Even with unchanged tax rates and relative prices, this measure will vary with real GDP if tax revenues are not unit-elastic with respect to income. However this problem would also afflict any alternative measure we might wish to consider, so that it is not a particular disadvantage of working with the tax ratio.

Another problem relates to the issue of discretionary changes in the tax element of fiscal policy. It may be that taxation policy is unstable, but revenue instability which is so directly policy-induced is not really what we have in mind. In principle, it would be highly desirable to take out these discretionary effects of taxation policy and focus completely on the automatic effects that arise with an unchanged tax regime. However, even in DMEs, direct estimates of discretionary effects are not attempted because of the complexity of tax systems; in LDCs the task would be virtually impossible because tax systems are frequently even more complex, with a large number of different taxes each subject to an uncertain degree of compliance (Tanzi, 1991, ch. 10). The DME approach of estimating automatic effects (either crudely, using proportional tax functions, or with much more highly developed models) and treating the discretionary element as the residual cannot easily be transferred to LDCs, where variation in relative prices (largely ignored in DME models) is likely to be a critical factor. Here, we have made no attempt to distinguish the automatic from the discretionary component of tax revenue instability; this needs to be borne in mind in interpreting our results.

Finally, there is the question of how to measure variability. The standard deviation of the tax ratio over the sample period would be artificially inflated in countries where the ratio exhibited a steady trend over the period with little year-to-year instability. A better approach would be to use the residual standard error from fitting a polynomial in time to the tax ratio, allowing the data to determine the estimated trend. Since such estimated trends have limited credibility, especially if extrapolated into the future, we preferred the simpler approach of working with the standard deviation of *changes* in the tax ratio, relying on the first-differencing process to deal with the trend.

Table 7.A1 in the Appendix presents data on the standard deviation of *changes* in central government tax revenue and grants as a proportion of GDP for fifty countries.[3] Note that the data refer only to central government, and not to local government. The results by country grouping are summarized in Table 7.1.

The figures given in Table 7.1 indicate that there is indeed a tendency towards greater instability of tax ratios in LDCs. The chosen measure averages 1.11 for DMEs, 1.15 for Asia, 1.88 for Latin America, 2.71 for Africa as a whole, and 2.85 for Sub-Saharan Africa. Moreover, in two-thirds of the SSA countries the measure exceeds 2. The difference between SSA

Table 7.1 Instability of tax revenue, by country grouping[4]

Grouping	*No. of countries*	*Instability measures*
Developed market economies	13	1.11
Asia	10	1.55
Latin America	9	1.88
Africa	17	2.71
Sub-Saharan Africa	15	2.85

Source: Calculated from Table 7.A1.

countries and other LDCs is statistically significant and remains so even if the two countries with exceptionally high values (Gambia and Swaziland) are excluded.

Sources of revenue instability

The foregoing analysis suggests that real tax revenues in LDCs exhibit greater variability than real tax revenues in DMEs. It also suggests that variability in SSA countries is greater than variability in non-SSA countries. What are the sources of this variability?

Revenue from a given tax (T_i), assuming no problems with compliance, can be written as:

$$T_i = r_i Q_i \tag{7.1}$$

where

r_i = tax rate; and
Q_i = tax base.

Thus, variations in T_i result from variations in the tax rate and/or variations in the tax base. In a simple model, the former would be the rate of income tax, or the rate of import duty and so on; the latter would be the number of wage earners, the value of dutiable imports. In the case of taxes, the bases for which involve foreign currency transactions (for example, taxes on imports), tax revenue may be represented as:

$$T_k = r_k e Q_k \tag{7.1'}$$

where e is the nominal exchange rate (in domestic currency per dollar) and Q_k is expressed in foreign currency terms. In principle, variations in e therefore provide an additional source of changes in tax revenues (in domestic currency terms). We have not pursued this empirically. On the one hand, nominal exchange rates remained stable over the sample period for our SSA countries. On the other hand, when changes occur they tend to be of a relatively large order of magnitude and could therefore produce a large shift in tax revenues in a particular year. If so, this could cause the tax instability index to be boosted by one (or a few) observations. However, inspection of our data does not suggest sharp, infrequent changes in revenue in an otherwise stable regime.

Generalizing, suppose that T_i represents indirect taxes and T_j direct taxes, with T_r denoting total revenue, then:

$$T_r = r_i Q_i + r_j Q_j \tag{7.2}$$

Clearly, changes in T_r result from changes in tax rates and or changes in tax bases. In principle, this could be decomposed further into those changes which are predictable, and those which are not. What grounds are there for supposing that tax rates and/or tax bases will be more variable in LDCs in general, and SSA countries in particular, than in DMEs?

One of the most striking features of tax structures in LDCs is their dependence on trade taxes (see Greenaway, 1980; Greenaway and Sapsford, 1987). This is particularly true of SSA countries (Greenaway and Milner, 1991). The reasons for this are well known and revolve around the fact that collection costs of trade taxes in LDCs are relatively low when compared with alternatives such as income taxes (see Gemmell, 1991). Perhaps, then, this characteristic is linked to revenue instability? The base for trade taxes is clearly the value of trade. Developing countries in general are small, open economies. Moreover, their import and export structures are typically rather more concentrated than those that characterize DMEs. This can result in greater vulnerability to external shocks. Again, this is especially so of SSA countries. There is a large literature which suggests that imports and exports of primary producers are more unstable than those of industrialized countries. The issue of whether this instability is caused largely by demand or supply shocks is a contentious one (see Riedel, 1984). Either way, the result is variability in the tax base. Whether this variability is greater than that associated with, say, income-based taxes, is an empirical question. On *a priori* grounds it is likely to be so, since changes in aggregate trade flows, in response to a given shock, are likely to be greater than changes in employment (because of the phenomenon of labour hoarding, as well as the fact that labour is employed in non-tradables as well as tradables).

In addition, there are grounds for expecting rates to be more variable than those applicable to income-based taxes. For the most part, tariff rates in LDCs are not bound under GATT, and unilateral changes are therefore possible. Moreover, variations in customs duty are easier to implement politically than variations in most alternatives, given the greater transparency of the latter. Finally, it is not unusual to find *de facto* that rates are altered by the introduction of new/additional import duties under alternative guises (surcharges, stamp duties, even statistical taxes).

Our empirical analysis, therefore, starts by looking at the role of the tax structure in generating revenue instability. We investigate the correlation of revenue instability, as measured by the figures given in Appendix Table 7A.1, with the share of total tax revenue taken by the three main tax categories: taxes on foreign trade; income taxes; and domestic indirect taxes. Within the category of income taxes we examined separately the role of individual and corporate income tax revenue. Although profits taxation can be a very important source of revenue in some countries (notably oil producers) and of low significance in others, it was not found to be correlated with revenue instability. The two variables that appeared to be important were the share of trade taxes and the share of domestic indirect taxes. Because the percentage shares of all taxes must add up to 100, these two variables tend to be negatively correlated with one another. To reduce any resulting collinearity, in the regressions presented in Table 7.2 the domestic indirect tax revenue variable (*itpntt*) is computed as the share of tax revenue excluding trade taxes, not of all tax revenue.

Our preferred regression relating revenue instability to tax structure variables is given in column 1 of Table 7.2. Revenue instability is positively correlated with trade tax dependence and negatively with the share of indirect taxes in the remainder.[5]

The positive coefficient on trade tax dependence is to be expected, given our previous discussion. The negative effects of domestic indirect tax dependence are more puzzling. Indirect tax revenue may perhaps be less sensitive to movements in relative prices of goods, or be less subject to changes in tax rates, the tax base, or tax compliance. Alternatively, the indirect tax share may have no significance of its own but may simply capture the effects of other variables with which it is correlated – there is some evidence of this, as we show below.

It is known that the relative importance of different taxes varies with economic variables such as the level of development. For this reason, the results reported in Table 7.2, column 1, do not necessarily mean that the tax structure influences revenue instability *independently* of these underlying economic factors. We turn therefore to economic explanations. The variables we look at are as follows,

(i) the level of development, as measured by the log of 1980 per capita GDP;

Table 7.2 Regression results for tax revenue instability

Sample	(1) *LDCs*	(2) *LDCs*	(3) *All*	(4) *LDCs*	(5) *LDCs*
Independent variables					
Constant	2.47	4.19	1.66	–0.0682	–0.096
	(3.89)	(2.84)	(1.77)	(–0.03)	(–0.26)
ttd	2.89			3.77	2.28
	(2.56)			(3.69)	(2.19)
itpntt	–2.58				
	(–2.40)				
infmax		0.00517	0.00316	0.00475	0.00498
		(3.16)	(2.46)	(3.41)	(3.98)
openness		2.26	1.53	1.42	1.44
		(4.58)	(4.37)	(3.30)	(3.73)
lypc		–0.570	–0.091		
		(–2.40)	(–0.80)		
dumssa					1.01
					(2.97)
F-statistic	9.09	7.67	10.67	11.47	12.92
Adjusted R^2	0.316	0.364	0.377	0.473	0.577
Standard error	1.08	1.04	0.971	0.950	0.852
Jarque-Bera statistic	2.77	8.13	28.6	4.99	3.43
Sample size	36	36	49	36	36

Notes:
Dependent variable: tax revenue instability as listed in Table 7.A1.
The variables are defined as follows:
ttd = Revenue from taxes on foreign trade as a proportion of total tax revenue.
itpntt = Indirect tax revenue as a proportion of total tax revenue other than firm taxes on foreign trade.
infmax = Maximum inflation rate recorded during the period.
openness = Imports plus exports as a proportion of GDP.
lypc = Log of per capita GDP.
dumssa = A dummy variable = 1 for Sub-Saharan African countries (other than South Africa), and 0 otherwise.
F-statistics are all significant at the 1% level. Significant points for the Jarque-Bera statistic, which tests for normality of the residuals, are 5.99 and 9.21 for the 5% and 1% significance levels respectively. Figures in brackets are t-statistics.

(ii) openness, as measured by the sum of exports and imports as a percentage of GDP;
(iii) size, as measured by the log of 1980 population; and
(iv) inflation variability, which is proxied by the maximum inflation rate recorded during the period (since it is well known that high inflation also tends to be much more variable).

Inflation variability is included because of the well-known Olivera – Tanzi effect, whereby inflation causes a reduction of real tax revenue because of lags in collection. These variables are not uncorrelated with one another; in particular, openness is correlated with population ($r = 0.65$). It was found that population did not add significantly to the explanation excluding population (the likelihood ratio statistic was 2.46 compared with a critical value at the .05 level of 3.84). The fitted equation, excluding population, for the same thirty-six LDCs is shown in column 2 of Table 7.2.

The signs of the coefficients conform to our *a priori* expectations. The results indicate that revenue instability is likely to be more of a problem in poorer, more open and more inflation-prone economies. If the sample is expanded to include the thirteen DMEs, then the results are as shown in column 3 of Table 7.2. All the coefficients become smaller, and in particular *lypc* becomes insignificant. This suggests that the LDC equation is underpredicting revenue instability in DMEs, with their high *per capita* GDP levels, and when DMEs are included in the sample the effect is to reduce the *lypc* coefficient.

Whether DMEs are included or not, there is evidence of non-normality of the residuals, as shown by the Jarque – Bera statistic. This may indicate that one or two outlying observations with large residuals are exerting disproportionate leverage over the results. For the regression shown in column 2, the two largest residuals are Swaziland (2.31) and Zambia (2.17). These are responsible for 40 per cent of the residual variance, and, as a test for robustness, the equation was re-estimated with these countries omitted. The results indicated that the estimated regression is robust, since the coefficients are little changed.

It is interesting to see how the tax variables used in column 1 of Table 7.2 relate to the economic variables in columns 2 and 3. Trade tax dependence (*ttd*) is strongly correlated with *per capita* GDP and openness (t-statistics of –4.34 and 3.45 respectively, when both are included as regressors, with an R^2 of 0.43), but is better explained if population is substituted for openness (t-statistic for population is –4.79; $R^2 = 0.54$). The share of indirect taxes in non-trade tax revenue (*itpntt*) is significantly explained only by openness (t-statistic of –4.44; $R^2 = 0.39$). One possible explanation for this negative correlation between the importance of indirect taxes and openness is that in the hierarchy of collection costs indirect taxes are more costly to collect than trade taxes, but less costly than income-based taxes. Thus, economies that are relatively closed, and therefore have limited access to trade taxes, raise relatively more from indirect taxes. Whatever the explanation, it might mean that *itpntt* is simply acting as a proxy for openness. If we allow ourselves to model revenue instability as a function of both tax and economic variables, then the best explanation is given by the specification shown in column 4 of Table 7.2.

In statistical terms, this is a significant improvement over column 2.[6] Column 4 suggests that revenue instability in LDCs can be related to inflation, openness and trade tax dependence. Although the last two are positively correlated, the equation indicates that, for the same degree of openness, greater trade tax dependence implies greater revenue instability, and vice versa. For Sub-Saharan African countries, these two variables are the basic explanation for the high degree of revenue instability recorded, since inflation is not as serious a problem as in Latin America. Other variables did not add significantly to the explanation. Using a non-nested testing procedure we can reject the substitution of *itpntt* for openness at the 5 per cent level ($\chi^2(1) = 3.92$ for the omission of openness from the encompassing regression, using a likelihood ratio test, whereas for the omission of *itpntt* the same statistic is 2.64, compared with a critical value of 3.84).

We have seen from Table 7.1 that revenue instability appears to be particularly great in Sub-Saharan Africa. Is this entirely explained by our analysis, or do there remain some special factors that render SSA tax revenues unstable? To investigate this we added a dummy variable for Sub-Saharan Africa (other than South Africa) to our preferred regression, with the result shown in Table 7.2, column 5. The dummy variable is significant, indicating the presence of a 'Sub-Saharan African effect', and the main impact of its inclusion is to reduce the importance of trade tax dependence. Why SSA should be noticeably different from other LDCs in this respect is less clear.[7]

A further explanatory variable we tested was export concentration, using the Gini – Hirschman coefficients for 1981 as given in UNCTAD (1984) *Handbook of International Trade and Development Statistics 1984*, table 4.5. It seemed likely that where exports are more concentrated, export revenues are more volatile. Given the evidence that openness affects revenue instability, volatility of export earnings is also likely to do so. However, the export concentration coefficient, though positive as expected, had a *t*-statistic of only 1.18 when added to the regression shown in column 2 of Table 7.2. There are two possible explanations for this finding. First, export taxes are a far less important source of revenue than import taxes. Second, even for those countries where export taxes are significant it matters a great deal what particular commodities countries specialize in exporting. If the supply of exports does not display great variance and the price is not too volatile, high export concentration will not imply great variation in export revenues. For example, Fiji has a high export concentration because of its sugar exports, but this tends to be a regulated market dominated by long-term agreements between exporters and importers. If Fiji is omitted from the sample the *t*-statistic for export concentration rises to 1.63, a result that suggests there is some truth to this explanation.

Consequences of revenue instability

Consider the government budget constraint:

$$G = T_i + T_j + \mathrm{d}M + B_f + B_h \tag{7.3}$$

where

G = total government spending;
T_i = tax revenues from source *i*;
T_j = tax revenues from source *j*;
dM = change in the money supply, inclusive of changes in foreign exchange reserves;
B_f = foreign borrowing; and
B_h = domestic borrowing.

If we take changes in (7.3) and rearrange, we get:

$$-\mathrm{d}T_i = -\mathrm{d}G + \mathrm{d}T_j + \mathrm{d}^2M + \mathrm{d}B_f + \mathrm{d}B_h \tag{7.4}$$

As before, suppose that T_i refers to trade taxes, and T_j to non-trade taxes. Furthermore, assume a relatively heavy dependence on trade taxes, and limited manoeuverability to vary non-trade taxes, because of institutional constraints, say. These are circumstances not untypical of SSA economies (where the average share of trade taxes in total taxes for our sample is 35 per cent). If we then have an exogenous shock in T_i, say, because of a commodity slump, the budget constraint can only be satisfied if one or more of the following consequences result:

(a) Government expenditure must be cut in line with the fall in T_i. Political economy considerations and empirical assessments of SAL programmes suggest that capital spending is more vulnerable to expenditure cuts than current spending (see Harrigan and Mosley, 1991). Thus both current and future output are affected by the revenue fall. Of course, one could argue that cuts in government expenditure, operating through reductions in real interest rates, 'crowd-in' private expenditure – both current and capital. Empirical evidence places a question mark against this. It has been noted, for example, by both World Bank (1990) and Harrigan-Mosley (1991) that adjustment lending programmes have been associated with investment slumps – cuts in government expenditure have failed to crowd-in private investment. Indeed, they may even have been associated with further reductions in private investment. One plausible explanation for why this occurs is policy incredibility. Reductions in tax revenues which result in reductions in government expenditure are less likely to crowd *in* private expenditure than increases in government expenditure associated with increases in taxation are likely to crowd *out* private expenditure. In other words, dG/dT_i is smaller when $dT_i < 0$ than when $dT_i > 0$. Thus, variations in T_i feed directly through to variations in G and thence to real output. In short, revenue instability results in output instability. We investigate below whether revenue instability is indeed associated with expenditure instability.

(b) If variations in both T_j and G are constrained variations in T_i could feed through directly to variations in the money supply. From Equation (7.4) we can see that $dT_i/d^2M < 0$. A decrease in tax revenues, with no commensurate decrease in government expenditure, may stimulate money creation with obvious inflationary consequences. Moreover, the relationship between T_i and M may be asymmetric – decreases in T_i result in monetary expansion, but increases in T_i fail to stimulate monetary contraction. Displacement/ratchet effects in government expenditure are well known. Thus, a clear potential danger of revenue instability is that it can feed inflationary dynamics.

(c) Of course, a revenue shortfall could be met by domestic borrowing. From an analytical standpoint, the interesting issue arising here is that of Ricardian equivalence. Because increased domestic borrowing implies a commitment to future tax obligations, domestic borrowing may have output effects that are little different to changes in government expenditure. In a SSA context this is unlikely to be a major concern. Quite apart from the conditions under which Ricardian equivalence holds, low domestic-savings ratios, thin capital markets and credibility problems combine to rule out recourse to voluntary domestic borrowing as a major offset to revenue instability. However, enforced borrowing from domestic institutions such as banks is widespread in LDCs, including SSA.

(d) The alternative to domestic borrowing is, of course, foreign borrowing, either through the private sector, or through the multilateral agencies.

> Although only a few SSA countries are in the World Bank's list of highly indebted countries (HICs), access to international capital markets is none the less restricted. Poor debt service ratios, low income *per capita*, and a narrow export base characterize the collateral of most SSA countries. The IMF can provide quick-disbursing funds through its upper tranche lending activities, some of which are earmarked to specific shocks. This is, however, conditional on appropriate adjustment and switching policies being agreed (some of which, in the short run at least, may exacerbate problems created by revenue shortfalls). Moreover, the repayment period is relatively short. The World Bank offers longer-term loans, of course. To an increasing extent these too are conditional (principally on supply-side reforms). Moreover, in general, they are not intended to operate as a quasi-contingency fund.

The above points raise interesting analytical issues for empirical research on the consequences of revenue instability, and are prominent in our ongoing research. We do not therefore undertake a detailed analysis here. Rather, we pursue the more limited objective of examining the relationship between revenue instability and expenditure instability, and whether any causal pattern (in the Granger sense of chronological priority) can be discerned in the expenditure–taxation–borrowing triangle in SSA countries. In our sample there are only a few SSA countries with a long enough run of data for the latter investigation to be possible, so that this aspect of the study is confined to Botswana, Ghana, Kenya, Malawi, Swaziland and Zambia.

It is not clear *a priori* that a correlation between revenue and expenditure instability is to be expected. If most of the variation in tax revenue is correctly recognized by governments to be caused by temporary shocks, expenditure is not likely to follow actual revenue closely, but rather to be based on the permanent component of revenue (Cuddington, 1989). Empirically, however, our data show a correlation between expenditure and revenue instability across LDCs. Measures of expenditure instability, calculated on an equivalent basis to our measure of revenue instability, are shown in Appendix Table 7.A1. The correlation between expenditure and revenue instability is 0.59, and is significantly different from zero at the 1 per cent level. Although SSA countries display significantly greater expenditure instability on average than other LDCs, this is entirely explained by the correlation with revenue instability. None of the explanatory variables that are correlated with revenue instability help to explain expenditure instability (over and above what is explained by revenue instability). However, Africa is characterized by an extremely wide dispersion across countries in the expenditure instability measure, much greater than for other LDCs.

The positive correlation of expenditure instability and revenue instability could be explained as an adjustment of expenditure to exogenous changes in revenue that are (at least partly) perceived as permanent, or as the effect of discretionary changes in tax policy according to the level of expenditure it is intended to finance.[8] A possible way of distinguishing between these is by use of the principle of Granger causality. If revenue changes precede expenditure changes, it seems likely that expenditures are reacting to exogenous changes in revenue, whereas in the opposite case it is probable that revenue changes reflect expenditure decisions.

Of the six SSA countries for which the data set contains enough observations to justify such Granger causality tests (Botswana, Ghana, Kenya, Malawi, Swaziland and Zambia), the three with the highest revenue variability (Botswana, Swaziland and Zambia) display no correlation between expenditure and revenue from year to year. For the other three there is a significant positive contemporaneous correlation. Only for Ghana, however, does the lagged value of one variable help to explain the other, and since this occurs in both directions, no inference about causality can be drawn.

As a further check on the interrelationship between tax shortfalls and borrowing, we also examined the relationship between budget deficits and (domestic plus foreign) government borrowing. This was dominated by very strong contemporaneous correlation, suggesting that the relationship is a near-identity. This no doubt reflects the low level of seigniorage revenue in most SSA countries, because of relatively low inflation rates. We therefore dropped domestic borrowing from the analysis, on the grounds that this is likely to be the residual form of financing and examined the relationship between foreign borrowing, expenditure and revenue. Again, the relationships were all simultaneous, but one interesting feature emerged. If revenue was regressed on expenditure and foreign borrowing, foreign borrowing was never significant. But with expenditure as the dependent variable and revenue as an explanatory variable, the foreign borrowing coefficient was significantly positive at the 5 per cent level for Botswana, Malawi and Swaziland, and at the 10 per cent level for Kenya and Zambia. Only in Ghana was it completely insignificant (and here foreign borrowing was very small throughout the period). This pattern is consistent with the 'euphoria' hypothesis that foreign borrowing tends to finance expenditure increases rather than tax reductions.

Policy implications

We have seen, then, that fiscal revenues tend to exhibit greater variability in LDCs than in DMEs. Moreover, this variability also appears to be greater in SSA countries. We have also seen that the variability appears to be connected to features of the tax structure – in particular, relative dependence on trade taxes, as well as other characteristics of the economy, such as inflation variability and openness. Finally, we have reviewed some of the likely consequences of tax revenue instability and undertaken some preliminary empirical investigations. While still at an early stage, our work thus far throws up some interesting policy issues.

First, revenue instability seems likely to feed through into expenditure instability (see Lim, 1983), in part because of the low contingency reserves carried by SSA countries and in part because of constraints on alternative funding sources. Moreover, the asymmetric impact of revenue booms and slumps on the pattern of government expenditure (booms often resulting in a disproportionate expansion of government consumption, while slumps result in a disproportionate contraction in capital expenditure) contributes further to expenditure instability. These effects also contribute to policy problems of macroeconomic stabilization in general, and stabilization of inflation in particular.

Another important consideration relates to commitment to conditionality. Adjustment lending programmes invariably involve trade policy reforms, and often fiscal reforms. A major source of slippage is budgetary pressures (see Mosley, 1987). Unstable revenues raise the probability of short-run budgetary pressures and therefore the likelihood of slippage.[9] Other things being equal, then, those countries with relatively unstable tax revenues may be most likely to renege on conditionality, a possible consequence of which is more limited access to a further source of contingency-type funds. The possible policy interactions here warrant further investigation.

The optimal policy response to revenue instability is a more speculative issue. If the root of the problem is that some governments are less capable of intertemporal optimization than others, perhaps because they are more susceptible to interest group pressures, then one finds oneself in the realms of constitutional reform. A more plausible starting point is the view that the facility for intertemporal optimization varies from one case to another. Thus, if the number of tax handles is limited and access to alternative sources of funds constrained, it is more difficult to optimize. This implies two things: the importance of fiscal diversification, and the importance of a commitment to contingency reserves. The key problem with the former lies in the absence of appropriate infrastructure to support non-trade taxes; in the case of contingency reserves, the problem lies in the availability of appropriate mechanisms for the maintenance of contingency funds specifically for this purpose. Both these problems offer important challenges to the multilateral lending agencies.

Appendix

Table 7A.1 Revenue and expenditure instability in a cross-section of countries (% GDP)

	(1) *No. of years*	*(2)* *Revenue**	*(3)* *Expenditure***
Developed countries			
USA 1973–88	16	0.73	
UK 1971–87	17	1.68	
Australia 1971–87	17	0.97	
Austria 1971–87	17	0.82	
Germany 1971–87	17	0.56	
Denmark 1971–88	18	1.31	
France 1973–87	15	0.98	
Finland 1973–87	15	1.38	
Italy 1974–87	14	1.44	
Netherlands 1974–88	15	0.93	
Norway 1973–87	15	1.38	
Spain 1971–86	16	0.67	
Sweden 1971–88	18	1.54	
Africa			
Botswana 1972–87	16	3.43	3.66
Burkina Faso 1974–86	13	1.31	2.02
Burundi 1974–81	8	2.47	1.83
Cameroon 1976–84	9	2.87	2.49
Gambia 1973–82	10	5.36	5.77
Ghana 1973–88	16	2.42	3.00
Kenya 1973–87	15	1.61	2.35
Liberia 1975–84	10	1.85	5.54
Malawi 1972–87	16	1.61	3.85
Morocco 1971–87	17	1.92	9.69
Sierra Leone 1975–85	11	2.69	3.82
South Africa 1973–86	14	0.70	1.20
Swaziland 1974–87	14	6.82	6.00
Tunisia 1973–84	12	1.33	2.04
Zaire 1972–82	11	3.99	7.06
Zambia 1973–86	14	3.60	10.37
Zimbabwe 1977–87	11	2.06	4.10

Table 7A.1 *(continued)*

	(1) No. of years	(2) Revenue*	(3) Expenditure**
Asia			
Fiji 1971–88	18	1.56	1.63
India 1975–87	13	0.76	1.04
Indonesia 1973–88	16	1.73	2.16
Korea 1971–88	18	0.87	1.76
Malaysia 1973–88	16	2.01	5.42
Pakistan 1974–86	14	0.81	1.96
Papua New Guinea 1978–87	10	2.25	1.81
Philippines 1973–87	15	1.56	1.89
Singapore 1971–87	17	3.05	3.39
Thailand 1973–88	16	*0.89*	1.79
Asia mean		**1.55**	
Latin America			
Argentina 1971–86	16	3.13	4.61
Brazil 1971–87	17	3.13	3.52
Chile 1973–88	16	2.35	2.35
Colombia 1972–84	13	0.69	0.96
Costa Rica 1973–86	14	1.73	2.73
Mexico 1973–87	15	1.48	3.18
Paraguay 1973–87	15	0.75	1.07
Peru 1971–86	16	1.85	1.87
Uruguay 1973–86	14	1.83	2.43

Notes:
* = Standard deviation of year-to-year changes in the tax revenue and grants received by central government as a percentage of GDP, as given in *International Financial Statistics*.
** = Standard deviation of year-to-year changes in government expenditure as a percentage of GDP, as given in *International Financial Statistics*.

Notes

1. Referring to the period 1974–81, Corden writes (1990, p. 68): 'In general, euphoria was characteristic of the whole period among many countries that had export booms, or countries that found it easy to borrow abroad even without such booms.'
2. This is true whatever threshold we choose to take as a definition of 'acute' inflation. According to IMF *International Financial Statistics* inflation in the developing world averaged 36.3 per cent p.a. over the period 1982–9, though this is a GDP-weighted measure that does not truly reflect the fact that the majority of LDCs have had relatively low inflation.
3. Grants are included because they are incorporated in tax revenue in *International Financial Statistics*. Obviously it would be preferable to exclude them. Grants are mostly less than 1 per cent of GDP but can be up to 5 per cent or 6 per cent for some African countries. However, such grants tend to be relatively stable over time.

4. The mean value for Sub-Saharan Africa is significantly different from that for other LDCs at the 1 per cent level.
5. Besides the taxes already mentioned there are wealth taxes and 'other taxes', but the share or these typically is small. The existence or these small taxes means that the share or direct plus indirect taxes in total revenue, excluding that from foreign trade taxes, does not add up to precisely 100, and a better fit was obtained using the indirect rather than the direct tax share.
6. Using a likelihood ratio test, addition of *lypc* to the column 2 regression is accepted; $\chi^2(1) = 7.26$ compared with a critical value at the .01 level of 6.63.
7. The data on these economies are known to be highly suspect in at least some respects (Yeats, 1990), but this seems unlikely to be the full explanation.
8. Borrowing constraints in the short-run may also contribute to the correlation (even if the revenue change is perceived as short-term).
9. SALs themselves have the potential to generate fiscal enhancement or fiscal depletion. This, however, is a separate issue. See Greenaway and Milner (1991).

References

Bevan, D. L., P. Collier and J. W. Gunning (1987) 'Consequences of a Commodity Boom in a Controlled Economy: Accumulation and Redistribution in Kenya 1975–83', *World Bank Economic Review*, vol. 1, no. 3, May, pp. 489–513.

Corden, W. M. (1990) 'Macroeconomic Policy and Growth: Lessons from Experience', *Proceedings of the World Bank Annual Conference on Development Economics*, pp. 59–84.

Cuddington, J. (1989) 'Commodity Export Booms in Developing Countries', *World Bank Research Observer*, vol. 4, no. 2, July, pp. 143–65.

Gemmell, N. (1991) 'Tax Collection Costs and the Choice of Tax Base in Developing Countries', CREDIT Research Paper, No. 91/3, CREDIT, University of Nottingham.

Greenaway, D. (1980) 'Trade Taxes as a Source of Government Revenue: An International Comparison', *Scottish Journal of Political Economy*, vol. 27, pp. 175–82.

Greenaway, D. and C. R. Milner (1991) 'Fiscal Dependence on Trade Taxes and Trade Policy Reform', *Journal of Development Studies*, vol. 27, pp. 95–134.

Greenaway, D. and D. R. Sapsford (1987) 'Further Econometric Analysis of the Relationship between the Fiscal Importance of Trade Taxes and Economic Development', *Public Finance*, vol. 42, pp. 309–19.

Harrigan, J. and P. Mosley (1991) 'Evaluating the Impact of World Bank Structural Adjustment Lending', *Journal of Development Studies*, vol. 27. pp. 63–94.

Lim, D. (1983) 'Instability of Government Revenue and Expenditure in Less Developed Countries', *World Development*, vol. II, pp. 447–50.

Mosley. P. (1987) 'Conditionality as Bargaining Process: Structural Adjustment Lending in 1980–86', *Essays in International Finance No. 168* (Princeton University: Princeton).

Riedel, J. (1984) 'Trade as an Engine of Growth in Developing Countries Revisited', *Economic Journal*, vol. 94, pp. 56–73.

Tanzi, V. (1991) *Public Finance in Developing Countries* (Aldershot: Edward Elgar).

World Bank (1990) *World Development Report* (World Bank, Washington, DC).

Yeats, A. J. (1990) 'On the Accuracy of Economic Observations: Do Sub-Saharan Trade Statistics Mean Anything?', *World Bank Economic Review*, vol. 4, pp. 135–56.

8

Analyzing the Incidence of Taxes in the Côte d'Ivoire[1]

Ngee Choon Chia, Sadek Wahba and John Whalley

Introduction

The question of who bears the burden of taxes has been a staple for public finance economists ever since Gregory King's analysis of the tax burdens of knights and earls in medieval England in 1688. Out of all of the work on tax incidence that has followed, a folklore has evolved concerning the effects of various taxes or tax systems. Over the years, this folklore has guided reformers in their efforts to achieve fairness and to minimize economic inefficiency in tax design. Thus, OECD tax systems are frequently perceived as achieving only limited redistribution, since the progressivity of the income tax is offset by the regressivity in sales, social security and other taxes (Pechman and Okner, 1974). Indirect taxes are viewed as being regressive (Musgrave, 1957; and Musgrave *et al.*, 1974); while corporate taxes are viewed as being sometimes progressive (because of backward-shifting to capital) and sometimes regressive (because of forward-shifting to consumers).

This chapter attempts to relate the above discussion to possible tax reforms in lower-income agrarian African economies. Implicitly, we ask whether tax incidence results obtained for OECD economies offer any guidance to economies with sharply different economic and social structures, with special reference to situation in the Côte d'Ivoire.[2] We use a numerical general equilibrium model of the Côte d'Ivoire developed as part of an ongoing World Bank project.

Since the model incorporates several specific Ivorian characteristics, this allows us to compare results of incidence analyses with and without such specific features.[3] Our results show how these features change tax incidence conclusions from conventional OECD-type analysis in important ways. One is that with narrow bases for each of the major taxes, typical of an agrarian African economy (for example, export taxes on cocoa and coffee, income tax on government employees), tax incidence effects are concentrated more by socioeconomic or sectoral groupings rather than by income range. Another is that, in a trade-restricted environment, changes in trade-related taxes (for examples tariffs, export taxes on commodity producers) have large incidence effects. Yet another is that with large inter-household transfers typical in African economies, taxes which might traditionally be viewed as being borne by one household group will be transmitted partially to others through induced changes in transfers, thus changing overall tax incidence conclusions. Hence, conducting OECD-type tax incidence analysis for the African economies, and concentrating on effects by income range may miss larger redistributions that are taking place elsewhere.

The broad conclusion we offer is that discussion of tax incidence in the African economies can only be guided by the results of incidence analyses for OECD economies with extreme caution. Specific and key characteristics of these economies need to be modelled explicitly, conventional analyses by income range mask larger redistributive effects of taxes among socioeconomic groups, and large inter-household transfers can further complicate results.

The economy and tax structure in Côte D'Ivoire

Côte d'Ivoire is a mid-sized African economy with a population of 12 million (1989) and income *per capita* of approximately $740 (1990). It is one of the key member countries of the West African Monetary Union (UMOA – Union Monétaire Ouest-Africaine)[4] that share a common freely-convertible currency. The Côte d'Ivoire accounts for 41 per cent of the Union's GDP and 23 per cent of the total population.

In the first two decades following independence, the Ivorian economy experienced strong economic performance, with rapid growth in both output and exports. The average annual growth rate of GDP for the period 1965–73 was 8.9 per cent. But in the second half of the 1970s, a series of shocks disrupted the economy. These began with a coffee price boom in 1976, following which revenues accruing to the government through the Stabilization Fund that regulates domestic coffee and cocoa prices received by producers were committed to finance a large investment programme. Although world prices fell immediately after 1976, the government continued its investment programme into the early 198Os, in the belief that the fall in world prices was temporary. But commodity prices continued to fall sharply, growth in the Ivorian economy slowed (and turned negative), and debt service became a major problem. By 1981, the budget deficit had reached 12 per cent of GDP (Chamley, 1991), by 1986 the terms of trade had fallen by 40 per cent, and by 1990 the country's external and internal outstanding debt had reached 125 per cent and 37 per cent of GDP respectively.

A series of structural adjustment programmes was implemented by the government in response to these developments, beginning in the early 1980s. Although there was an improvement in performance between 1984 and 1986, resulting from a rise in world prices of coffee and cocoa and an appreciation of the dollar, since 1986 earlier declines in real output have continued, with real GDP falling by more than a quarter. Along with this deterioration in economic performance, government revenues have also steadily fallen as a percentage of GDP, from 31.1 per cent in 1984 to 23.6 per cent in 1990, with this fall mainly reflecting declining commodity Stabilization Fund revenues. Coffee and cocoa no longer have the majority share of exports, although in 1990 they still accounted for 35 per cent of total exports of goods and services.

The tax system

The Ivorian tax system has also undergone substantial change since the 1960s. Initially limited in revenue-raising capabilities, both government expenditure and revenues grew in the 1960s as commodity exports grew, because of the pre-eminent role of trade taxes (both export taxes and import duties) in the tax system. But as small-scale manufacturing developed, with urbanization and an expansion of government employment, personal income taxes (largely on government employees), and corporate taxes (heavily on foreign-owned subsidiaries) grew. Indirect taxes also became more important, and today a manufacturing level value added tax (VAT)[5] now operates alongside specific excise taxes on petroleum, tobacco, liquor, and other items as a major government revenue source.

The tax system in the Côte d'Ivoire has traditionally been strongly biased against exports, with price stabilization policies operating, against the traditional export sectors, especially in the mid-1980s. In 1986, export taxes and contributions to the Stabilization Fund provided almost 17 per cent of total taxes collected. Changes aimed at reducing the burden of taxes borne by the export sector have been a major feature of recent reforms. Falling world cocoa prices have also meant that in recent years the Stabilization Fund has subsidized rather than taxed exports.

The present day tax system in the Côte d'Ivoire is a hybrid, seemingly including all the major elements of a typical OECD tax system (income,

Table 8.1 Composition of tax revenue in Côte d'Ivoire, selected years (%)[a]

	1980	*1983*	*1986*	*1987*	*1988*	*1989*	*1990*
Percentage of total revenue:							
Production taxes	25.6	29.7	27.7	30.7	31.9	33.9	38.5
Import duties	32.0	30.6	35.9	33.6	34.3	37.8	32.7
Export taxes	10.5	8.7	11.9	11.8	8.6	3.7	1.5
Income taxes	32.0	31.1	24.5	24.0	25.2	24.7	27.4
Tax revenue as percentage of GDP	23.0	22.2	20.4	21.5	20.3	19.1	19.4

Note: [a] = columns do not always add up to 100 because of rounding.
Sources: World Bank (1987, 1991); Chamley (1991).

corporate, sales and so on), while maintaining features commonly found in other developing economy tax systems. First, as Table 8.1 indicates, there is a continuing heavy dependence on import duties.[6] Second, the base of each of the major taxes remains narrow (income tax on government employees, corporate tax heavily on foreign subsidies, VAT restricted to manufacturing level and so on), which leads to relatively high tax costs for certain sectors of the economy. Third, the tax system operates in an often turbulent macro environment, with large debt service costs and domestic government payments further complicating incidence analyses.

Production taxes (VAT and other indirect taxes)

Most manufactured goods and services are subject to value added tax.[7] The system, however, contains considerable cascading. Exporters of certain commodities cannot, for example, recover VAT paid on their inputs, which effectively makes the VAT for these producers a tax on exports. Excises on petroleum products are also especially important.[8]

As Table 8.1 indicates, production taxes now represent the largest source of revenues in the Côte d'Ivoire. According to Chia, Enoh and Wahba (1991), the production VAT represented 27.7 per cent of tax revenues in 1986, and increased to 38.5 per cent by 1990. Their data also imply that, in 1986, the service sector paid 47 per cent of total production taxes, partly explaining the relatively high cost of services in the Côte d'Ivoire.

Income (direct) taxes

Income taxes in the Côte d'Ivoire cover direct taxes on income and corporate profits, as well as taxes on wages and salaries (payroll tax). As a share of total tax revenues, these have remained relatively constant, with a fall relative to previous years only in 1989 and 1990. As in other Sub-Saharan African countries, the tax is effectively sector-specific, since formal-sector households pay most of the tax (19 per cent for private-sector households and 46 per cent for government employees).[9]

Trade taxes

The share of tariffs in total tax revenue in the Côte d'Ivoire remained relatively stable throughout the 1980s. Under the 1987 Structural Adjustment Programme, the government attempted to simulate a devaluation (caused by the overvalued real exchange rate) by providing the same level of incentive for exports (through export premia) as protection for import substitutes. The premia were to be financed through a special tariff on imports. This proved unsustainable, in part because of the discretionary powers the authorities had to exempt products.

The Stabilization Fund

The Ivorian Stabilization Fund derives its revenues from the difference between the prices paid to producers of coffee and cocoa, and world prices. In 1986, the value of the Stabilization Fund was 40 per cent of the value added of the traditional export sector, although since then the Fund has subsidized rather than taxed exports. The value of the Fund has varied from a high of 145 billion CFA in the 1980s to a low of 159 million (deficit) in 1989.

In our later modelling discussion, we treat net payments to or received from the Stabilization Fund (or Caisse de Stabilization) as a tax (or subsidy), and the flow transactions of the Fund as part of the Ivorian tax system. In affecting producer decisions of producers of key export crops (coffee and cocoa), this component of the wider tax subsidy system has substantial impact on a large portion of the population in a key agricultural sector.

Overall, then, the Ivorian tax system has grown and matured since independence, but is still relatively narrow in coverage and is distorted in its impacts on the economy, until recently being heavily biased against non-traditional exports, as well as production. The existence of a series of tax rates and exemptions in the indirect component of the tax system has complicated collection and encouraged evasion. Reforms proposed in the context of a competitiveness programme[10] aimed to broaden the scope of the VAT, further reduce the anti-export bias in the tax system, reduce tariffs (and especially their dispersion), and achieve relative equality in the tax treatment of traded and non-traded goods sectors.

Several specific features of the Ivorian economy and the tax system that are important for tax incidence analysis are especially worth noting. One is large inter-household transfers, typically operating between urban households and rural family members. These imply that taxes usually thought of as being borne by one group of households may have part of their burden transmitted to other households through reduced transfers. A second is the narrow base of key taxes, which implies more specificity in tax incidence than in countries with broadly-based taxes, since taxes primarily affect more narrowly-defined socioeconomic groups (government employees, cocoa farmers and so on), rather than income ranges. A third is the economy's relationship to the external sector, and the tax implications which follow. Significant revenues are raised through trade taxes, and hence in a protected environment and with such a large portion of foreign exchange earnings from commodity exports, tax and subsidy arrangements related to trade have large incidence effects.

Tax incidence analysis in developed and developing countries

Who then bears the burden of these Ivorian taxes? What is their impact on the distribution of income, and what guidance do studies of tax incidence in other economies offer? Studies of the redistributive effects of taxes for various economies around the world[11] typically produce numerical calculations of annual tax incidence based on various assumptions (or model-based treatments) as to how components of tax systems are shifted[12] on to consumers, producers, owners of assets, and other agents.

They typically focus on five key tax groups: personal income; corporate; sales and excise; property; and social security taxes. In these analyses, each has sources and/or uses side-effects. These reflect either assumptions as to how any given tax is either partially or fully borne by one or more components of income on the sources side (that is, capital income, labour income and transfers), or by various household groups on the uses side (that is, according to savings and expenditure patterns by household); or the outcome of calculations made in an explicit modelling framework. Numerical general equilibrium models are the main tool used in such model-based analyses (see Shoven and Whalley, 1984).

Using annual data, three main income sources are assumed to bear the burden of taxes in such studies: capital income; labour income; and transfers. Transfers are heavily concentrated in the lower end of the income distribution, capital income in both the upper and lower ends (because of the presence of retirees), while labour income is closest of the three to being proportional to income. Thus, depending upon whether the sources side-effects of a tax apply to capital income, labour income, transfers, or income in general, progressive or regressive incidence can result. The key feature on the uses side is differential savings rates by income range. In OECD countries, around 40 per cent of household savings is typically concentrated in the top 10 per cent of the income distribution, and taxes that are treated as being borne by consumers of taxed products produce regressive incidence effects.[13]

Sources and uses effects of taxes in incidence calculations thus largely reflect their allocation to components of annual household budget constraints, which for simplicity we can write as (deleting household subscripts):

$$C + S = K + L + Tr - PT \tag{8.1}$$

where C and S denote consumption and savings; and K, L, Tr and PT are capital and labour income, transfers, and personal taxes, respectively. Sources side-effects arise because the composition of income is different by income range. Uses side-effects primarily arise across households as consumption to savings ratios differ by income range.

A sample of the shifting assumptions used in some of the more prominent incidence studies on developed countries (as summarized in Whalley, 1984; and Shah and Whalley, 1991) are set out in Table 8.2, along with an indication as to which produce progressive or regressive incidence results. As can be seen, the major areas of disagreement centre on the corporate, property, and sales and excise taxes. The income tax is treated as paid by income recipients and is progressive due to increasing average tax rates. Social security and related contributions are treated as payroll taxes on labour and, outside of the lower tail of the income distribution, are regressive due to the ceilings on contributions. Corporate and property taxes are regressive if assumed shifted forward to consumers, but progressive if assumed shifted backwards to recipients of capital income. Corporate taxes are even more progressive if assumed borne by capital income specific to taxed industries rather than capital income in general, because of light tax treatment of widely held housing capital. In some literature, this motivates the use of dividends rather than all capital income (which includes dividends) as a more progressive distributive series for allocating corporate taxes. Sales and excise taxes are regressive if borne by consumers, and progressive if borne by recipients of factor

Table 8.2 Incidence assumptions used in developed country tax incidence calculations and on tax incidence patterns

Incidence pattern	*Most progressive*	*Most regressive*	*Shifting assumptions by tax*	*P/O most redistributive case*[a]	*P/O least redistributive basic case*[a]	*Gillespie's basic case*[b]	*B/J competitive case*[c]	*B/J alternative case*[c]
P			A) Individual income tax: (not shifted) allocated to taxpayers according to income taxes paid	X	X	X	X	X
			B) Corporation income tax:					
P			– to capital income in general				X	
P	X		– half to capital income in general; half to dividends (stockholders)			X		
A		X	– half to capital income in general; half to total consumption		X			
P			– half to capital income in general; half to factor incomes	X				X
A			– half to dividend income; half to total consumption					
			C) Property taxes:					
			(i) on land					
P	X		– to capital income in general			X	X	
P			– to landowners	X	X			
P			– to capital owners					
P		X	– half to capital income in general; half to factor income					X
			(ii) on structures and improvements					
P	X		– to capital income in general	X			X	
R		X	– to shelter and consumption		X	X		
P			– half to capital income in general; half to factor income					X

Table 8.2 (continued)

Incidence pattern	*Most progressive*	*Most regressive*	*Shifting assumptions by tax*	*P/O most redistributive case*[a]	*P/O least redistributive basic case*[a]	*Gillespie's basic case*[b]	*B/J competitive case*[c]	*B/J alternative case*[c]
			D) Sales and excises					
R		X	– to consumer of taxed goods	X	X	X		
P	X		– to factor incomes				X	X
			E) Social security					
			(i) on employee					
A			– to employee compensation	X	X	X	X	X
			(ii) on employers					
A			– to employee compensation	X		X	X	
A		X	– half to employee compensation; half to consumption		X			
P	X		– half to employee compesnation; half to factor income					X

Notes: The first column of the table indicates whether a particular shifting consumption results in a progressive (*P*), regressive (*R*) or ambiguous (*A*) pattern; ambiguous being when two opposite patterns occur across income classes.

[a] = P/O refers to Pechman and Okner (1974).

[b] = Gillespie refers to Gillespie (1980).

[c] = B/J refers to Browning and Johnson (1979).

Sources: Whalley (1964), and Shah and Whalley (1991).

incomes. Estimates of the incidence of whole tax systems reflect separate incidence calculations by income range for each tax, which are then summed across taxes.

Studies of tax incidence for developing countries are more typically on a tax-by-tax basis rather than of the whole tax system. By and large, they adopt the same shifting assumption as in developed country incidence analyses, and in a relatively uncritical way.[14] The studies generally find the overall system to be broadly progressive (pro-poor), showing either a U-shaped [see e.g. Malik and Saqib (1989) for Pakistani], or a progressive [see e.g. Jayasundera (1986) for Sri Lanka] incidence pattern. Exceptions to this include Wasylenko (1985) for Jamaica, who finds an inverted U-shaped incidence pattern for the overall tax system, implying that the tax system redistributes from the middle income groups to the poor and the rich.

On a tax by tax basis, the main themes emerging from these studies are as follows:

Value added taxes (VAT)

Developing incidence country analyses of VAT generally reflect an assumption of full forward shifting. The tax is usually simply allocated among income ranges using data on consumption expenditures. Most studies find VAT to be regressive, while also arguing that this regressivity could be reduced through the use of differential tax rates by commodity and excises on 'luxury goods'. Some studies use input–output data to take into account differential rates and exemption of commodities (see Bird and Miller, 1989) while continuing to (implicitly) assume full forward shifting.

Other sales taxes

Incidence effects of manufacturer and wholesale level sales taxes in developing countries are also usually found to be regressive. Full forward-shifting, again, is generally assumed. It is claimed that in many developing countries, despite the widespread use of forward-shifting, producers and wholesalers typically apply a fixed percentage mark-up to prices, and full forward-shifting does not occur. Econometric studies, such as Jeetun's (1978) study of Pakistan, tend to support this point of view.

Excises

Incidence analyses of excise taxes are also based on full forward-shifting, with progressive incidence usually found, since taxed products are bought more heavily by higher income groups. Taxes on tobacco and cheap liquor usually have a regressive incidence pattern, as in developed countries, because of relatively heavier consumption by the poor. Tobacco taxes have been found to be regressive in Colombia (McLure and Thirsk, 1978) in Argentina, Guatemala and Greece (see Bird and Mil1er, 1989), but progressive in Lebanon (Cnossen, 1977). Cnossen (1977) finds regressive incidence and Asher and Booth (1983) progressive incidence in the Philippines.

Import duties

Import duties are usually assumed to be fully forward-shifted to consumers of imported products, with a regressive or proportional incidence outcome being the standard result (see Jeetun, 1978). Most studies ignore the implications of quotas and import licensing for the shifting assumptions used.

Export taxes

Most incidence studies assume the incidence of export tax falls on producer–exporter groups. This yields a progressive incidence pattern, since these groups are in the higher income ranges. A study for Sri Lanka (Jayasundera, 1986) also considered implicit subsidies to domestic consumers associated with export taxes on tea and rubber, and found these also have pro-poor incidence effects.

Personal income taxes

Developing-country incidence studies generally show personal income taxes to be progressive, since these taxes are assumed to be borne by those individuals who pay them. These studies ignore complications stemming from effects on labour migration (urban – rural, for example) or tax evasion.

Corporate income taxes

The shifting assumption most commonly used is that 50 per cent of the tax is shifted forward to consumers, and 50 per cent is borne by owners of capital in the economy. A common finding here is regressive incidence for the lowest income ranges, and a progressive incidence profile for higher income groups.

Urban property taxes

The incidence of the property tax emerges as progressive from most developing country studies (see Bahl and Linn 1985). For owner-occupied residential, commercial and industrial properties, the usual shifting assumption is that the tax falls on capital owners, with no forward-shifting. For rental properties, varying degrees of forward-shifting are assumed. In general,[15] property taxes on owner-occupied property are progressive, while the tax collected from rented property is regressive.

Agricultural land taxes

The usual incidence assumption for agricultural land taxes is that taxes on large farms fall on land owners, and that taxes on subsistence agriculture induce increased marketable surpluses, resulting in a decline in agricultural product prices. An implication of this (see Qureshi, 1987) is that landowners bear more than just the burden of tax. As land ownership is generally concentrated in a few hands in most developing countries, a progressive incidence impact results.

A general equilibrium model of the Côte d'Ivoire for tax incidence analysis

Rather than simply make a series of assumptions on which to base our tax incidence analyses for the Côte d'Ivoire, we have instead used a numerical general equilibrium model which allows us to also incorporate various factors specific to the Côte d'Ivoire which potentially affect tax incidence analysis for the country.[16] The model we use is a numerical open economy general equilibrium model of the Côte d'Ivoire, which forms part of an ongoing World Bank project, and is in the tradition of the computable general equilibrium tax models deriving from Shoven and Whalley (1972 and 1984).

The model captures the main features of the Ivorian economy: production sectors, household sectors, the government sector (which includes the public enterprises) and the rest of the world, along with the institutional setting within which tax policy is conducted (the wider fiscal system, stabilization of domestic producer prices through the Stabilization Fund, inter-household and government–household transfer mechanisms). The model is calibrated to a 1986 benchmark equilibrium data set for Côte d'Ivoire; it also uses Cobb–Douglas and CES functions and literature-based elasticity estimates.

Production

The production side of the model includes seven tradable and eight non-tradable sectors. Tradable sectors include: the food crop sector; the traditional export sector; the non-traditional export sector; the food-processing sector; and the manufacturing sectors. Non-tradable sectors include: gas and electricity; construction; transport; financial services; government services; and other services.

Given the importance of agriculture in the Côte d'Ivoire, (46 per cent of GDP and 91 per cent of exports in 1986), considerable detail is incorporated for the agricultural sector. We disaggregate this sector into the food crop sector, the traditional export sector (which include coffee and cocoa), and the non-traditional sector (for example, sugar, palm oil, rubber). The model also incorporates a distinction between formal and informal sectors in the Ivorian economy; the informal sector is defined as activities under-represented in the annual financial survey of enterprises, and those that do not pay taxes or receive subsidies (Chia, Enoh and Wahba, 1991).

All sectors are assumed to be competitive; labour is assumed to be mobile across sectors; capital is immobile in the short run, but mobile in the longer run; and capital is assumed to be internationally immobile. Firms determine factor demands and output supplies by maximizing profits. Production functions in each sector are nested; the top level nest is a Leontief function of intermediate demands and value added; intermediate demands are a CES function of domestically-produced and imported goods; value added is a nested CES function of capital and labour, the latter being further disaggregated.

Households

Unlike the case in tax incidence studies for developed countries, which group households according to income range, households in our study are stratified by socioeconomic group. Classifying households in this manner allows us to identify the impacts of alternative policy scenarios on different segments of the economy. The seven household groups are export households; food crop households; households in the Savannah region; households who are administrative government employees; households in the formal sector; households engaged in independent trades or in the informal sector; and inactive households.[17] These are listed in Table 8.3, along with data on household group characteristics, including shares of population, household income, savings rates and net transfers paid or received.[18]

Households are assumed to maximize a nested utility function subject to their budget constraint. In the top nest, the utility function is a Cobb–Douglas function defined over goods. In the lower nest, each good is a CES function defined over domestic and imported goods. In our static model, household shares of consumption and savings in post-tax income are assumed to be constant. All household savings are treated as being paid into a savings pool, which finances domestic investment.

Table 8.3 Key characteristics of Ivorian household groups identified in the model

Household types	*Population share*	*Poverty[a] index (%)*	*Per capita income (CFA)*	*Savings as percentage of total income*	*Income tax as percentage of total income*	*Transfer payments to other households (as percentage of total income)*	*Transfer income received from other households (as percentage of total income)*
Food croppers in Savannah	11.03	63.68	132 972	0.33	0.80	0.00	24.00
Export croppers	20.28	44.04	173 722	0.57	0.50	15.60	0.00
Small businesses	21.48	46.81	187 600	0.91	1.02	0.00	0.00
Other food croppers	12.77	34.46	202 176	0.37	0.45	32.75	0.00
Inactive	15.10	37.07	220 629	0.75	2.81	0.00	67.86
Government employees	11.80	8.69	423 085	0.89	5.86	11.24	0.00
Households in formal sector	7.60	1.79	622 807	0.80	2.48	16.96	3.50

Note: [a] = This index indicates the fraction of the household population within each cell who are below the official poverty line.

Each household thus consumes the fifteen types of consumer goods identified in the model, is endowed with an exogenous and fixed amount of both mobile factors (labour and capital) and sector-specific factors, and preferences differ by household. Besides income from endowments, households also receive transfers from the government, from abroad and from other households. Unlike in developed countries, as Table 8.3 indicates, inter-household transfers play a major role in the economy with its strong rural–urban linkage.

Labour market

The model structure includes a treatment of the labour market that is more detailed than in many other general equilibrium models. To capture labour market segmentation in the Côte d'Ivoire, labour is disaggregated into three types: agricultural; skilled; and unskilled. Skilled and unskilled labour move freely across sectors, while agricultural labour is sector-specific. In the agricultural sector, unskilled labour, skilled and agricultural labour enter a CES aggregation function. In the non-agricultural formal sectors, labour is a nested CES function of skilled labour and unskilled labour. The informal sector uses only unskilled labour.[19] With unskilled and skilled labour mobile across sectors, this treatment of the labour markets captures movements between formal and informal sectors, as well as migration between agricultural and non-agricultural sectors (that is, rural–urban migration).

Government

In the model, the government provides various services, such as public administration, economic and social planning, defence and security services to the public without charge (or with only a small user fee). They are decided upon through government utility maximization defined over inputs (mainly labour) used to provide these service: that is, there is no mechanism for households to articulate demands for public goods.

In addition to real goods and services used by government to provide public services, public-sector transfers to households for education and other objectives also enter the model. All these government activities are financed by the taxes that are modelled explicitly and whose incidence provides the subject matter of this chapter. Finally, the government sector also includes the Caisse de Péréquation (marketing board for rice) and Caisse de Stabilization (marketing board for cocoa, coffee), whose activities are modelled as tax or subsidies depending upon whether or not revenues are raised by the fund on a net basis.

External sector

The treatment of the external sector in the model embodies the Armington (1969) assumption that imports are imperfect substitutes for comparable domestically-produced goods. Tariffs apply to imported products. Domestic-import composites enter both intermediate demands and household final demands. The model departs from the 'price taker' on imports and 'price maker' on exports assumption, and assumes small, open, price-taking behaviour for both imports and exports. Exported products are homogeneous across domestic and foreign markets.

Numerical implementation and calibration of the model

The model is implemented following the procedures outlined in Mansur and Whalley (1984). We use a benchmark equilibrium data (BED) representing the Ivorian economy for 1986.[20] The BED is used to calibrate a basic variant of the model as well as other variants used in sensitivity and other analyses, and also provides a benchmark for counterfactual analysis with the model. The specification used for the central case variant of the model is outlined in Table 8.4.

Table 8.4 Model specifications, central case variant, Côte d'Ivoire model

A	**PRODUCTION**
	Fifteen sectors
	Nested CES function
	Leontief function of value-added and intermediate demand
	Value-added is CES function of capital and labour
	Intermediate demand is a CES function of domestically-produced and imported
	Two categories of capital
	Non-agricultural capital – fully mobile
	Sector-specific agricultural capital
	Three labour types
	Skilled labour
	Unskilled labour in agricultural sector
	Unskilled labour in non-agricultural sector
B	**CONSUMPTION**
	Seven household types
	CES utility function defined over Armington goods
C	**KEY FEATURES**
	Inter-household transfers
	Small open price-taking economy
	Goods distinguished between domestically-produced and imported

Table 8.5 Elasticity of substitution assumptions, Côte d'Ivoire model

Sectors[1]		*Elasticity of substitution between capital and labour*	*Elasticity of substitution between qualified and non-qualified labour*
1	Food crop	0.4	0.6
2	Traditional export	0.4	0.6
3	Non-traditional export	0.5	0.6
4	First transformation (F)	0.8	0.4
5	First transformation (I)	0.9	0.8
6	Manufacturing (F)	0.8	0.4
7	Manufacturing (I)	0.9	0.8
8	Gas, electricity	0.8	0.4
9	Construction (F)	0.3	0.4
10	Construction (I)	0.4	0.8
11	Transport	0.5	0.4
12	Financial services	0.8	0.4
13	Services (F)	0.8	0.4
14	Services (I)	0.9	0.8
15	Government services	0.0	0.0

Note: [1] F and I denote formal and informal sectors.

Following Harberger (1962), a unit's convention is used to separate the benchmark equilibrium data into separate price and quantity observations. For example, assuming the net-of-tax price of labour to be one, the quantity of labour demanded by sector *i* is determined simply from the value added data on labour in sector *i*. With this separation complete, model calibration is straightforward for Cobb–Douglas functions[21] and is implemented for the CES functions in the ways described in Mansur and Whalley (1984), using elasticity parameters from related literature.[22] The key elasticity parameters used in the model on the production side for capital-labour and qualified–non-qualified labour substitution are set out in Table 8.5. MPS/GE, a software package developed by Rutherford (1989) is used to solve the model.

Côte d'Ivoire incidence analyses from the general equilibrium model

As Musgrave (1957) long ago pointed out, there is no unique way to execute tax incidence analyses, since the counterfactual needs to be carefully specified. He suggested three different tax incidence concepts: 'absolute', 'differential' and 'budget' incidence. In differential incidence analysis, the most widely used of his concepts, the tax being examined is

Table 8.6 Incidence impacts of Ivorian taxes, central case model variant (Hicksian EVs expressed as percentage of benchmark gross income)

Households		*Introducing an equal yield, non-disturbing consumption tax to replace:* Personal income tax	Production taxes	Export taxes	Import duties	Stabilization fund	Subsidies
		1	*2*	*3*	*4*	*5*	*6*
Poor ↓	Food croppers in Savannah	–0.65	–6.44	0.25	0.67	0.46	–3.58
	Export croppers	–0.26	4.51	1.12	24.11	27.87	0.86
	Small businesses	–1.58	1.24	0.09	–0.18	–1.60	0.22
	Other food croppers	–1.52	–7.93	0.04	0.16	–3.03	–3.20
	Inactive	2.66	–2.53	0.42	1.12	5.35	–2.79
	Government employees	3.44	2.59	–0.61	–8.50	–10.33	1.52
↑ **Rich**	Households in formal sector	–0.63	3.48	–0.38	–10.8	–8.73	1.73

replaced by a yield-preserving neutral alternative tax. The counterfactual analyses we perform with our model use this differential incidence concept, as in Shoven and Whalley (1977). We substitute a yield-neutral broadly-based sales tax for each major component of the tax system, such that total real government revenues (and hence expenditure) are kept constant in each of our analyses.[23]

Table 8.6 reports tax incidence results for various components of the Côte d'Ivoire tax system using 1986 data and the central case specification of our model. We analyze the effects on the seven household groups in the model, which we rank from richest to poorest.[24] For each household group we report welfare impacts by household for the tax change involved, in terms of Hicksian-equivalent variations expressed as a fraction of the base case gross income of the household group. A positive number indicates a gain from the tax change, and a negative number a loss from the change, from the present tax regime to one containing an equal-yield, broadly-based sales tax in place of the replaced tax.

Personal income taxes

Our results in Table 8.6 generally produce a progressive incidence profile for the Ivorian income tax, but not for the top income group in the formal sector, where the use of tax loopholes and avoidance changes the incidence profile. Other developing country incidence studies using partial equilibrium generally show personal income taxes to be progressive, since these taxes are assumed to be borne by those individuals who pay them. These studies ignore complications stemming from effects of labour migration (urban–rural, for instance), or tax evasion,[25] and inter-household transfers which (as will be shown) can alter the tax-incidence profile.

Production (sales, value-added and excise) taxes

Column 2 in Table 8.6 presents incidence results for production taxes, finding their incidence profile to be neither progressive nor regressive, with the major effects of removing these taxes operating against the non-export agricultural sector (food croppers in the Savannah, and other food croppers), and with exporters and urban dwellers gaining from the removal of the tax (and its replacement by a yield-neutral alternative). A series of factors account for these results. Food croppers are largely tax free in the base-case situation, and are adversely affected by the broadly-based, equal-yield tax which they, along with all households, pay. Urban dwellers are heavy payers of the manufacturing level VAT in the Côte d'Ivoire.

These results also differ from other incidence analyses of production taxes in developing countries, which generally reflect an assumption of full forward-shifting. Because these taxes are usually simply allocated among income ranges using data on consumption expenditure, such studies usually find that these taxes are regressive, while also arguing that this regressivity could be reduced through the use of differential tax rates by commodity, and excises on 'luxury goods'. Here, the incidence profile is a mix of negative and positive effects by household group. Larger redistribution occurs than with income tax because of the large relative price effects stemming from removal of selective sales taxes, including VAT and border tax adjustments.

Export taxes

Incidence results in Table 8.6 for export taxes show a pro-poor effect from the removal of export taxes in the Côte d'Ivoire, suggested that these taxes are regressive. Indeed, current reforms aim at eliminating these taxes gradually (The World Bank, 1991). In part, these incidence effects from the model reflect the impact of the replacement taxes in also applying to urban households consuming imported products. These results are in contrast to those from other incidence studies, which assume that the incidence of export taxes falls exclusively on producer–exporter groups, and which yield a progressive incidence pattern, since these groups are in the higher income ranges. One study consistent with our findings is that of Sri Lanka by Jayasundera (1986) who also considered implicit subsidies to domestic consumers associated with export taxes on tea and rubber, and found that these have pro-poor incidence effects.

Import duties

Results in Table 8.6 also suggest that incidence effects of import duties in the Côte d'Ivoire are large, with mixed effects across household groups ranked by income range. Removing duties positively and substantially affects agricultural export sectors, since import duties operate in a similar way to export taxes. Since prices of domestic import competing products increase behind the tariff wall, removing tariffs raises domestic prices of exportables relative to import substitutes, which affects returns to fixed factors in export sectors. Subsistence food croppers selling food products to the domestic and urban market suffer as agricultural wages are bid up by agricultural exporters.

Government workers lose since they must pay the new replacement tax. In other developing country incidence studies, import duties are usually assumed to be fully forward-shifted to consumers of imported products, with a regressive or proportional incidence outcome being the standard result (see Jeetun, 1978).

Stabilization payments

Results in Table 8.6 also reveal large incidence effects for the Stabilization Fund covering coffee and cocoa. In part, this is a reflection of the 1986 base-year data used in the model, since in that year large net receipts accrued to the Fund, which acted as a tax on export croppers. In the early 1990s, the Fund was close to break-even if not a net payer of revenues, and hence in model terms more like a subsidy. The gain to export croppers from removing the 1986 tax is nearly 30 per cent of income. Interestingly, inactive households share in this gain because of the large inter-household transfers operating in Côte d'Ivoire. Government employees and households in the formal sector lose due to the introduction of the yield-neutral alternative tax which they must pay.

Subsidies

The elimination of subsidies, like other experiments considered in Table 8.6, has a mixed incidence pattern, with both positive and negative effects across households. Food croppers tend to lose because of the direct benefits they forego from agricultural and other subsidies; the inactive loss because of reduced inter-household transfers; and other groups gain because of reduced financing requirements (reflected in a replacement by a yield-neutral, broadly-based subsidy).

A theme that emerges strongly from these results is that the Ivorian tax system has large redistributive effects, but they criss-cross the rich–poor spectrum of household mean incomes in a number of ways. Removing import duties benefits export croppers substantially. Government employees and formal-sector households gain from removing subsidies to the poor because of lowered taxes, and from removing progressive personal income taxes. Low-income food croppers lose because of the effective broadening of the VAT base, and the removal of subsidies. And finally, given the 1986 data we used, in which the Stabilization Fund appears as a tax, export croppers benefit from its removal, while higher income groups lose from the equal-yield replacement tax introduced in its place.

The overall incidence effects are, however, not graduated from rich to poor, as is the case in OECD-style incidence analyses. Positive and negative signs appear alternately in incidence profiles as one moves from mean income poor to rich households. In part, this is because incidence effects by tax, in contrast to developed countries, are more heavily concentrated on particular socioeconomic groups than they are by income range. The importance of the external sector, given high protection, is another factor.

Tax incidence with no inter-household transfers

A further reason is the role that inter-household transfers play in determining tax incidence in the Côte d'Ivoire. As Table 8.3 suggests, they are large, and as a result taxes thought to be borne by one household group are indirectly borne by others through reduced transfer incomes.

Although our data and model do not capture the full pair-wise flows of inter-household transfers, the net flows (or receipts) we capture are still large enough to affect results. Table 8.7 reports incidence results for taxes in the Côte d'Ivoire, where all inter-household transfers are treated in the model as, instead, being paid directly to the government, so as to remove the direct effects of inter-household transfers on incidence results.

Compared to Table 8.6, incidence effects change sign for some household groups (such as the inactive) in the production tax case, and the general incidence picture is substantially different for each tax. The mechanism underlying these differences in results is that payers of transfers are little affected by the model modification, paying transfers in the central-case model variant to other households, and in the new model variant to the government. But receivers of transfers (such as the inactive) now receive a larger overall proportional share of government revenues, rather than directly from other households, substantially weakening

Table 8.7 Incidence effects of Ivorian taxes when interhousehold transfers are eliminated from the model (Hicksian EVs expressed as percentage of benchmark gross income)

Households		*Introducing an equal yield non-distorting consumption tax, to replace:*					
		Personal income tax	*Production taxes*	*Export tax*	*Import duties*	*Stabilization fund*	*Subsidies*
		1	*2*	*3*	*4*	*5*	*6*
Poor ↓	Food croppers in Savannah	–1.17	–8.06	0.21	0.62	–0.88	–3.97
	Export croppers	–0.05	3.99	1.20	24.43	29.43	0.36
	Small businesses	–1.63	1.26	0.08	–0.17	–1.40	0.24
	Other food croppers	–1.25	–9.00	0.21	0.58	–0.49	–4.39
	Inactive	0.16	0.61	0.07	–0.43	–1.36	0.06
	Government employees	4.62	2.10	–0.54	–8.13	–8.92	0.97
↑ **Rich**	Households in formal sector	0.22	2.89	–0.29	–10.38	–7.06	1.06

inter-household linkage in transfer activity and its influence on tax incidence results. The differences in results between Table 8.6 and 8.7 thus suggest the importance of inter-household transfers in assessing the incidence of taxes in economies such as the Côte d'Ivoire.

Sensitivity analysis

We have also investigated the sensitivity of our incidence results to model features and parameters, conducting a series of further incidence analyses under a variety of alternative model specifications. One of the resulting sets of results is reported in Table 8.8, the case where we set all capital labour substitution elasticities equal to 0.5 (see Table 8.5). Another is reported in Table 8.9. This reports on various changes in substitution elasticities between domestic and foreign products in consumption and production in the context of the removal of import duties case analyzed in Table 8.6. While these are, admittedly, relatively small changes in model specification, results in Table 8.8 and 8.9 show little sensitivity in incidence findings to these elasticity variations. Generally, this is the case with other elasticity variations, but for changes in model structure (such as variations in the relative size of fixed-to-variable factors by industry) more variation is obtained.

Thus the theme that emerges from these incidence analyses is that mechanical application of partial equilibrium incidence analysis based on

Table 8.8 Incidence analyses of the Ivorian taxes, using capital–labour substitution elasticity of 0.5 (Hicksian EVs expressed as percentage of benchmark gross income)

Households		*Introducing an equal yield, non-distorting consumption tax, to replace:* Personal income tax 1	Production tax 2	Export tax 3	Import duties 4	Stabilization fund 5	Subsidies 6
Poor ↓	Food croppers in Savannah	−0.64	−6.41	0.27	0.77	0.56	−3.58
	Export croppers	−0.25	4.68	1.18	24.20	28.01	0.87
	Small businesses	−1.57	1.32	0.12	−0.06	−1.45	0.23
	Other food croppers	−1.50	−7.82	0.08	0.39	−2.76	−3.17
	Inactive	2.65	−2.58	0.39	1.01	5.18	−2.82
	Government employees	3.40	2.37	−0.71	−8.98	−10.89	1.50
↑ **Rich**	Households in formal sector	−0.62	3.39	−0.40	−10.77	−8.71	1.71

Table 8.9 Import duty removal incidence, sensitivity to various substitution elasticities between domestic and imported goods in consumption and production (Hicksian EVs expressed as percentage of benchmark gross income)

Households		*Introducing an equal yield, non-distorting consumption tax, to replace:* Personal income tax 1	Production tax 2	Export tax 3	Import duties 4	Stabilization fund 5	Subsidies 6
Poor ↓	Food croppers in Savannah	0.14	0.23	0.67	1.13	1.96	3.61
	Export croppers	26.33	25.15	24.11	23.48	22.60	21.29
	Small businesses	0.02	−0.05	−0.18	−0.30	−0.50	−0.87
	Other food croppers	0.34	0.21	0.16	0.11	−0.04	−0.51
	Inactive	−0.23	0.13	1.12	2.12	4.01	8.01
	Government employees	−10.03	−9.29	−8.50	−7.88	−6.81	−4.72
↑ **Rich**	Households in formal sector	−11.45	−11.01	−10.80	−10.75	−10.74	−10.80

shifting assumptions to African economies should only be undertaken with extreme caution. Country-specific features such as inter-household transfers can affect results substantially; narrowness in tax bases implies concentrated and localized incidence effects which may not be reflected in effects across income ranges; and tax burdens may be transmitted to other groups through changed behavioural patterns.

Concluding remarks

This chapter has discussed tax incidence in the Côte d'Ivoire, reporting results from a numerical general equilibrium model of the Côte d'Ivoire recently developed with World Bank support. It made the argument that, for lower income agrarian African economies, country-specific features need to be incorporated in any tax incidence analyses performed, since mechanical transfer of OECD-style incidence analysis can potentially be highly misleading. Here, we evaluate incidence effects for various Ivorian taxes (as well as the whole tax system). Model results suggest important effects on incidence findings from large inter-household transfers (taxes thought to affect one group also affect others through changed transfers); from taxes which are much more marked in their impact across socioeconomic groups than income ranges, because tax bases are narrow and largely sector- (or group-) specific; and tax burdens are potentially substantially affected by trade-related tax changes.

Notes

1. This chapter is a revised draft of a paper originally prepared for a Conference on African economic policy reform, organized by the Centre for the Study of African Economies, Oxford University, and the Centre for Research in Economic development and International Trade, Nottingham University held in Oxford, 6–8 January 1992. The views expressed in this chapter do not reflect those of the organizations with which the authors are affiliated. We are grateful to Conference participants for helpful comments.
2. A paper by Shah and Whalley (1991) also highlights the pitfalls in applying OECD-type incidence analyses to developing countries in which there are extensive price and quantity interventions in place.
3. For a full discussion of the model structure and different policy options see Chia *et al.* (1992).
4. The UMOA includes six other countries: Bénin, Burkina-Faso, Mali, Niger, Sénégal and Togo.
5. See the more detailed discussion of the VAT in the Côte d'Ivoire in Heian and Monson (1987).
6. Export taxes were reduced sharply throughout the late 1980s.
7. See Heian and Monson (1987).
8. In 1990 the tax on petroleum products averaged 167 per cent of the ex-factory price, making the price of petroleum products in the Côte d'Ivoire among the highest in the world (World Bank, 1991).
9. See Chia, Enoh and Wahba (1991), who estimate the distribution of the burdens across different households from government budget data as well as household surveys.

10. See World Bank (1991).
11. See, for example, Gillespie (1980), Pechman and Okner (1974), Musgrave *et al.* (1974), and Browning (1978).
12. In the literature, the terms 'shifting assumptions', 'incidence assumptions' and 'sources and uses side-effects' all refer to procedures used in the allocation of tax burdens. These terms are used interchangeably here, although we predominantly use the term 'shifting assumption'.
13. This is the case with the conventional treatment of sales and excise taxes. Uses side-effects can also occur, which are product-specific, such as with excise taxes on alcohol and tobacco.
14. A few recent studies have examined developing country tax incidence using general equilibrium techniques (see, for example Habito, 1984; Bovenburg, 1987; and Chowdhury, 1990), although the important country specific features of individual developing countries which we stress in this paper do not receive any significant attention in this work.
15. These studies all ignore tax capitalization effects, under which property taxes lead to a fall in the market value of assets (see Chaudry-Shah, 1988). With such effects included, a properly administered property tax is likely to be somewhat more progressive than it appears under traditional assumptions.
16. A more detailed description of the model structure and its implementation is given in Chia, Piggott, Wahba and Whalley (1991).
17. See Chia, Enoh and Wahba (1991) for a more detailed discussion of this household classification.
18. See Chia, Enoh and Wahba (1991) for more detail on the data on transfers. These are estimated by using household data on financial savings to which regression estimates on acquisition of financial assets are applied. The difference is taken to be net transfers, which across all household groups are constrained to sum to zero.
19. For a more detailed description of the structure of the value-added functions, see Chia *et al.* (1992).
20. The year 1986 was chosen because it had the most reliable national accounts data available (that is, final accounts rather than provisional accounts), as well as having a Living Standard Measurement Survey (LSMS) (see Chia, Enoh and Wahba, 1991); 1986, however, was a year in which the Stabilization Fund raised significant net revenues (that is, acted as a tax), unlike the late 1980s and the 1990s.
21. See also, Bond (1983) and Benjamin and Devarajan (1985), and especially the modèle de prévision macro-éonomique used by the planning department in the Côte d'Ivoire.
22. Scale parameters in the Cobb–Douglas function are determined from the input shares of factors.
23. See de Wulf (1975) for a review of tax incidence analysis in developing countries.
24. Note, however, that this classification from poor to rich is not identical to what would be used in a more traditional income range tax-incidence analysis, since the use of socioeconomic criteria rather than income deciles mean that the poor and the rich households in the economy are distributed across all these groups. The poor-to-rich household ranking shown in Table 8.6 is by the mean incomes of each group.
25. For anecdotal evidence on tax evasion see, for example, Klitgaard (1988).

References

Armington, P. S. (1969) 'A Theory of Demand for Products Distinguished by Place of Production', *International Monetary Fund Staff Papers, no. 16*, pp. 159–76.

Asher, M. G. and A. Booth (1983) *Indirect Taxation in ASEAN* (Singapore University Press).

Bahl, R. and J. Linn (1985) *Urban Public Finance and Adminstration in Developing Countries* (New York: Oxford University Press).

Benjamin, N. and S. Devarajan (1985) 'Oil Revenues and Economic Policy in Cameroon', World Bank Staff Working Paper, no. 745.

Bird, R. M. and B. D. Miller (1989) 'Taxation, Pricing, and the Poor', in R. M. Bird and S. Horton (eds), *Government Policy and the Poor in Developing Countries* (University of Toronto Press).

Bond, M. E. (1983) 'Agricultural Responses to Prices in Sub-Saharan African Countries', *IMF Staff Working Papers*, vol. 30, no. 4, December.

Bovenberg, A. L. (1987) 'Indirect Taxation in Developing Countries: A General Equilibrium Approach', *IMF Staff Papers*, vol. 34, no. 2, June, pp. 333–73.

Browning, E. K. (1978) 'The Burden of Taxation', *Journal of Political Economy*, vol. 86, pp. 649–71.

Browning, E. K. and W. R. Johnson (1979) *The Distribution of the Tax Burden* (Washington, DC: American Enterprise Institute for Public Policy Research).

Chamley, C. (1991) 'Côte d'Ivoire: The Failure of Structural Adjustment', in *Restructuring Economies in Distress. Policy Reforms and the World Bank*, V. Thomas *et al.* (eds), (Oxford University Press).

Chamley, C. and H. Ghanem (1991) 'Fiscal Policy with Fixed Nominal Exchange Rates', *Working Paper Series*, no. 658, Washington, DC: World Bank.

Chaudry-Shah, A. (1988) 'Capitalization and the Theory of Local Public Finance: An Interpretive Essay', *Journal of Economic Surveys*, vol. 2, December, pp. 209–43.

Chia, N. C., E. Enoh and S. Wahba (1991) 'Improving the Macroeconomic Data Base: A SAM for Côte d'Ivoire, 1986', mimeo (Washington DC: World Bank).

Chia, N. C., J. Piggott, S. Wahba and J. Whalley (1991) 'A General Equilibrium Modelling Capacity for Côte d'Ivoire,' mimeo (Washington DC: World Bank).

Chia, N. C., S. Wahba and J. Whalley (1992) 'A General Equilibrium-Based Social Policy Model for Côte d'Ivoire', *Poverty and Social Policy series* (Washington DC: World Bank).

Chowdhury, O. (1990) 'Tax Policy Analysis in Bangladesh: A Computable General Equilibrium Approach', Ph.D. dissertation, University of the Philippines, Manila.

Cnossen, S. (1977) *Excise Systems: A Global Study of the Selective Taxation of Goods and Services* (Baltimore, Md: Johns Hopkins University Press).

de Wulf, L. (1975) 'Fiscal Incidence Studies in Developing Countries: Survey and Critique', *International Monetary Fund Staff Papers*, vol. 22, no. 1, pp. 61–131.

Gillespie, W. I. (1980) *The Redistribution of Income in Canada* (Ottawa: Gage Publishing).

Habito, C. F. (1984) 'Equity and Efficiency Tradeoffs in Philippine Tax Policy Analysis: A General Equilibrium Approach', Ph.D. dissertation, Harvard University, Cambridge, Mass.

Harberger, A. (1962) 'The Incidence of the Corporate Income Tax', *Journal of Political Economy*, vol. 70, June, pp. 215–40.

Heian, B. and T. Monson (1987) 'The Value-Added tax in Côte d'Ivoire', Discussion Paper Report No. DRD227 (Washington DC: World Bank).

Jayasundera, P. B. (1986) 'Economic Growth, Income Distribution, and Welfare Expenditure: The Case of Sri Lanka', Ph.D. dissertation, Boston University.

Jeetun, A. (1978) 'Incidence of Taxes in Pakistan', *Research Report 10*, Applied Economics Research Centre, University of Karachi.

Klitgaard, R. (1988) *Controlling Corruption* (Berkeley, Calif.: University of California Press).

Malik, M. H. and N. Saqib (1989) 'Tax Incidence by Income Classes in Pakistan', *The Pakistan Development Review*, vol. 28, no. 1, Spring, pp. 13–26.

Mansur, A. and J. Whalley (1984) 'Numerical Specification of Applied General Equilibrium Models: Estimation, Calibration and Data', in H. E. Scarf and J. B. Shoven (eds), *Applied General Equilibrium Analysis* (New York: Harper & Row).

McLure, Jr, C. E. and W. Thirsk (1978) 'The Inequity of Taxing Inequity: A Plea for Reduced Sumptuary Taxes in Developing Countries', *Economic Development and Cultural Change*, vol. 26, pp. 487–503.

Michel, G. and N. Michel (1984) 'Short Term Responses to Trade and Incentive Policies in the Ivory coast: Comparative Static Simulations in a Computable General Equilibrium Model', *World Bank Staff Working Paper*, no. 647.

Musgrave, R. A, (1957) *The Theory of Public Finance*. (London: McGraw-Hill).

Musgrave, R. A., E. E. Case and H. B. Leonard (1974) 'The Distribution of Fiscal Burdens and Benefits', *Public Finance Quarterly*, vol. 2, pp. 259–311.

Pechman, J. A. and B. A. Okner (1974) *Who Bears the Tax Burden*? (Washington DC: Brookings Institutions).

Qureshi, S. K. (1987) *Agricultural Pricing and Taxation in Pakistan: Some Policy Issues* (Islamabad: Pakistan Institute of Development Economics).

Rutherford, T. F. (1989) *General Equilibrium Modeling with MPS/GE (University of Western Ontario).*

Shah, A. and J. Whalley (1991) 'Tax Incidence Analysis of Developing Countries: An Alternative View', *The World Bank Economic Review*, vol. 5, no. 3, September, pp. 535–52.

Shoven, J. B. and J. Whalley (1972) 'A General Equilibrium Calculation of the Effects of Differential Taxation of Capital in the U.S.', Cowles Foundation Discussion paper no. 328 and *Journal of Public Economics*, vol. 1, pp. 281–322.

Shoven, J. B. and J. Whalley (1977) 'Equal Yield Taxes: A Computation Procedure and an Existence Proof ', *Journal of Public Economics*, vol. 8, pp. 211–224.

Shoven, J. B. and J. Whalley (1984) 'Applied General Equilibrium Models of Taxation and International Trade: An Introduction and Survey', *Journal of Economic Literature*, September.

Wasylenko, M. (1985) 'The Distribution of Tax Burden in Jamaica', Metropolitan Studies Program, The Maxwell School, Syracuse University, New York.

Whalley, J. (1984) 'Regression or Progression: The Taxing Question of Incidence Analysis', *Canadian Journal of Economics*, vol. 4, pp. 654–82.

World Bank (1987) *The Côte d'Ivoire in Transistion: From Structural Adjustment to Self-Sustained Growth*, Report no. 6051-IVC, vol. IV, Statistical annexes.

World Bank (1991) *Competitiveness and Regulatory Reform Adjustment Program Program* (Washington DC: World Bank).

9
Tax Reform in Tanzania

Nehemiah E. Osoro

Introduction

Tanzania's economic failure since the 1970s is often identified with inappropriate policies. The tax system, which constitutes an assortment of policy tools, has been applied to many kinds of government operation. Consequently, the Tanzanian tax system has been continually changed and become increasingly complex and distorted.

Tax policies, however, do not seem to have been very effective in achieving their intended objectives. First, since the general base of the overall tax is gross domestic product (GDP), the slow growth in GDP experienced from the late 1970s would imply a possible failure of the tax system to generate sufficient revenue. Second, tax administration has been inefficient. Third, the level of compliance on the part of taxpayers has, in general, been very low. In view of such reasons, despite the numerous and frequent discretionary changes in the tax system, the tax policy has not succeeded in raising revenue productivity (Osoro, 1991a). In addition, the tax policies seem not to have been successful in achieving equity objectives either. In a nutshell, tax policy, in effect, was not considered to be at the core of economic policy-making in Tanzania until very recently.

The general economic and social situation has changed considerably over the years; however, there is no credible reason to believe that the effectiveness of tax policy has increased significantly. Thus, the recent appearance of tax reform issues on the central stage of political and policy debates seems to reflect changes in the economic and political environment in Tanzania. The government's ability to exercise direct influence over the process of resource allocation has been declining gradually. Equity goals which were given top priority in tax policy in the past are now being treated comparatively lightly. By and large, the effective demand for tax reform has increased recently.

The objective of this chapter is to present an overview of the 1992 tax reforms issues in Tanzania. To do justice to this, a general overview of the Tanzanian tax system is provided. The next section reviews the historical changes in Tanzanian tax policy and the tax structure, then the current tax system and structure is outlined in the following section 9.3. A few important structural problems with the Tanzanian tax system will also be identified. Recent theory and issues in tax reform are reviewed in the following section. Finally, the 1992 tax reform issues and tax reforms to be carried out in following years are discussed in the last two sections.

Historical overview of Tanzanian tax policy and reform

Virtually every year since independence in 1961 some changes have been made in the tax system. Among these changes, the reforms in 1964, 1969, 1976, 1978, 1979, 1980, 1981, 1985, 1986, 1988, 1989, 1990, 1991 were undertaken on a larger scale than other reforms, and they were linked directly to Tanzania's economic, political and social policies. Thus Tanzanian tax policy has been part and parcel of the country's development policy. Invariably, revenue and equity objectives have dominated in practically all these reforms at the expense of efficiency objective of a tax policy (Osoro, 1991b).

To discuss the policy changes it is appropriate to break down the period from independence to the time of writing into three subperiods: (i) the pre-Arusha Declaration period; (ii) the Arusha Declaration period to the collapse of the East African Community (EAC); and (iii) the collapse of the EAC to June 1992.

The pre-Arusha declaration period (1961–6)

Tanzania became independent in December 1961 and a United Republic in 1964. The government of the new, independent government had inherited the British tax system, which was embodied in relatively few tax legislations. The pre-decentralization government maintained a lean administration from 1961 to 1970. A moderate degree of intervention in the economy backed up by sound budgetary responsibility allowed the government to keep a small and simple administrative structure. Accordingly, only very minor changes in the tax system were effected after independence. These were the introduction of a tax on motor vehicles and beer in 1964, and the introduction of the development levy of 5 per cent on all persons earning not less than TShs 200 per month and a turnover of most significant agricultural products (Osoro, 1992).

The Arusha Declaration period to the collapse of the East African Community (1967–77)

Several major events took place in Tanzania during this period. These were Arusha Declaration (1967); decentralization (1971); the first oil-price shock wave (1973–4), the nationwide drought (1974–5); and the Villagization Programme (1975). All these events generated rapid expansion in government expenditure, which called for increased revenue. Since Arusha Declaration policies were intended to discourage dependence on foreign finance, the obligation to raise revenue rested on domestic sources, particularly taxation. To this end, several tax policy changes were made to meet additional revenue needs.

The major tax reforms that took place during this period was the introduction of sales tax in 1969, income tax in 1973, and significant amendments of the original Sales Tax and Customs Tariff Acts, in 1976. The major objective of introducing sales tax and income tax were revenue and equity. Thus the motive behind tax reform during the 1967–76 period were revenue generation and equity considerations. However, the reform generated complexities in the tax structure. Towards the end of the 1970s, both the rate structure of import duty and sales tax had become very complex.

The collapse of the East African Community, structural adjustment and trade liberalization period (1977–1980s)

Major events surfaced during this period. First, the East African Community collapsed in July 1977, forcing Tanzania to set up its own national corporations to run the services that were formerly run by the Community.[1] Second, in 1978–9 Tanzania fought a war with Uganda which took an indeterminate financial and social toll that official estimates put at US$500 million. Third, the situation was further aggravated by the intensification of the Southern Africa struggle, the second oil shock wave of 1978 coupled with deterioration in agricultural export performance in the wake of the drought, and flooding during the later part of 1979. These crises resulted in the country running huge fiscal and balance-of-payments deficits from 1979. Unfortunately, foreign funds were not forthcoming.

Yet further events emerged in the 1980s. It was a decade of economic crises. Again, the early 1980s were characterized by drought. Consequently, the country registered huge deficits in the fiscal budget and balance-of-payments accounts. The crises intensified when government attempts to negotiate with the International Monetary Fund (IMF) failed. Thus the government had no option but to rely on domestic sources of finance. To this end, the major domestic source of deficit financing was through running the printing press.

Tax reforms before 1985 were aimed at raising revenue. For example, import duty rates were raised as high as 1100 per cent. Once again, these reforms led to a complex tax structure. While in 1969, there had been no more than five *ad valorem* and half a dozen specific rates of sales tax, by the early 1980s the numbers had increased to twenty-five of each, some of which were most 'odd' and inconvenient.

From 1984, the country's policy assumed a rather different dimension, when the government launched trade liberalization. Negotiations with the IMF were concluded in 1986, which opened the door to foreign financial resources. The first Economic Recovery Programme (ERP) was launched in the same year. These developments generated a new look at government economic policies. Several studies of the tax system were undertaken by the World Bank, the IMF and local experts for the government. Most of these studies recommended, among other things, simplification and rationalization of the major taxes (that is, import duty, income tax and sales tax) through reduction of rates and rate categories with a view to improving compliance and tax administration. Nevertheless, it should be pointed out that these studies were undertaken at the behest of the World Bank and the IMF.

As a result of these studies, the rates of sales tax and import duty were reduced. However, a more significant rate reduction and rationalization occurred in 1988 with respect to import duty, and in 1989 with respect to sales tax. Excise duty was reintroduced in 1989 to facilitate rationalization and simplification of sales tax structure and administration.

In the area of income taxation, marginal rates were reduced for the first time from a range of 20–95 per cent to a range of 15–75 per cent in 1986; to a range of 15–55 per cent in 1989; and finally to a range of 7.5–40 per cent in 1991. These rate reductions were aimed primarily at enhancing the take-home pay of workers, whose real income has been declining since the 1980s.

It is now clear from the ongoing analysis that tax reform and tax policies since the 1960s were largely focused on revenue objectives. Efficiency objectives hardly featured on the agenda, objectives of simplicity only came into the picture during the second half of the 1980s.

The tax system in the 1990s

Structure and characteristics

The Tanzanian tax system includes over thirty-five different taxes, with consumption and income taxes being the major revenue sources. An important feature of the Tanzanian tax structure is heavy dependence on indirect taxes, with a lesser reliance on income and property taxes (see Appendix, Table 9.A1). This is a common characteristic in most developing countries (Appendix, Table 9.A2). As shown in Table 9.A2, about 72 per cent of total tax revenue is from indirect taxes. In particular, sales tax has become a major source of revenue since its introduction in 1969. The introduction of sales tax was non-neutral in the sense that it led to both an increase in the overall tax burden and heavier reliance on indirect taxes for government revenue.[2]

In the area of direct taxation, the role of company tax is significant. In the fiscal year 1989/90 company tax accounted for 19 per cent of total tax revenue (Appendix, Table 9.A1). The role of personal income tax in raising revenue is relatively insignificant in Tanzania. Only 6.4 per cent of total tax revenue or about 18 per cent of sales tax revenue is collected from personal income tax. In 1989 only 1.5 per cent of GDP was collected as personal income tax (Appendix, Table 9.A2); in most Western countries the level is around 10 per cent (Appendix, Table 9.A3). The low contribution of individual income tax to tax revenue is attributable to three factors. First, although the marginal tax rates have been very high and progressive, the exemption or threshold income has also been high, and fewer than 50 per cent of workers pay tax. Second, tax evasion among individual businesses is a common phenomenon, since they do not keep records. Third, capital gains from financial assets transactions are not taxed effectively, as those who dispose off their assets normally understate the sale price to avoid paying high taxes. Most importantly, the general level of personal income tax compliance is very low. Specifically, proprietors' income is notorious for escaping taxation.

During the colonial period, the African countries relied heavily on customs duties as a major revenue source. While this reliance has been declining, it still remains high in many countries (Appendix, Table 9.A4).[3] In contrast, in Tanzania, taxes on international trade transactions, import duty and foreign travel levy[4] have not been the most significant source of revenue. This has been one of the unique characteristics of the country's tax system. Nevertheless, since the fiscal year 1986/7 the relative importance of import duty in revenue contribution has been rising gradually.[5]

Taxation of income

The present income tax structure dates back to 1937, when the tax was imposed in Kenya in the form of a diluted replica of the United Kingdom Tax Act of 1920. Similar statutes were enacted in Tanganyika, Zanzibar and Uganda as late as 1940. Common legislation was introduced in the three territories in 1952.

Individual income tax in Tanzania is global in the sense that all incomes are included in the global income calculation. Global income consists of business income, wage and salary incomes, and dividends, and is taxed progressively from 5 to 30 per cent. Capital gains tax, introduced in 1974, is levied on the gains realized on the sale of premises (including land and parts of the buildings, if occupied separately) in the United Republic. The rates of capital gains are graduated, ranging from 20 to 30 per cent.[6] Capital gains of less than TShs 100,000 are not taxed.

Corporate profits are taxed under the co-operation tax legislation. Resident companies' profits are subject to 35 per cent corporation tax, while non-resident companies' profits attract 40 per cent tax. Non-exempt co-operatives are taxed at 25 per cent. Dividends received from companies are included in their incomes and taxed, but dividends received by companies in which the recipient is a corporate body and has a shareholding interest of more than 25 per cent of paid-up capital are exempt. Tax is withheld at 10 per cent from dividend payments to residents, and is credited against their final liability. For non-residents, the rate of withholding is 20 per cent.[7]

Other taxes on income include shipping tax, excess profit tax, single trade transaction tax, and windfall tax.

Consumption taxes

Sales tax ranks first among consumption taxes in terms of revenue yield, followed by import duty and excise duty, in that order. Other consumption taxes are entertainment tax, business licences, motor vehicle taxes and licences, hotel levy and other licences.

The Tanzanian sales tax is a manufacturer sales tax type, applying to imports and goods sold by domestic manufacturers. It is also levied on a few selected services (for example, telephones, electricity and catering). The major objective of this tax is revenue, though equity is another objective. Sales tax is currently levied at *ad valorem* rates of zero, 10, 20 and 30 per cent. The major problem with this tax has been that the Sales Tax Act provides for generous exemptions, either statutory and discretionary, the latter being granted by the Minister for Finance. However, most of these exemptions were abolished on 19 June 1992.

Import duty is one of the oldest indirect taxes in Tanzania. It is levied on imports. The objective of the duty is protection and revenue. The current rate structure is zero, 10, 20 and 40 per cent. Like sales tax, import duty has suffered from generous exemptions.

Excise duty is another consumption tax. It was introduced into East Africa by the British in the 1950s and was a replica of the excise duty found in Britain. This duty was abolished in 1979/80. However, an excise duty was reintroduced in June 1989. When it was reintroduced, it was initially levied on domestic commodities and imports. At the time of writing, domestically-produced commodities such as sugar, soap, textiles, matches, foam mattresses and cement are no longer subject to the duty. Excise duty is the only indirect tax in Tanzania with a uniform rate (20 per cent). The major objective of excise duty is to raise revenue and discourage the consumption of luxury goods and those that might be injurious to health. Nevertheless, the duty is designed to achieve the two objectives without making it prohibitive, which would encourage tax avoidance and evasion.

Taxes on property ownership

Taxes on property in Tanzania include land rent, estate duty and motor vehicle transfer tax. Taxes on capital gains from real estate property transactions can also be classified as taxes on property transfers. By and large, taxes on property have a negligible revenue contribution to total central government tax revenue. This is because of the existence of a narrow base coupled with evasion through underdeclaration of sales value of the asset in question.

At present, land rent is payable under the Land Ordinance Cap 113 of the laws enacted in 1923, when title deeds to land were first granted. The main objective of land tax is to regulate ownership of land. In addition, the tax aims at making land ownership conform with national land policy under which land in Tanzania belongs to the state, and is occupied by people as leaseholders. The other objective, of course, is revenue. Land used exclusively for worship, burial or cremation is exempt from land rent.

The rent charges on land in urban areas are fixed by land valuers, and depend on the size of the plot, its use, and location, having regard also to vicinity, infrastructure, its proximity to the city centre and amenities available. Thus land rent on urban land is not uniform. Agricultural registered land is charged at Shs 3.00 per acre, while the rate for pastoral land is Shs 1.00 per acre. These rates are obviously too low to be meaningful.

Estate duty is imposed on the property of all deceased persons, on all other properties which are passed on, and on certain benefits which arise on death and on property disposed of as a gift within three years of death. Foreign immovable properties are exempt, as are certain properties on the death of husband or wife, where some properties were previously taxed.

Allowances are granted in case of quick succession to property. Deductions are allowed for funeral expenses, debts and similar duties in other countries. The objective of this duty is to achieve equity in the distribution of wealth by discouraging accumulation of wealth by the heirs of deceased wealthy individuals. The other objective is revenue. The current rates of the estate duty range from 9 per cent on the excess over Shs 2 million to 54 per cent on the excess over Shs 3.1 million. The present exemptions are such that only the estate of a comparatively wealthy person, by Tanzanian standard, is taxed. Estate duty is one of the most unpopular taxes in the country, hence it suffers considerable evasion.

Theory and issues in tax reform

The literature on tax reform has been growing rapidly, indicating the theoretical and practical importance of the subject. Much of the literature on tax reform has been more descriptive than analytical; and besides this, the techniques applied to evaluating success or failure of tax reform are not well documented. Thus, generally, the analysis of tax reform has tended to focus on evaluating the objectives the tax reforms were attempting to achieve. These objectives were revenue adequacy, economic efficiency, equity, and simplicity. The need for tax reform has been the result of the deficiency of the existing tax system in achieving these objectives (McMahon and Berrios, 1991, p. 5).

Revenue adequacy is the basic elementary standard a tax system ought to achieve. The existing budget deficits in many developing countries suggest that the tax systems are not revenue productive (McMahon and Berrios, 1991, p. 5). Some may overlook this and attribute the cause of deficits to excessive spending, or to temporary adverse economic conditions. This may bear some truth, yet in situations where budget deficits persist for long periods, one must ask whether more revenue should not be an objective of the tax reform. The answer is bound to depend on the circumstances of each country. Certainly, few, if any, developing countries can afford to adopt tax reforms, no matter how desirable on other grounds, if they might lead to substantial revenue losses. Goode (1987) argues that it is hard to gain serious consideration for revenue-neutral reform proposal. By and large, in Africa, most finance ministers consider revenue gain as the primary motive for tax reform.

Trends in tax reform in the 1980s

The 1980s were certainly an important period for tax reforms world-wide, from which clear patterns are observable. Significant elements of these trends have included the increasing introduction of a uniform-rate value-added tax system (VAT) as a standard model of commodity taxation; there has been a change in the direction of broader personal and corporate income tax bases; there is more emphasis on improving tax administration; and more indexation has been adopted for the income tax system. As regards income taxation, the inclination has been to broaden the tax base to reduce the tax rate, both of which have had important effects on the efficiency of the system and on vertical equity. Buchanan (1987) argues that, for some taxpayers, the rate reductions do not fully offset the greater revenue raised by broadening the tax base. Despite the reduction in their excess burden, they will suffer net utility losses.

The focus on the redistributive role of the tax system is gradually waning, as a direct consequence of perversive tax evasion. Conceptually, progressivity still scores high on the political agenda. None the less, the political will to enforce income tax compliance is frequently not forthcoming, and vertical equity increasingly is being accorded a lower order of priority in tax reform (Khalilzadeh-Shiraz and Shah, 1991, pp. 459–71).

Income taxation, as the main instrument used to achieve the goal of vertical equity, seems to have been declining in importance. The combination of base-broadening and higher tax revenue from tax reform appear to be far more effective tools for meeting equity goals. Base-broadening clearly contributes to restriction, because excluded income is largely received by high-income families. But the role of high tax revenue in income redistribution deserves special comment. Studies on the impact of the budget on income distribution in the USA, Colombia, Malaysia and Chile strongly indicate that if the budget is to serve redistributive purposes effectively, the primary emphasis must be placed on expenditure, not on the tax side of the budget.[8] In a nutshell, the incidence studies suggest that the expenditure side of the Indonesian budget has been a much more effective means of shifting income and services to the poor than the tax side (Gillis, 1985, p. 235).

In the area of commodity taxation, there has been a trend to replace the turnover sales tax by value-added taxes. Trade liberalization policies in many developing countries have led to a persistent and discernible trend towards reduced dependence on narrowly-based trade taxes. Thus, to overcome revenue shortfalls inherent in such policies, there has been increased emphasis on broadly-based, hybrid value-added taxes (Khalilzadeh-Shiraz and Shah, 1991, p. 60). In Musgrave's opinion, these trends suggest certain implications: a change in perceiving income tax as the main instrument of progressive taxation; an increasing acceptance of consumption as the tax base; and the emergence of VAT as the appropriate means for income tax reform (Khalilzadeh-Shiraz and Shah, 1990). These changes have occurred in the context of an academic preference for consumption as the tax base. Musgrave argues that important factors in promoting this process were the complexities of direct taxation, distortions introduced by incentive effects, and the shifting political attitude towards equity (McMahon and Berrios, 1991, p. 7).

Reform of tax administration

A single obvious conclusion the recent tax reform has demonstrated has been the need for a simple and manageable tax system. Tax administration plays a key role. Ironically, justice has not been done to tax administration in the literature on the subject (McMahon and Berrios, 1991, p. 7).

The 1980s obviously exhibited the importance of the administrative limits of tax systems in developing countries. Admittedly, a sharp contrast between the real conditions for implementing tax systems and the degree of complexity with which the structures have been designed are observable. Accordingly, tax reform should stress the need to look for ways of setting clear and simple tax structures and having real administrative capacity on hand to implement them.

Bird, 1990, pp. 1–20, identifies three different approaches to reforms of tax structures and administration. The first approach considers the reform of tax structure as the central concern, after which administrative changes should take place. A second approach views administrative changes as the primary concern of tax reform and should come first. A third approach considers administrative changes and reform of tax structure as being independent. The third approach is the commonly accepted view at present.

Basic issues of tax reform

Tax reform raises four basic questions (Messere, 1988, p. 277): Why do it? When should it be done? In what directions should it go? How should it be implemented?

Why do it

Tax reform has many objectives. However, broad objectives include simplicity, economic efficiency and equity, along with that ever-conflliciting pair: the promotion of economic and social goals, and the achievement of tax neutrality. Specific goals are improving labour supply, encouraging private saving, and reducing the attraction of the underground economy. In Tanzania, the major objective of tax reform has primarily been to raise revenue. Other objectives have been secondary. Specifically, governments adopt techniques they believe will achieve these objectives, and announce their intention, for example, to cut rates of particular taxes, to broaden the tax base of those taxes, and to abolish some taxes and replace them with new ones.

When should it be done?

There are long-term and short-term considerations. In the long term it is generally agreed that when the economy is healthy (for example, in the 1960s and 1970s) it is not necessary to carry out reforms, since the would-be winners will not react and the potential losers will be resentful. In the 1960s and 1970s there was enormous confidence in the government's ability to guide the economy, at both macro and micro levels. Accordingly, extensive application of tax instruments was common. However, the government policies and fiscal instruments of the 1960s and 1970s were no longer considered appropriate in the 1980s (Asher, 1989, pp. 39–40).

In the 1980s, characterized by recession, lower levels of growth, employment and inflation, as well as the feeling that the tax system was unfair, inefficient and unnecessarily complicated, governments have been convinced that tax reform may be a vote winner rather than a vote loser. This view has been reinforced by the experience of the USA, and it now scores highly on the political agenda of almost all OECD countries (Messere, 1988, p. 278).

Some developing countries, (for example, the East Asian developing countries) have had to respond to tax reforms in the major industrial countries, particularly the USA and the UK (Asher, 1989, p. 41). By and large, tax reforms in industrial countries in the 1980s generated substantially lower nominal rates of personal and corporate income taxes. Also there were attempts to broaden the tax base of income tax and to reduce differentials of property income. Reforms in the industrial countries signal that due attention must be paid to an appropriate tax mix and the design and structure of major taxes in developing countries.

The argument that conservative macroeconomic policies, including fiscal policy, are often necessary for sustained economic growth, especially for open economies, is now increasingly receiving acceptance. There is more need for domestic resources, including taxation, to finance public expenditure. Since increases in nominal rates, particularly for income tax, are no longer feasible because of tax reforms in industrial countries, base-broadening and efficient tax administration has received more attention.

Short-term considerations refer to the election cycle. The USA began reform early in the cycle; Australia seem to have been prevented from getting its broad-based sales tax by beginning too late in what is an exceptionally short (three years) parliamentary term; Canada began late in its election cycle on its VAT proposals; France, Italy, the Netherlands, Sweden and the UK appear to be delaying changes. These are political choices.

In what directions should it go?

Most governments seem, in theory, to be dedicated to rate-cutting and flattening, base-broadening, and improving tax compliance and administration. In practice, much depends on where a country takes off from in terms of tax levels, tax structure and tax system, and so on, and where it has recently been moving. For example, base-broadening and rate-reducing seem to have limited possibilities.[9] This may have arisen because, with revenue-neutral constraint, which is very common, base-broadening will probably not attract sufficient revenue to lower rates significantly. The need to attract saving is probably frustrated by the favourable tax treatment given in a country for borrowing in relation to saving (Messere, 1988, p. 279).

How should it be implemented?

The crucial issue is how to get tax reform through legislation. It can be done in many ways. The form of constitution and institution of a country, as well as its perceptions and habits, will pay a major role. Elements such as a high or low profile, universal or selective consultation, and the extent of prior consultation, vary from country to country. Thus, the more ambitious the reform, the higher the profile that may have to be taken and the greater the risk that it will not work. In other words, tax reform projects are a gamble that may not come to fruition.

The 1992 tax reform issues

Recent policy changes

The period between the mid-1980s and 1992 may be considered to be a turning point in Tanzanian economic and political history. During this period, considerable shifts in the economic environment were demonstrated, several policy changes took place. The major policy changes include the trade liberalization of 1984 along with deconfinement policy and price decontrol; an active foreign exchange rate policy adopted in 1986; and the liberalization of the foreign exchange market in 1992 through the establishment of foreign exchange bureaux. Further, some of the Arusha Declaration policies have been shelved, if not relaxed. Finally, the CCM government adopted multipartism. The new environment has paid serious attention to the importance of the private sector in the economy. There is no doubt that these new policy changes have had a positive effect on the economy.

Tax reform under a new environment

These policy changes have exerted an enormous influence, both on the policy-making process and the policy objectives themselves. Thus recent tax reforms reflect these changes.

Income taxation and equity

As was pointed out earlier, income tax is not a significant revenue source in developing countries. Only Botswana, Cameroon, Gabon, Malawi, Swaziland, Zambia and Zimbabwe obtain over 40 per cent of their tax revenues from this source, and in several of these, most of the revenue is from mining complexes (Appendix, Table 9.A4).

One major inherent problem with income taxation in most African countries, and particularly in Tanzania, is that the great majority of the people are not easily reached by the tax, in view of the dominance of subsistence income, the relatively limited income in excess of bare poverty levels, and the poor levels of education and record-keeping. Seldom more than 20 per cent of population is reached, and any attempt to broaden the coverage would add large number of taxpayers who would yield little revenue but add materially to enforcement costs. For example, in the Sudan, in 1973–4, well over half of all employees fell into the lowest tax bracket (S£170 to S£299), but this bracket yielded only 1.8 per cent of tax revenue (Due, 1977). Over time, of course, more and more families will become subject to the tax as their incomes rise, but there is little to be gained in broadening the coverage of the tax materially in the immediate future.

The 1992 reform has finally reduced personal income tax marginal rates to a range between 5 and 30 per cent, a process begun 1986. Reducing the tax burden of low-income workers and enhancing the take-home pay of workers, however, appears to be a powerful and attractive political move.

The 1992 tax reforms on personal income tax, while designed to help low-income workers, has, in effect, undermined the already weak base of the income tax system and may have contributed negatively to redistributive equity. First, by reducing the tax rates without any other compensatory measures, the income tax burden on upper-bracket workers will visibly be reduced. Second, most allowances and fringe benefits paid to workers are not taxed, and these allowances often far exceed the basic salary of a worker. For example, out of the total monthly pay of a university professor, (excluding other income from 'income-generating activities') allowances which are untaxed, constitute over 70 per cent. Thus the taxed income is less than 30 per cent, since the remaining portion will have the threshold income of TShs 3250 deducted from it. For some top civil servants and top executives in public and private companies untaxed allowances may be more than 80 per cent of the total pay. It is obvious that under such an income policy, rate reduction is not likely to achieve distributive equity. Finally, it is apparent that tax revenue in general would be reduced. In fact, the contribution of personal income taxes to GDP has been declining since the mid-1980s (Appendix, Table 9.A2).

Commodity taxation

The 1992 tax reforms in the area of commodity taxation focused on: (i) having a tax system that would enhance compliance and discourage tax evasion and people requesting exemption; (ii) having a tax system that does not have a negative effect on production in the industrial and other sectors; (iii) having a tax system that increases efficiency in production, and leads to the production of high-quality goods that are affordable by domestic and foreign consumers; and (iv) having a tax system that would attract foreign investors to invest in Tanzania.

In the face of these considerations, in June 1992 the government decided to reduce the tax rates, abolish and modify exemptions, and abolish some taxes that had outlived their usefulness. In this connection, the 1992 reform reduced the customs duty rates from zero, 10, 20, 30, 40 and 60 per cent to zero, 10, 20, 30 and 40 per cent. In respect of sales tax, the rates have been reduced to zero, 10, 20, and 30 per cent. Further, excise duty, which previously had eight different rates, ranging from zero to 85 per cent, were reduced to a uniform rate of 20 per cent, and, as stated earlier, excise duty on sugar, soap, matches, foam mattresses and cement has been abolished.

Perhaps one of the most important elements of the 1992 reform was the removal of taxes on raw materials used by domestic industries to produce final goods. The objective of this reform was to enable domestic industries to have easy access to raw materials, and to reduce the cost of production, thereby enabling companies to compete in domestic and foreign markets.

Another very important aspect of the 1992 tax reform in the area of commodity taxation was exemption. The previous tax reforms had not paid much attention to exemption, which had been eroding the indirect tax base continuously. In June 1992 the government decided to abolish all tax exemptions that had been formally granted to central government, local governments, political parties (CCM), commercial entities, and religious and charitable organizations. This was a very crucial reform in the Tanzanian tax system. If properly implemented, there is great likelihood this will increase the commodity tax base and consequently enable more revenue collection.

However, although the 1992 tax reform reduced the commodity tax rates, the tax bill (which is important to the taxpayer) on imports will still be high because of a rapid depreciation on the Tanzanian shilling. Thus the scope for evasion may still exist.

Value added tax (VAT)

There has been increasing acceptance of the principle of VAT in developing countries, and Tanzania has been no exception. Some recent official studies on taxation in Tanzania, particularly those undertaken by the IMF and the World Bank, have recommended adoption of the 'credit system', or adoption of VAT. Similarly, the Tax Commission also recommended the introduction of VAT, which the government accepted and introduced in January 1994. These studies argue that the introduction of VAT would expand the indirect tax base and consequently raise more revenue. The introduction of VAT is the most pervasive feature of tax reform in many developing countries. First, pre-retail VATs generate significant amounts of distortion and administrative complexities, and in consequence are not worth adopting. Second, all services (except health care, education, social welfare, banking and insurance) should be included in the base. Third, rate differentiation should be minimized, although protecting the poor may call for reduced rates for food, essential consumer items, drugs, electricity and fuel, newspapers and books, and public transportation. If luxuries are to be taxed at a high rate, special excises should be levied instead of increasing the VAT or applying multiple rates. Finally, VAT is a suitable tax for large, integrated economies characterized by sophisticated production and distribution channels. It is relatively less suitable for small, island-type economies that have a narrow manufacturing base and depend on cross-border trade (Khalilzadeh-Shiraz and Shah, 1991, p. 465).

There was apparent pressure on the Tanzanian government from the IMF and the World Bank to introduce VAT. VAT was introduced in 1994, at the manufacturing level. Since retailing in Tanzania is of a small scale nature such that control of retail tax is almost impossible, there is unlikely to be a significant difference between this form of VAT and the existing manufacturing sales tax. Moreover, the above experiences with VAT seem to work against the introduction of VAT in Tanzania.

Tax reforms and fiscal incentives

The attraction of foreign investors is an aspect that came out clearly in the 1992 tax reform. It was the government's intention to attract foreign investors through fiscal incentives (for example, tax holidays, exemption of sales tax and import duty and so on).

However, the basic question to be raised about fiscal incentives is: Are the gains from additional investment significant enough to warrant the loss of revenue? No general answer is available, but there is increasing belief that the gains are limited. One of the problems with these incentives, particularly tax holidays, is that they make countries become competitive. One country in a region provides liberal holidays, and others feel they must do likewise or lose industry, which may well occur. Yet all the countries in the region might well be better off without the holidays.

Some citizens, of course, would like the investment codes to be abolished. They are basically used largely because others have got them. For all practical purposes, it is very difficult to advise a country to go it alone, abolishing its investment codes, while countries it competes with still offer incentives.

Muten (1987, p. 30) argues that, although it is certain that the objective of these incentives is to promote investment, there are other factors or more incentives that are even more important. They are: (a) economic and political stability; (b) a good and well-trained labour force; (c) adequate infrastructure; (d) closeness to markets; and (e) a reasonable tax system.

On the basis of the experiences of a large number of developing countries, many tax experts are now strongly opposed to the use of tax incentives.[10] They are seen to breed corruption and rent-seeking activities, and have a negative effect on the quality of a good tax system (Tanzi and Shome, 1990, pp. 42–5). Tax incentives are also likely to lead to substantial revenue losses if not properly legislated. For some countries the trend has been to reduce or abolish tax incentives and reduce income tax rates. Low tax rates will improve compliance and administration, which may result in increased tax collection. However, the 1992 tax reform reduced income tax rates while still retaining tax incentives. Tax incentives are not expected to play a significant role in relieving these inherent problems.

Tax administration and compliance

Efficient tax administration and compliance have been increasing in importance in recent years. Reform of the tax structure, if undertaken without a corresponding reform of tax administration, may not achieve desired goals. As pointed out earlier, the reform of tax administration should emphasize the need to look for ways of setting up a realistic integration between the design of clear and simple tax structure and the real administrative capacity on hand to implement them. The 1992 tax reform put emphasis on strengthening tax collection. This will involve restructuring the present Customs and Sales Tax Department, not only for improving administration but also to make preparation for the introduction of VAT. (URT, *Budget Speech* 1992/3).

None the less, such efforts are not likely to achieve the intended goals unless the government seriously considers improving the remuneration of the tax departments' staff; improving their overall working conditions; and providing them with working facilities, not to mention adequate office space.

Taxation of property

As discussed earlier, property taxes are an insignificant revenue source. This is because of the Arusha Declaration policy which discouraged private property ownership. However, since the mid-1980s the construction industry has been booming. The relaxation of certain aspects of the Arusha Declaration policies has even encouraged private property ownership, so that private ownership of real estate is no longer something to be looked into by the 'Anti-corruption squad'. Nevertheless, the 1992 tax reform appeared to be silent on the taxation of property. The problem arises because some of the policy-makers are themselves property owners, and therefore would find it rather difficult to pass a law that taxes property.

Pending issues and prospects

The Tanzanian economy faces serious issues in the 1990s. The industrial sector is in rehabilitation mode and needs to increase capacity utilization. From the short-run and medium-run perspective, achieving macroeconomic stability is crucial but difficult. There is a labour surplus situation while real wages are declining, and the government is required to pay its civil servants adequate wages and salaries if efficiency has to be achieved.

At the same time, major financial sector reforms are implemented. It is estimated that the financing of the reforms will require about Shs 46 billion. Even if the financing comes from donor agencies, there is no doubt that it will have a significant impact on the fiscal budget. Finally, the multiparty system has formally been adopted by the CCM government. The country's political and socioeconomic policies are likely to change to suit the new political environment. The government relies too heavily on foreign sources of finance since the existing tax system is not yet capable of generating revenue to finance even recurrent expenditure.[11]

Under such circumstances, tax policy in the coming years (under multiparty system) should first of all clearly demonstrate commitment by the government to 'reform'. There is only a remote chance of achieving this goal through the reform of income taxation, as personal incomes – particularly wages and salaries – have been declining in real terms. Therefore, income tax reform is not likely to increase revenues substantially.

Equity objectives, while crucial as a policy goal, are rather difficult to achieve through tax policy: taxation has not proved to be a proper instrument for achieving equity.[12] The goals of equity may better be pursued by expenditure policy (that is, by increasing transfer expenditures and other social programmes).

Efficiency, like equity, objectives are important but difficult to achieve through tax policy. There is often a trade-off between the two. For many years, the tax policy in Tanzania has emphasized equity at the expense of efficiency: efficiency has been sidelined. Yet a tax system which promotes efficiency in the economy is likely to be more desirable than one that achieves equity alone. The 1992 tax reform recognized for the first time the importance of efficiency. That is why the reform abolished taxes on raw materials and reduced sales tax and import duty rates. Nevertheless, lower rates of tax alone are not enough, particularly when sales tax and import duty attract multiple rates, which are distortive. The tax reform in the coming years needs to focus much more seriously on efficiency. One way of bringing about greater efficiency is through imposing uniform tax rates, as uniform rate commodity taxes are usually less distortive.

In recent years the government has attempted to raise the tax-to-GDP ratio, without much success (Appendix, Table 9A.2). The failure has been caused by the narrowness of the tax base, which has mainly been eroded by the granting of generous exemptions; and by inefficient tax administration resulting in poor compliance and tax evasion. The 1992 tax reform abolished exemption, as was pointed out earlier. However, as long as tax legislation continues to bestow discretionary exemption powers on the minister of finance, it is doubtful if the exemptions will be abolished effectively. And effective abolition of exemptions calls for serious government commitment.

It is not certain that the current government will reform the tax system to raise substantial revenue in the near future mainly because of risks, corruption, inefficiencies, and probably apparent lack of seriousness. The VAT introduced in 1994 is likely not to generate substantial revenue, in view of the experiences outlined in the previous section.

In the coming years, under the multiparty system, tax reform should be directed towards taxation of real estate. Real estate stands out as a potentially important tax base. Most of the demand for reform can be met if real estate is taxed effectively. However, taxation of property in Tanzania is very difficult and will remain so for some time if the current administration continues in power. Success in this area will require the government's commitment to tax property. Such commitment may be possible under a multiparty system. Thus, the most challenging and most important issues in the area of tax policy under multipartism will concern how to operate a property-related tax system effectively, and how to enforce them, as opposed to what new systems are to be introduced (Kwack and Lee, 1990).

To improve tax collection from, in particular, personal income tax, in the coming years, the income policy in place should be overhauled. That is, the system of paying civil servants and other workers low salaries but paying relatively high allowances in form of fringe benefits must be abandoned.[13]

Tax policies in the coming years should focus on reform of tax administration to improve compliance and thereby reduce tax evasion, which is one of the major problems of the tax system.[14] The reform of tax administration will need the future government to spend relatively more money on tax collection. Currently, the government spends less than 2 per cent on total tax collection. This does not mean that the tax system is efficient. All it means is that the personnel in tax departments are working under very difficult conditions. The government will have to improve the remuneration of the tax personnel, improve their working conditions, provide them with a reasonable office space and with working facilities.

Finally, in order to improve revenue collection, the future multiparty government should ensure that the tax authorities cease to look at faces when assessing or collecting taxes. The tax liability should be paid irrespective of the status of the person in the society or in the government. Currently, this is one of the major problems in the existing tax administration.

Appendix

Table 9A.1 The tax structure in Tanzania, 1980–90

	1980/1	*1984/5*	*1987/8*	*1989/90*
Tax revenue	100.0	100.0	100.0	100.0
Domestic taxes	89.0	91.1	86.8	85.5
Taxes on income and wealth	34.4	29.1	28.8	27.6
Income taxes	33.5	27.8	27.4	27.5
Pay-as-you-earn (PAYE)	9.2	9.0	6.4	4.3
Individuals[1]	3.2	2.4	1.8	2.1
Company	20.2	15.7	16.9	19.0
Other	0.9	0.6	1.2	2.1
Property taxes	0.6	1.1	0.3	0.4
Land rent	0.5	0.8	0.2	–
Estate duty	0.03	0.0	–	10.4
Motor vehicle transfer taxes	0.1	0.2	0.1	0.6
Payroll or manpower taxes	0.2	0.2	1.1	1.8
Payroll tax	–	–	0.9	1.0
Training levy	0.2	0.2	0.1	0.8
Domestic taxes on goods and services	54.4	60.0	53.3	54.2
Sales tax – local	48.3	51.2	41.3	25.4
Sales tax – imports	5.0	7.3	11.5	10.7
Entertainment tax	0.2	0.2	0.1	0.4
Business licences	0.2	0.3	0.1	0.2
Motor vehicle taxes and licences[2]	0.6	0.8	1.3	1.5
Hotel levy	–	–	0.7	0.9
Other licences	–	0.1	0.1	0.1
Excise duty – local	–	–	–	12.0
Excise duty – imports	–	–	–	3.0
Taxes on international transactions	11.0	8.9	13.2	14.5
Customs duty	10.8	8.9	12.9	14.3
Import duty	8.2	8.8	12.9	14.3
Export duty	2.6	0.1	–	–
Foreign travel levy	0.3	0.1	0.2	0.2
Other taxes	0.3	2.0	–	3.7
Stamp duty	0.3	2.0	3.5	3.7

Notes:
1 In 1987/8 individual tax includes single trade transaction tax (TShs. 12.1 million).
2 Motor vehicle taxes and licences include motor vehicle licences, motor vehicle registration tax, motor vehicle road licences and road tolls.
Source: Computed by the author from URT (various years), *Financial Statement and Revenue*, and *National Accounts of Tanzania 1976–89*.

Table 9A.2 Central government tax revenue 1980/81–1989/90[1] (% GDP)

	1980/1	*1981/2*	*1982/3*	*1983/4*	*1984/5*	*1985/6*	*1986/7*	*1987/8*	*1988/9*	*1989/90*
Tax revenue	10.3	18.8	19.1	20.0	20.4	17.9	19.8	21.7	15.5	23.4
Income taxes	6.5	6.6	6.5	6.0	5.6	5.9	4.9	5.9	8.4	6.4
Individuals[2]	2.4	2.4	2.4	2.2	2.3	2.0	1.9	1.8	3.7	1.5
Company	3.9	4.0	4.0	3.7	3.2	3.8	2.9	3.7	4.1	4.4
Other[3]	0.2	0.2	0.1	0.1	0.1	0.1	0.1	0.2	0.2	0.2
Payroll or manpower taxes[4]	–	–	–	–	–	0.2	0.2	0.2	0.2	0.2
Taxes on property[5]	0.1	0.1	0.1	0.2	0.2	0.1	0.0	0.0	0.0	0.0
Domestic taxes on goods and services	10.5	10.6	10.6	11.9	12.2	9.9	11.1	12.0	12.5	12.5
Sales tax	10.3	10.4	10.4	11.6	11.9	9.5	10.8	11.4	11.2	8.4
Local	9.3	8.9	8.9	9.4	10.4	8.1	8.3	8.9	8.5	5.9
Imports	1.0	1.5	1.5	2.2	1.5	1.4	2.5	2.5	2.7	2.5
Excise duty	–	–	–	–	–	–	–	–	0.0	3.5
Local	–	–	–	–	–	–	–	–	0.0	2.8
Imports	–	–	–	–	–	–	–	–	0.0	0.7
Motor vehicle taxes[6]	0.1	0.1	0.1	0.2	0.2	0.2	0.2	0.3	0.3	0.3
Other[7]	0.1	0.1	0.1	0.1	0.1	0.1	0.1	0.2	0.3	0.3
Taxes on international transactions	2.1	1.4	1.7	1.5	1.8	1.4	2.9	2.8	3.0	3.4
Import duties	1.6	1.4	1.2	1.4	1.8	1.4	2.7	2.8	2.9	3.3
Foreign travel levy	–	–	0.4	0.1	–	–	0.2	0.1	0.1	0.1
Stamp duties	0.1	–	0.2	0.5	0.4	0.5	0.6	0.7	0.5	0.9

Notes:
1 Tax revenue by fiscal year; GDP by calendar year.
2 Includes pay-as-you-earn (PAYE) and individuals.
3 Includes withholding tax, capital gains tax, shipping tax and transport tax.
4 Includes training levy, as of 1985/86 and payroll tax.
5 Includes land rent and service charges, estate duty and motor vehicle transfer tax.
6 Includes motor vehicles registration and licences.
7 Includes business licences, entertainment tax and hotel levy.
Sources: Computed from URT (various years) *Financial Statement and Revenue Estimates, National Accounts of Tanzania, 1976–1989.*

Table 9A.3 Tax revenue structure by types of tax: an international comparison, 1985 (% to GDP)

	Income		*Consumption*				
	Total	*Personal*	*Total*	*General*	*Property*	*Social security*	*Total*
Canada	15.0	12.0	10.7	4.5	3.2	4.5	33.9
West Germany	13.1	10.8	9.7	6.0	1.1	13.8	37.8
Sweden	21.2	19.5	13.3	7.0	1.2	14.7	50.5
UK	14.8	9.9	12.0	6.0	4.6	6.7	38.1
USA	12.3	10.3	5.1	2.1	2.9	8.4	28.7
Japan	13.0	7.0	4.0	–	2.7	8.5	23.3
Tanzania (1989)	6.4	1.5	16.8	8.4	0.1	–	23.3

Sources: OECD, *Revenue Statistics of OECD Member Countries 1965–1985*, table 1.

Table 9A.4 Revenue from various taxes as a percentage of total tax revenue, selected African countries

	Income tax	*Individual income tax*	*Corporation tax*	*Property tax*	*Domestic taxes on goods and services*	*Sales tax*	*Excises*	*Taxes on internal trade transactions*	*Import duty*	*Export duty*	*Other taxes*	*Indirect taxes*
Botswana	75.52	5.7	62.97	0.12	1.65	1.28	n.a.	22.41	22.37	0.03	0.02	24.08
Burkina Faso	21.08	11.72	5.33	3.53	30.37	17.26	9.69	29.39	26.14	1.55	15.63	75.39
Burundi	25.10	11.26	12.54	9.99	32.19	n.a.	30.65	26.91	25.17	1.71	5.81	64.91
Cameroon	47.65	9.41	38.25	1.62	21.26	11.76	8.69	14.71	11.55	3.11	14.76	50.73
Comoros	14.99	3.93	10.48	1.44	10.92	9.43	n.a.	71.96	54.40	16.05	0.69	83.57
Gabon	64.21	4.31	57.87	0.40	9.43	7.49	n.a.	23.55	21.26	2.29	2.41	35.39
Ghana	31.12	10.04	21.07	0.04	30.63	9.34	20.68	38.13	19.48	18.65	0.08	68.84
Kenya	31.15	n.a.	n.a.	n.a.	47.75	35.64	8.82	19.90	18.77	1.13	1.20	68.85
Lesotho	12.01	8.04	3.96	0.02	25.17	21.32	2.39	62.68	62.55	0.13	0.12	87.97
Liberia	35.67	29.46	5.51	1.33	33.47	2.72	13.51	28.19	28.07	0.06	1.34	63.00
Malawi	42.99	13.18	28.84	0.07	39.09	37.38	3.20	17.41	17.91	–0.50	0.44	56.94
Mali	10.07	5.17	4.33	2.72	27.13	21.40	4.19	34.40	28.81	4.89	25.68	87.21
Mauritius	14.00	6.05	7.94	5.32	22.76	8.32	8.61	52.81	43.65	8.72	5.11	80.68
Sénégal	20.21	13.03	5.29	2.25	29.28	22.94	4.68	42.49	42.02	0.34	5.77	77.54
Seychelles	18.82	1.33	17.49	0.15	6.07	0.05	n.a.	56.68	56.68	–	18.28	81.03
Sierra Leone	20.58	9.64	10.90	0.02	22.38	n.a.	17.20	56.62	54.07	1.89	0.40	79.40
Swaziland	43.54	10.64	30.61	0.24	14.73	13.67	n.a.	41.20	38.12	3.07	0.29	41.49
Tanzania	27.21	10.52	16.39	1.10	60.47	58.99	n.a.	9.05	8.90	0.08	2.17	71.69
Togo	39.79	10.16	26.48	0.86	10.75	7.45	1.49	39.55	32.47	1.12	9.05	59.35
Uganda	7.06	0.36	6.70	n.a.	25.38	19.99	3.94	67.52	10.54	46.59	0.04	92.94
Zaire	37.25	24.50	12.68	0.26	12.37	7.60	3.59	47.20	31.78	15.41	2.92	62.49
Zambia	41.65	8.51	30.45	0.20	40.46	25.70	14.21	17.27	17.03	0.13	0.42	58.15
Zimbabwe	48.96	29.71	17.78	0.25	29.02	20.32	8.46	20.91	20.32	–	0.80	50.73

Source: Computed by the author from IMF (various years) *International Financial Statistics*.
n.a. = Not available.

Notes

1. These services included port and harbours, airlines, railways, postal and telecommunications, and so on.
2. The most important change in the tax structure resulting from the introduction of sales tax was that the Tanzanian indirect tax system became more reliant on the general consumption tax rather than on selective excise taxes and import duties.
3. Particularly Lesotho (73% of total tax), Seychelles (57%), Sierra Leone and Comoros (54%), and Mauritius and Sénégal (over 40%).
4. Foreign travel levy until 19 June 1992 was a 20 per cent levy on foreign air tickets. However, it was then abolished because people travelling to foreign countries can now purchase foreign exchange with which to buy air tickets.
5. The rise has mainly resulted from an increase in the volume and value of imports arising from trade liberalization, export retention schemes, and self-funded imports.
6. In computing a gain, for the original cost of premises, the 'adjusted cost' is used. The adjusted cost is arrived at after adjusting for inflation and devaluation at the exchange rates applicable at the time of sale.
7. In practice, dividends payments are comperatively rare, and shareholders take their money through other routes, such as directors' remuneration, which is allowable in compiling the chargeable profits of the paying company.
8. For evidence on the relative roles of tax and expenditure sides of the budget in income redistribution in LDCs, see (for Chile) Foxley *et al.* (1979, ch. 6); for Columbia, Selowsky (1979, ch. 1); and for Malaysia, Snodgrass (1974).
9. Base-broadening and rate-reduction seem to have limited possibilities in Italy and the Netherlands.
10. Of course, it remains an open question to ask what would have happened in the absence of those tax incentives.
11. According to official estimates, about 45 per cent the recurrent budget and over 75 per cent of the development budget are financed by foreign funds.
12. Instead, taxation, if not properly desired, can result in to serious distortions in the economy.
13. Most of these fringe benefits are currently exempt from personal income tax. The justification often given for doing so is that, since salaries are low, taxing fringe benefits would not enhance the take-home pay of civil servants. However, this argument does not seem to be at all convincing.
14. For details of tax evasion in Tanzania, see Osoro (1991b).

References

Asher, M. G. (1989) 'Tax Reforms in East Asian Developing Countries: Motivations, Directions and Implications', *Asian-Pacific Economic Literature*, vol. 3, no. 1, March, pp. 39–63.

Buchanan, J. M. (1987) 'Tax Reform and Political Choice', *Journal of Economic Perspective*, vol. 1, no. 1, November, pp. 29–35.

Due, J. F. (1977) 'The Tax Structure of the Democratic Republic of the Sudan, with Emphasis on the Indirect Taxes and Posible Reforms', University of Illinois College of Commerce, Working Paper No. 420, July.

Foxley, A., E. Aminat and J. P. Arellano (1979) *Redistribution Effects of Governmental Programs: The Chilean Case* (New York: Pergamon Press).

Gillis, M. (1985) 'Micro and Macroeconomics of Tax Reform: Indonesia', *Journal of Development Economics*, vol. 19, no. 3, December, pp. 221–54.

Goode, R. (1987) 'Implementing Tax Reform in Sub-Saharan Africa', in *Tax Policy for Sub-Saharan Africa, Papers and Proceedings*, Bureau for Africa Agency for International Development, October 29–30, pp. 2–34.

Khalilzadeh-Shiraz, J. and A. Shah (eds) (1990) *Tax Policy in Developing Countries* (Washington DC: World Bank Symposium).

Khalilzadeh-Shiraz, J. and A. Shah (1991) 'Introduction: Tax Policy Issues for the 1990s', *World Bank Economic Review*, vol. 5, no. 3, September, pp. 459–73.

Kwack, T.-W. and K.-S. Lee (1990) 'Tax Reform in Korea', Paper presented at a conference on the Political Economy of Tax Reforms and the Implications for Interdependence, Seoul, Korea; June 14–16.

McMahon, G. and M. Berrios (1991) 'Tax Reform and Macroeconomic Policy in Developing Countries', mimeo.

Messere, K. C. (1988) 'Overview', in J. A. Pechman (ed.) *World Tax Reform: A Progress Report* (??).

Muten, L. (1987) 'Some Remarks Based on Experiences of IMF Technical Assistance Work', in *Tax Policy for Sub-Saharan African, Paper and Proceedings*, Bureau for Africa Agency for International Development, October 29–30, pp. 122–38.

Osoro, N. E. (1990) 'The Revenue Generating Potentials of the Tanzanian Tax System', *Tanzania Journal of Economics*, vol. 2, no. 1, January, pp. 53–62.

Osoro, N. E. (1991a) 'Revenue Productivity Implications of Tax Reform in Tanzania', A Final Report submitted to the African Economic Research Consortium, September.

Osoro, N. E. (1991b) 'Tax Reform in Tanzania: Motivations, Directions and Implications, A Research Proposal presented at AERC Workshops, Nairobi, December 7–11.

Selowsky, M. (1979) *Who Benefits From Government Expenditure*? (New York: Oxford University Press).

Snodgrass, D. R. (1974) 'The Fiscal System as Income Redistribution in West Malaysia', *Public Finance*, vol. 29, n. 1, pp. 56–76.

Tanzi, V. and P. Shome (1990) 'The Role of Taxation in the Development of East Asian Economies', Paper presented at the Conference on the Political Economy and their Implications for Interdependence, Seoul, Korea, June 14–16.

United Republic of Tanzania (URT) (1969) *The Sales Tax Act 1969* (Dar es Salaam: Government Printer).

United Republic of Tanzania (URT) (1973) *Income Tax Act 1973* (Dar es Salaam: Government Printer).

United Republic of Tanzania (URT) (1976a) *Sales Tax Act 1976* (Dar es Salaam: Government Printer).

United Republic of Tanzania (URT) (1976b) *Customs Tariff Act 1976* (Dar es Salaam: Government Printer).

United Republic of Tanzania (URT) (1989) *Hali ya Uchumi 1989* (Dar es Salaam: Government Printer).

United Republic of Tanzania (URT) (1990a) *National Accounts of Tanzania 1976–1989* (Dar es Salaam: Central Statistical Bureau).

United Republic of Tanzania (URT) (1990b) *Investment Promotion Policy* (Dar es Salaam: Planning Commission), February.

United Republic of Tanzania (URT) (various dates) *Budget Speech* (Dar es Salaam: Government Printer).
United Republic of Tanzania (URT) (various dates) *Financial Statement and Revenue Estimates* (Dar es Salaam: Government Printer).

Part III

Trade and Fiscal Interfaces

10
Fiscal Implications of Trade Liberalization

David Bevan

Introduction

There is now a considerable amount of literature devoted to the theory and practice of trade liberalization,[1] and a rapidly growing literature devoted to fiscal reform in developing countries.[2] To a surprising extent, these two types of policy reform have either been considered in isolation from each other, or as two separate types of exercise that might interfere with each other, and hence pose a sequencing problem. Relatively few studies[3] have focused on the extent to which trade liberalization exacerbates the government's existing budgetary problems, or the reverse. Yet this is a consideration which often makes developing country governments wary of embarking on a liberalization programme, and which can lead to the collapse of a programme once adopted.

The problem is that liberalization typically involves wholesale movements in both relative and nominal prices, including the exchange rate itself, and consequential shifts in output and expenditure. It is very much a general equilibrium type of problem, for which partial equilibrium reasoning may be highly misleading. In addition, liberalization in practice is always partial, rather than complete, so the usual second best types of ambiguity abound. The consequence is that the relationship between the trade policy regime and the budget is complex and not well understood, depending in a detailed way on the fiscal structure, substitution possibilities in production, and the pattern of preferences. The budgetary impact of liberalization cannot reliably be signed without specifying this structure in some detail.

The purpose of this chapter is to throw some light on this relationship. To the extent that trade liberalization has budgetary implications, these can be absorbed in three different ways, possibly in combination. First, the fiscal structure may itself be altered to accommodate the changes. Second, there may be a change in net capital inflow to the government, that is a change in the foreign financing of the deficit. Third, there may be a change in the domestic financing of the deficit; in the present context, where domestic capital markets are supposed to be undeveloped, this involves changes in the amount of the deficit which has to be monetized and hence changes in the inflation tax. In practice, the size of fiscal impact that can be absorbed via the inflation tax is fairly limited, so the compatibility of trade liberalization must be ensured either by being part of a self-financing package, or by accommodating inflows.

This chapter examines the issue under each of these mechanisms. In both cases use is made of a simple CGE model, whose structure is given in Appendix 1. While simplified, the model attempts to capture the salient features of the economy, with a sufficiently rich characterization of the structure of production, preferences, and particularly government, to permit computation of the budgetary impact of the relative price changes involved in liberalization. It can be used to compare the relative (stationary) equilibria under alternative (compatible) trade regimes, and can also track the path between them, since it captures the main macroeconomic channels of impact (monetization of the deficit, exchange rate changes and inflation, as well as real changes) other than transitional unemployment. The next section of the chapter attempts to estimate the actual impact of a given liberalization package, using Kenya as an illustration, (Appendix 2 details how the model was calibrated on Kenya data). It turns out that simple quota removal is substantially budget-improving in this case, so that compatible liberalization can combine this with tariff reduction. The section focuses on a number of packages, including an aid-assisted package, that are compatible in a comparative, static sense (that is, they generate steady-state inflation rates roughly comparable to the pre-liberalization rate); in particular, it examines the characteristics of dynamic adjustment under these reforms. Even when the reform is compatible and welfare-improving in a comparative static sense, the transition path may be unacceptable to the government. For example, it may involve unacceptably high transitional rates of inflation; in these circumstances there might indeed be a role for temporary additional aid to accompany the liberalization, even though this will ultimately be at least self-financing.

The following section further examines the relationship between fiscal structure, economic structure and liberalization. It again provides illustrative calculations, but in this case of stylized economics. It is concerned with the relative (stationary) equilibrium under different trade regimes, rather than the path between them, so it suppresses the dynamic and monetary features that figured importantly in the previous section. The budgetary impact of various changes is now assessed directly by calculating the change in net capital inflow that would be required to accommodate it. This provides a first cut at the scale of the fiscal adjustment that would be required in the absence of variable capital inflow. In other words, it takes into account the relative price changes consequent directly on the liberalization, in isolation from any further changes that may be induced by the associated financing requirements.

Liberalization and the Kenyan budget

In this section, the impact on the Kenyan budget of a hypothetical liberalization package is considered, starting with a simple foreign-exchange budget calculation, then importing relative price changes from the CGE exercise, and concluding with the CGE simulations themselves. It should be stressed the assumption is maintained throughout that the pre-liberalization regime is sustainable though inefficient; the liberalization package is not embedded within a stabilization programme. Whether or not it is practicable to combine liberalization with stabilization, as opposed to deferring the liberalization until stabilization is achieved, it is clearly inappropriate to attribute fiscal changes required for stabilization to the liberalization programme itself.

In practice, different components of the budget will be affected by the liberalization/devaluation package in different ways. To obtain a rough idea of the overall impact, it is helpful to disaggregate both the revenue and expenditure sides of the budget into tradable, non-tradable and wage components. The procedure is illustrated in Table 10.1, where data for 1988/9 and 1989/90 are averaged to provide an estimate of calendar 1989 values. The disaggregation between tradable and non-tradable expenditures is fairly crude, based on the relatively highly aggregated breakdown provided in the economic analysis of expenditure tables in the statistical abstract: it could be refined considerably by using the appropriation accounts. However, given the impossibility of accurate calculation of these general equilibrium effects, such refinement is probably not worthwhile.

First, consider the fiscal implications of devaluation. Discussions of this often focus heavily on the 'foreign exchange budget' to ascertain whether the government is a net seller or purchaser of foreign exchange. From the table, direct transactions in foreign exchange involve inflows from external grants (K£202 million) and net foreign financing (K£251

Table 10.1 Central government revenue and expenditure, 1989 (K£ millions)

Expenditure	
Labour costs[1]	896
Transfers[2]	192
Non-tradables[3]	490
Tradables[3]	476
(of which Imports)	142
Domestic interest	323
Foreign interest	159
	2536
Revenue	
Income tax	556
Indirect taxes	
Sales tax (domestic)	338
Excise	143
Sales tax (imports)	277
Import duties	285
Export duties	14
	1057
Other revenue[4]	352
External grants	202
	2167
Financing	
Net foreign	251
Net domestic	118
	369

Notes:

1 Labour costs from table 6.9 of source text, plus cost of teachers' salaries from forward budget figures in World Bank (1989) *Kenya: Public Expenditure Issues*, table 23.

2 Capital transfers plus current transfers less cost of teachers' salaries as Note 1.

3 Tradables is share of transport expenses, purchase of stores, food rations, uniforms, other consumable stores, maintenance, military construction and equipment in 'Other goods and services' in current expenditure plus share of plant, machinery, and equipment and transport equipment in Gross fixed capital formation in Capital expenditure. Non-tradables is residual of 'Other goods and services' and Gross fixed capital formation. Shares calculated from breakdowns in *Statistical Abstract 1990*, tables 195(b) and 196(b), using averages for 1984/5–1987/8. Share of tradables is computed at 71 per cent for 'Other goods and services' and 20 per cent for 'Capital formation'.

4 Business and trading licences, licenses and fees under the traffic act, other licences and duties on production or sale, other revenues and income.

Source: Government of Kenya (1991) *Economic Survey 1991*, tables 6.1, 6.4 and 6.9, from figures for 1988/9 and 1989/90 by simple averaging.

million); and outflows for direct imports (K£142 million) and foreign interest payments (K£159 million). For 1989, the government was a net seller of foreign exchange to the tune of K£152 million. Evidently, these components of the budget would be revalued by the full amount of any

Table 10.2 Foreign exchange budget, 1984–8 (K£ millions)

	1984	*1985*	*1986*	*1987*	*1988*
External grants	84.0	90.5	120.7	131.1	233.6
Net foreign financing	87.6	–20.3	12.8	148.5	255.9
Inflows	**171.6**	**70.2**	**133.5**	**279.6**	**489.5**
Direct imports	57.9	53.9	99.4	249.2	230.3
Foreign interest payments	69.4	82.6	96.6	111.5	138.7
Outflows	**127.3**	**136.5**	**196.0**	**360.7**	**369.0**
Net flow[1]	44.3	–66.3	–62.5	–81.1	120.5

Note: Minus sign = outflow.
Source: Research Department of Central Bank, except for foreign interest payments, which were obtained from simple averaging of data in Economic Survey, table 6.9.

devaluation, and to that extent would improve the net budgetary position.

There are two important caveats to this conclusion. First, the underlying flows are very volatile, so that, for a country such as Kenya, not only the magnitude but also the sign of the foreign exchange budget varies from year to year. Table 10.2 gives the main components of the foreign exchange budget for the five years before 1989. For three of the five years, the government was a net buyer of foreign exchange, and for the remaining two, a net seller. The move into surplus in later years was partly a consequence of increased external grants and loans directly associated with the liberalization programme. There are a number of drawbacks to aid-financed liberalization. However, current levels of aid do appear to ensure that the impact effect of devaluation on the budget would be positive.

The second reason for caution in using the foreign exchange budget is more general. It is, at best, only an impact measure which uses a partial equilibrium approach to address a general equilibrium question. A liberalizing devaluation will result in wholesale shifts in relative prices. For a small country, the cif price of imports and the fob price of exports will move, in domestic currency terms, by the full amount of the devaluation. The movement in the implicit-tariff inclusive domestic price of importables, the price of non-tradables, and the wage rate is much harder to estimate, depending on the precise nature of the package, and the ease of substitution in production and consumption.

The obvious way to generate numbers for these relative price changes is via a CGE simulation, which also produces estimates of the associated volume shifts and the composite fiscal consequences of both. Since appropriate CGE models are not routinely available, however, it is of some interest to consider price and quantity effects separately. While the net consequences depend on both, and they are intimately related, it is possible to draw some inferences from the likely relative price movements, even when the quantitative responses to these are unknown. Here we focus on the impact of changes in four prices, as faced by the government (that is, net of various explicit and implicit taxes), denominated in domestic currency terms. They are the price of foreign exchange $1/e$, the wage rate (w), the producer price of non-tradables (p_n) and the producer price of domestically-produced importables (p_m).

The first step is to recompose the numbers in Table 10.1 into groups whose values depend on movements in these four prices. We assume[4] that expenditure on imports and foreign interest, revenue from sales tax on imports, import duties, export duties, and receipts of external grants and net foreign financing all move with the cost of foreign exchange. Labour costs and transfers, income tax[5] and other revenue are assumed to move with the wage rate. Expenditure on non-tradables, and 80 per cent of the sum of domestic sales tax and excise taxes[6] are assumed to move with the price of non-tradables. Expenditure on domestically-manufactured tradables, and 20 per cent of revenues from domestic sales tax and excise taxes are assumed to move with the price of importables. Finally, the domestic currency cost of domestic interest payments is assumed to move with the wage rate, as a proxy for inflation. The alternative would be to assume this component invariant to the various liberalization packages. However, this seems to be an extreme assumption when liberalization markedly increases the inflation rate. The assumption made here is conservative: that is, it probably overestimates the adverse impact of liberalization.

The attributions in Table 10.3 are to some extent arbitrary, but the general picture conveyed in the net column of Panel B appears to be fairly robust for the case of Kenya. It is that the directly foreign-exchange-sensitive budgetary operations run at a substantial surplus, largely offset by deficits in the other three categories. An immediate implication of this is that an augmented foreign-exchange budget calculation is considerably more favourable than the direct exercise reported earlier. That is, if the exchange rate alone were to change, leaving the wage rate and price of non-tradables invariant, and the importable price to rise by the full amount of the devaluation, then the base for the budgetary gain would not be net direct foreign exchange sales of K£152 million, but K£491 million (K£728 – K£237). This reflects the fact that the government obtains substantially greater (*ad valorem*) revenue on tradable goods than its expenditure n them. The surplus on tradable activities in general is much greater than that on direct foreign exchange transactions.

Table 10.3 Central government revenue and expenditure by price category

A: Categories

Price applied to category	*Revenue*	*Expenditure*
Foreign Exchange (*1/e*)	Import duties Sales tax on imports Export duties External grants Net foreign financing	Direct imports Foreign Interest
Wage rate (w)	Income tax Other revenue	Government Wages Transfers Domestic Interest
Non-tradables (p_n)	Domestic sales tax + Excise taxes (80 per cent)	Government expenditure on non-tradables
Domestically-produced importables (p_m)	Domestic sales tax + Excise taxes (20 per cent)	Government expenditure on importables

B: Values (1989, (K£ millions))

	Revenue	*Expenditure*	*Net*
Foreign exchange	1029	301	728
Wage rate	908	1411	–503
Non-tradables	384	490	–106
Importables	97	334	–237
	2418	**2536**	**–118**

Source: Table 10.1 above, and discussion in text.

More generally, the combination of trade liberalization and depreciation is likely to have still more positive budgetary effects. Broadly, we would expect the price of foreign exchange to rise and the domestic price of importables to fall, relative to the wage rate and the price of non-tradables. This is borne out by price paths generated in the simulations reported later in the chapter. Table 10.4 gives a sample of these, together with the net budgetary impact when they are confronted with the budgetary structure of Table 10.3.

While the actual paths tabulated are very different, they all share the property discussed above, ($1/e > w$, $p_n > p_m$). Hence, in all cases, the budgetary impact is favourable, ranging from the elimination of the domestically-financed component of the deficit (Panel A) to its reversal from K£118 million to a surplus of similar magnitude (Panels B), (C) and (D). These latter figures are misleading, however, since they take no account of the tax and tariff changes in the package. For example, in Panel B the tariff cut would reduce revenue (on unchanged volumes) by around

Table 10.4 Price following liberalization (%) relative to non-liberalization prices

	Year 1	*Year 2*	*Year 3*	*Year 4*
A) Abolition of quotas				
Foreign exchange (1/*e*)	107	86	66	48
Wage rate (*w*)	100	79	60	44
Non-tradables (p_n)	100	79	60	44
Importables (p_m)	75	60	46	34
Net deficit (K£ millions)	**+8**	**–3**	**–6**	**–1**
B) Abolition of quotas with reduction of tariffs to uniform low (compatible) rate				
Foreign exchange (1/*e*)	118	127	134	139
Wage rate (*w*)	103	111	117	121
Non-tradables (p_n)	103	100	115	119
Importables (p_m)	57	61	65	67
Net deficit (K£ millions)	**–97**	**–105**	**–111**	**–118**
C) As (b) but with transitional aid of K£50 million in Years 1 and 2				
Foreign exchange (1/*e*)	116	116	114	118
Wage rate (*w*)	102	102	100	103
Non-tradables (p_n)	102	101	97	100
Importables (p_m)	56	56	55	57
Net deficit (K£ millions)	**–141**	**–142**	**–94**	**–100**
D) Abolition of quotas and tariffs, with increased uniform sales tax for compatibility				
Foreign exchange (1/*e*)	119	129	137	142
Wage rate (*w*)	103	112	119	123
Non-tradables (p_n)	102	110	115	119
Importables (p_m)	54	59	62	65
Net deficit[1] (K£ millions)	**–112**	**–119**	**–130**	**–135**

Note: 1 Takes enhanced capital inflow in Years 1 and 2 into account.
Source: Simulation exercises reported later in this chapter.

K£130 million. Overall, the pure price plus tax effects of these packages would imply a very substantial reduction, but not a reversal of the domestic deficit.

This discussion has suppressed all volume responses. Tables 10.5 to 10.9 present the main quantity, price and budgetary effects of a number of liberalization packages, obtained by simulation using the model whose structure is given in Appendix 1, and whose calibration to Kenyan data is described in Appendix 2. Results are presented for the first four years of the adjustment path, and for the new steady state to which the system is converging. The model is calibrated for the pre-liberalization equilibrium to involve a level of deficit financing sufficient to sustain steady state inflation at 9 per cent per annum, the historical average. Four types of package are considered, in three variants of the model. The four packages are as follows.

First, quantitative restrictions are abolished in Year 1, but no accompanying fiscal changes are made. This is a large and abrupt trade reform: the implicit tariff on competing imports falls by 55 per cent (from 1.20 to 0.54), amounting to a 30 per cent fall in the domestic price before we consider induced exchange rate changes. Subsequently, trade policy is constant. It turns out, given the fiscal structure described in Table 10.1 and Appendix 2, that this is powerfully budget-surplus enhancing. This is partly because of the relative price effects discussed earlier (see Table 10.4, Panel A). It is also because the quantity-constrained imports also carry very high tariff rates. Hence the expenditure shifts into competing imports are strongly revenue-enhancing. These effects are strong enough to drive the domestic budget into substantial surplus unless foreign capital inflows are reduced. Indeed, restoration of a domestic deficit of the pre-liberalization magnitude (so that the system reverts to a 9 per cent inflation rate) requires the capital inflow to be eliminated (K£230 million net inflow to K£30 million net outflow).

While this outcome is clearly sustainable, we assume here that the government wishes to maintain net capital inflow at something like its historic level. In consequence, this first liberalization package would, in practice, be accompanied by other fiscal changes to take up the budgetary slack. We consider three such packages on the base model, and the figures are given in Tables 10.5, 10.6 and 10.7. Each package is designed to have the property of long-run fiscal neutrality, in the sense that the new equilibrium has a steady-state inflation rate in the broad vicinity of 9 per cent. The liberalization-cum-harmonization package (Table 10.5) supplements the abolition of quotas with a massive cut in the tariff rate on competing imports to equal the much lower rate on non-competing imports (a cut from 54 per cent to around 6 per cent). This cut also takes place in Year 1; it generates a steady-state inflation rate of 8.2 per cent per annum. The complete liberalization package (Table 10.6) abolishes quotas and all tariffs, compensating for this by raising sales taxes from 16 per cent (non-tradables, competing imports and domestically-produced importables) and 11 per cent (non-competing imports) to a uniform rate of 18 per cent. Once again, these changes all take place in Year 1 and are maintained thereafter; in this case, the new steady-state inflation rate is 9.7 per cent p.a. Governments of developing countries are liable to negotiate for additional transitional aid to 'finance' the liberalization process. The last package considered, the aid assisted liberalization

Table 10.5 Liberalization-cum-harmonization[1]

	Pre-liberalization equilibrium	*Year 1*	*Year 2*	*Year 3*	*Year 4*	*Post-liberalization equilibrium*
Q_m	0.116	0.074	0.069	0.064	0.060	0.001
Q_n	0.811	0.808	0.814	0.818	0.820	0.813
Q_x	0.470	0.540	0.546	0.551	0.555	0.589
E_m	0.147	0.221	0.221	0.221	0.221	0.213
E_n	0.696	0.693	0.699	0.703	0.705	0.697
E_f	0.487	0.440	0.442	0.442	0.441	0.425
$E_m - Q_m$	0.031	0.146	0.152	0.157	0.161	0.211
L_m	0.110	0.039	0.036	0.034	0.031	0.001
L_n	0.440	0.437	0.436	0.435	0.434	0.431
L_x	0.239	0.313	0.317	0.320	0.323	0.357
K_m	0.120	0.120	0.110	0.101	0.092	0.001
K_n	0.290	0.290	0.297	0.302	0.305	0.301
K_x	0.021	0.021	0.025	0.027	0.028	0.034
K	0.431	0.431	0.432	0.429	0.426	0.335
I_g	0.037	0.038	0.035	0.033	0.032	0.029
I_n	0.016	0.016	0.014	0.012	0.011	0.012
ri_m	0.089	0.003	0.004	0.005	0.006	0.089
ri_n	0.089	0.099	0.095	0.093	0.092	0.089
ri_x	0.089	0.146	0.123	0.111	0.103	0.089
ri_{av}	0.089	0.074	0.074	0.074	0.074	0.089
e	1.000	0.780	0.664	0.577	0.509	*
w	1.000	0.875	0.876	0.875	0.873	0.838
P_n	1.000	0.872	0.864	0.858	0.852	0.819
P_{mc}	2.544	1.231	1.231	1.231	1.231	1.231
P_{nc}	1.157	1.009	1.000	0.992	0.986	0.948
P_{fc}	1.179	1.179	1.179	1.179	1.179	1.179
g_{exp}	0.184	0.170	0.169	0.168	0.167	0.164
g_{wag}	0.211	0.185	0.185	0.184	0.184	0.177
d_{rev}	0.094	0.081	0.081	0.081	0.081	0.078
i_{rev}	0.226	0.189	0.192	0.194	0.195	0.192
aid	0.054	0.054	0.054	0.054	0.054	0.054
def	0.021	0.030	0.026	0.023	0.022	0.016
gdp	1.747	1.508	1.508	1.506	1.502	1.432
gdp_w	1.608	1.503	1.503	1.501	1.498	1.432
m_1	0.159	0.135	0.135	0.136	0.135	0.130
u_2	1.292	1.350	1.357	1.361	1.363	1.328
u_c	1.067	1.121	1.145	1.160	1.170	1.153
ex	1.537	1.307	1.309	1.308	1.306	1.249
P_{kap}	1.000	0.814	0.811	0.808	0.805	0.791
P_{con}	1.000	0.813	0.810	0.807	0.805	0.790
infl^n	9%	4.2%	17.1%	14.7%	13.0%	8.2%

Note: 1 Abolition of quota, tariffs harmonized at low uniform rate of 6.4 per cent.
Source: Simulation using model detailed in the Appendices (post-equilibrium exchange rate is arbitrary, depending on adjustment path, so given as *).

Table 10.6 Complete liberalization[1]

	Pre-liberalization equilibrium	*Year 1*	*Year 2*	*Year 3*	*Year 4*	*Post-liberalization equilibrium*
Q_m	0.116	0.071	0.066	0.062	0.058	0.001
Q_n	0.811	0.803	0.811	0.816	0.819	0.812
Q_x	0.470	0.547	0.554	0.560	0.564	0.596
E_m	0.147	0.226	0.227	0.227	0.227	0.219
E_n	0.696	0.688	0.695	0.700	0.704	0.697
E_f	0.487	0.439	0.441	0.442	0.442	0.425
$E_m - Q_m$	0.031	0.154	0.160	0.165	0.169	0.218
L_m	0.110	0.036	0.033	0.031	0.029	0.000
L_n	0.440	0.432	0.431	0.430	0.429	0.425
L_x	0.239	0.322	0.326	0.329	0.332	0.364
K_m	0.120	0.120	0.110	0.101	0.092	0.000
K_n	0.290	0.290	0.299	0.306	0.310	0.307
K_x	0.021	0.021	0.025	0.028	0.030	0.036
K	0.431	0.431	0.434	0.434	0.432	0.344
I_g	0.037	0.041	0.037	0.035	0.033	0.030
I_n	0.016	0.019	0.016	0.013	0.012	0.013
ri_m	0.089	–0.000	0.001	0.002	0.003	0.089
ri_n	0.089	0.101	0.097	0.094	0.092	0.089
ri_x	0.089	0.157	0.128	0.114	0.105	0.089
ri_{av}	0.089	0.076	0.075	0.074	0.074	0.089
e	1.000	0.770	0.650	0.564	0.499	*
w	1.000	0.864	0.866	0.865	0.864	0.832
P_n	1.000	0.857	0.847	0.840	0.834	0.802
P_{mc}	2.544	1.180	1.180	1.180	1.180	1.180
P_{nc}	1.157	1.011	1.000	0.991	0.984	0.946
P_{fc}	1.179	1.180	1.180	1.180	1.180	1.180
g_{exp}	0.184	0.168	0.167	0.166	0.165	0.162
g_{wag}	0.211	0.182	0.183	0.182	0.182	0.175
d_{rev}	0.094	0.080	0.080	0.080	0.080	0.078
i_{rev}	0.226	0.185	0.189	0.191	0.193	0.187
aid	0.054	0.054	0.054	0.054	0.054	0.054
def	0.021	0.031	0.026	0.023	0.021	0.018
gdp	1.747	1.488	1.490	1.489	1.487	1.424
gdp_w	1.608	1.488	1.490	1.489	1.487	1.424
m_1	0.159	0.133	0.134	0.134	0.134	0.129
u_2	1.292	1.350	1.360	1.366	1.368	1.335
u_c	1.067	1.105	1.135	1.154	1.167	1.156
ex	1.537	1.254	1.257	1.257	1.255	1.203
P_{kap}	1.000	0.781	0.777	0.774	0.771	0.757
P_{con}	1.000	0.808	0.804	0.801	0.798	0.783
$infl^n$	9%	5.0%	17.9%	14.8%	12.6%	9.7%

Note: 1 Abolition of quotas and tariffs: sales taxes raised to uniform rate of 18 per cent.
Source: As Table 10.5 above.

Table 10.7 Aid-assisted liberalization-cum-harmonization[1]

	Pre-liberalization equilibrium	*Year 1*	*Year 2*	*Year 3*	*Year 4*	*Post-liberalization equilibrium*
Q_m	0.116	0.074	0.069	0.064	0.060	0.001
Q_n	0.811	0.812	0.819	0.820	0.821	0.813
Q_x	0.470	0.536	0.543	0.551	0.555	0.589
E_m	0.147	0.223	0.224	0.221	0.221	0.213
E_n	0.696	0.697	0.704	0.704	0.706	0.697
E_f	0.487	0.446	0.447	0.442	0.441	0.425
$E_m - Q_m$	0.031	0.150	0.155	0.157	0.161	0.221
L_m	0.110	0.038	0.036	0.034	0.031	0.001
L_n	0.440	0.441	0.440	0.435	0.434	0.431
L_x	0.239	0.310	0.314	0.321	0.323	0.357
K_m	0.120	0.120	0.110	0.101	0.092	0.001
K_n	0.290	0.290	0.298	0.304	0.306	0.301
K_x	0.021	0.021	0.024	0.027	0.028	0.034
K	0.431	0.431	0.433	0.431	0.427	0.335
I_g	0.037	0.039	0.036	0.033	0.032	0.029
I_n	0.016	0.017	0.014	0.011	0.010	0.012
ri_m	0.089	0.002	0.003	0.005	0.006	0.089
ri_n	0.089	0.100	0.096	0.092	0.091	0.089
ri_x	0.089	0.144	0.122	0.112	0.104	0.089
ri_{av}	0.089	0.075	0.074	0.073	0.074	0.089
e	1.000	0.791	0.728	0.678	0.601	*
w	1.000	0.880	0.880	0.874	0.873	0.838
P_n	1.000	0.881	0.871	0.855	0.851	0.819
P_{mc}	2.544	1.231	1.231	1.231	1.231	1.231
P_{nc}	1.157	1.019	1.008	0.989	0.984	0.948
P_{fc}	1.179	1.179	1.179	1.179	1.179	1.179
g_{exp}	0.184	0.171	0.170	0.168	0.167	0.164
g_{wag}	0.211	0.186	0.186	0.184	0.184	0.177
d_{rev}	0.094	0.081	0.081	0.081	0.081	0.078
i_{rev}	0.226	0.191	0.195	0.194	0.195	0.192
aid	0.054	0.066	0.066	0.054	0.054	0.054
def	0.021	0.018	0.013	0.023	0.021	0.016
gdp	1.747	1.516	1.515	1.505	1.502	1.432
gdp_w	1.608	1.511	1.511	1.501	1.498	1.432
m_1	0.159	0.137	0.137	0.136	0.135	0.130
u_2	1.292	1.362	1.371	1.363	1.364	1.328
u_c	1.067	1.127	1.154	1.165	1.173	1.153
ex	1.537	1.326	1.327	1.308	1.306	1.249
P_{kap}	1.000	0.818	0.814	0.807	0.805	0.791
P_{con}	1.000	0.817	0.813	0.806	0.804	0.790
infl^n	9%	3.3%	8.1%	6.4%	12.5%	8.2%

Note: 1 As Table 10.5 above, but with increased capital inflow to government in first two years of liberalization programme.
Source: As Table 10.5 above.

(Table 10.7), replicates the liberalization-cum-harmonization package of Table 10.5, with the addition of an enhanced capital inflow of K£50 million in each of the first two years.

All these exercise are conducted within the confines of the base model calibration given in Appendix 2. This is characterized by relatively slow depreciation and hence rather slow adjustment of the capital stock. Table 10.8 reworks the case of Table 10.5 under the assumption of a much faster potential transition (depreciation is at 20 per cent p.a. instead of 5 per cent). The new steady-state inflation rate is 7 per cent p.a. A more radical alternative is depicted in Table 10.9, which utilizes the counterfactual assumption that all protection of domestic importable production takes the form of quotas, so that all tariff revenue is levied on non-competing imports. This turns the simple quota abolition from being powerfully revenue-enhancing to being mildly detrimental (the steady-state inflation rate rises to 11.6 per cent p.a.).

The model is described in Appendix 1. In brief, it has four goods; three produced using a fixed factor, labour (mobile between sectors, fixed in aggregate) and capital (mobile between sectors, variable in aggregate), and three consumed. There is an importable good and a non-tradable good (produced and consumed); an exportable good (produced but not consumed); and a foreign good (consumed but not produced). These are indexed by m, n, x and f. The distinction between competing and non-competing imports is particularly important in capturing the structure of trade policy in many developing countries. Production sectors share the same elasticity of substitution between capital and labour, but differ in their capital intensity (and in reliance on the fixed factor). In consumption, any pair of the three goods may be specially related (either as substitutes or complements) *vis-à-vis* the third. Government volume purchases are taken to be independent of relative prices: hence, relative price changes translate directly into public expenditure changes. Taxes are *ad valorem* so revenues respond to private expenditure changes, whether emanating from price or quantity changes. The government may also make discretionary tax changes as part of its liberalization programme. Except for 'aid-assisted' cases, it is assumed that capital inflows are fixed in foreign-currency terms. The residual budget deficit is monetized and via a simple transactions demand for money this generates a variable inflation rate. Gross investment in each sector is linearly related to the gap between the immediately previous sectoral rate of return and a target rate, subject to it being non-negative. Two further assumptions are made about investment. First, it has the same sectoral composition as consumption expenditure. Hence the split of private spending between consumption

Table 10.8 Liberalization-cum-harmonization, rapid depreciation case[1]

	Pre-liberalization equilibrium	*Year 1*	*Year 2*	*Year 3*	*Year 4*	*Post-liberalization equilibrium*
Q_m	0.116	0.074	0.060	0.049	0.040	0.001
Q_n	0.811	0.808	0.816	0.819	0.820	0.813
Q_x	0.470	0.540	0.552	0.561	0.567	0.589
E_m	0.147	0.221	0.220	0.219	0.218	0.213
E_n	0.696	0.692	0.700	0.704	0.705	0.697
E_f	0.487	0.441	0.440	0.438	0.436	0.425
$E_m - Q_m$	0.031	0.146	0.160	0.170	0.178	0.211
L_m	0.110	0.039	0.032	0.026	0.021	0.001
L_n	0.440	0.437	0.435	0.434	0.433	0.431
L_x	0.239	0.314	0.323	0.330	0.335	0.357
K_m	0.120	0.120	0.092	0.071	0.055	0.001
K_n	0.290	0.290	0.300	0.304	0.306	0.301
K_x	0.021	0.021	0.026	0.028	0.030	0.034
K	0.431	0.431	0.418	0.404	0.391	0.335
I_g	0.102	0.088	0.085	0.082	0.081	0.079
I_n	0.016	0.002	0.001	0.002	0.003	0.012
ri_m	1.181	–0.055	–0.047	–0.038	–0.029	0.181
ri_n	0.181	0.206	0.193	0.185	0.182	0.181
ri_x	0.181	0.337	0.259	0.225	0.207	0.181
ri_{av}	0.181	0.140	0.144	0.149	0.154	0.181
e	1.000	0.783	0.684	0.611	0.554	*
w	1.000	0.875	0.870	0.865	0.860	0.838
P_n	1.000	0.872	0.855	0.844	0.837	0.819
P_{mc}	2.544	1.231	1.231	1.231	1.231	1.231
P_{nc}	1.157	1.009	0.990	0.977	0.969	0.948
P_{fc}	1.179	1.179	1.179	1.179	1.179	1.179
g_{exp}	0.184	0.170	0.168	0.166	0.166	0.164
g_{wag}	0.211	0.185	0.184	0.182	0.181	0.177
d_{rev}	0.090	0.077	0.077	0.077	0.077	0.076
i_{rev}	0.226	0.194	0.195	0.195	0.195	0.192
aid	0.058	0.058	0.058	0.058	0.058	0.058
def	0.021	0.025	0.021	0.018	0.017	0.014
gdp	1.747	1.508	1.497	1.487	1.477	1.432
gdp_w	1.608	1.503	1.493	1.483	1.474	1.432
m_1	0.159	0.136	0.135	0.134	0.133	0.130
u_2	1.292	1.350	1.355	1.355	1.353	1.328
u_c	1.067	1.155	1.169	1.174	1.174	1.153
ex	1.537	1.307	1.301	1.293	1.286	1.249
P_{kap}	1.000	0.814	0.807	0.802	0.799	0.791
P_{con}	1.000	0.813	0.806	0.801	0.798	0.790
$infl^n$	9.0 %	3.9 %	13.5 %	11.2 %	9.8 %	7.0 %

Note: 1 As Table 10.5 above, but with capital depreciating at 20 per cent per annum, rather than 5 per cent per annum.
Source: As Table 10.5 above.

Table 10.9 Quota abolition with counterfactual representation of initial trade regime[1]

	Pre liberalization equilibrium	*Year 1*	*Year 2*	*Year 3*	*Year 4*	*Post liberalization equilibrium*
Q_m	0.116	0.071	0.066	0.062	0.057	0.001
Q_n	0.811	0.805	0.811	0.815	0.817	0.809
Q_x	0.470	0.545	0.552	0.557	0.560	0.592
E_m	0.147	0.228	0.228	0.229	0.228	0.220
E_n	0.696	0.690	0.696	0.700	0.702	0.693
E_f	0.487	0.435	0.437	0.437	0.437	0.420
$E_m - Q_m$	0.031	0.157	0.162	0.167	0.171	0.219
L_m	0.110	0.035	0.033	0.031	0.029	0.000
L_n	0.440	0.434	0.433	0.433	0.432	0.428
L_x	0.239	0.319	0.323	0.326	0.329	0.361
K_m	0.120	0.120	0.110	0.101	0.092	0.000
K_n	0.290	0.290	0.297	0.302	0.305	0.300
K_x	0.021	0.021	0.025	0.027	0.029	0.034
K	0.431	0.431	0.431	0.429	0.426	0.335
I_g	0.037	0.038	0.035	0.033	0.032	0.029
I_n	0.016	0.016	0.014	0.012	0.011	0.012
ri_m	0.089	–0.002	–0.001	0.000	0.001	0.089
ri_n	0.089	0.098	0.095	0.093	0.092	0.089
ri_x	0.089	0.151	0.125	0.111	0.104	0.089
ri_{av}	0.089	0.073	0.072	0.072	0.073	0.089
e	1.000	0.769	0.660	0.577	0.511	*
w	1.000	0.867	0.869	0.868	0.867	0.834
P_n	1.000	0.862	0.855	0.849	0.844	0.814
P_{mc}	2.543	1.156	1.156	1.156	1.156	1.156
P_{nc}	1.156	0.997	0.989	0.982	0.976	0.941
P_{fc}	1.252	1.252	1.252	1.252	1.252	1.252
g_{exp}	0.184	0.169	0.168	0.167	0.166	0.163
g_{wag}	0.211	0.183	0.183	0.183	0.183	0.176
d_{rev}	0.093	0.078	0.078	0.078	0.078	0.076
i_{rev}	0.245	0.209	0.212	0.213	0.214	0.207
aid	0.035	0.035	0.035	0.035	0.035	0.035
def	0.021	0.029	0.025	0.023	0.022	0.020
gdp	1.747	1.493	1.495	1.493	1.491	1.427
gdp_w	1.608	1.493	1.495	1.493	1.491	1.427
m_1	0.162	0.136	0.136	0.136	0.136	0.131
u_2	1.294	1.348	1.355	1.359	1.361	1.325
u_c	1.074	1.124	1.148	1.163	1.172	1.154
ex	1.572	1.318	1.320	1.320	1.318	1.262
P_{kap}	1.000	0.805	0.802	0.799	0.797	0.784
P_{con}	1.000	0.804	0.801	0.798	0.796	0.783
infl^n	9.0%	4.6%	16.0%	14.0%	12.6%	11.6%

Note: 1 Simple quota abolition; counterfactual specification of initial trade regime has importable production protected solely by quotas and all tariffs on non-competing imports.
Source: As Table 10.5 above.

and investment has no impact on the composition of output. The second, and closely related, assumption is that the same function that determines the substitutability of goods in producing utility also determines their substitutability in producing units of capital. It is a consequence of the assumed fixity of financial capital inflows that changes in the private domestic investment rate must be financed domestically. The target rate of return reflects domestic time preference, rather than any assumed perfect international capital market.

Each table gives data for the common pre-liberalization year, assumed to be in steady state, the first four years of liberalization, and the steady state to which the economy converges following liberalization. Data are given for output volumes (Q_i), private expenditure at constant prices (E_i), the volume of competing imports of the private sector ($E_m - Q_m$), sectoral labour force (L_i) and capital stock (K_i), aggregate gross and net real investment (I_g, I_n), and sectoral (ri_j) and average (ri_{av}) real rates of return. The wage rate (w), producer price of non-tradables (p_n), and consumer prices (p_{ic}) are all given in terms of their foreign exchange values, using the current exchange rate (foreign currency obtained per unit of domestic currency, *e*). The same convention is adopted in reporting the budgetary magnitudes (g_{exp}, g_{wag}, d_{rev}, i_{rev}, aid and the domestically-financed deficit, *def*); the value of GDP at factor cost (*gdp* where importable production is valued at distorted domestic relative prices, gdp_w where it is valued directly at world prices); the real value of the money stock (m_1) and the value of private expenditure at producer prices (*ex*); and the prices of a composite unit of capital and of consumption (p_{kap}, p_{con}; u_2 is the real value of private expenditure, and u_c the representative level of utility generated by private consumption. (No allowance is made for the benefits of government expenditure, but this is modelled as being stationary.) Finally, the true rate of inflation of consumer prices is given as the rate of change of the domestic currency value of p_{con} ($infl_n$). For the pre- and post-liberalization equilibrium, the steady-state inflation value is given, for Years 1–4, the year-on-year value.

All the cases tabulated have an immediate abolition of quantitative restrictions as one component. As is clearly noted, this is a large and abrupt trade reform; the exchange rate falls by around 22 per cent compared to its usual depreciation of 9 per cent. Most dramatically, the sector producing importables sheds two-thirds of its labour force in the first year of transition. This is partly a reflection of the fact that in the model as calibrated to Kenyan data there is really no future for a domestic sector producing importables in the absence of substantial protection. In the model, all this released labour is immediately absorbed entirely in the exportable sector, since non-tradable employment is stable or falls slightly. In practice, this rate of reabsorption would be extraordinarily difficult to achieve, even in those African economies with very high rates of circular migration between rural and urban sectors. In consequence, abrupt liberalization is likely to be more disruptive and slower to achieve beneficial resources reallocation than the present simulations portray.

Once this substantial initial switch takes place, the transition appears to become somewhat becalmed on a plateau, even when the system is some way from the final equilibrium. For example, in Table 10.5, L_m falls in Year 1 to 35 per cent of its initial value; but by Year 4 has fallen only to 28 per cent, or one fifth of the remaining adjustment. This plateau effect is common to all the main quantity variables other than those involving capital.

The second relatively systematic feature to note is that aggregate investment falls, and hence so does the capital stock. This is a feature of adjustment programmes which has been much remarked upon.[7] In the present context it arises simply because the contracting sector is far more capital-intensive than the expanding sector. Although the real price of capital falls, and also falls relative to the wage, so that sectoral capital intensity actually rises, this is not enough to offset the sectoral switch, and aggregate desired capital and gross investment fall. In the low depreciation case, the fall in net investment is fairly modest, roughly to its new equilibrium value (Table 10.5). In the high depreciation case, the effect is much more dramatic, with net investment nearly being eliminated during the four transitional years depicted (Table 10.8). One consequence of this is that welfare actually overshoots its new equilibrium value during the transition. (Of course, transitional unemployment and other costs of the transition which are reflected here might overturn this result.)

The third feature is the time path of the budget deficit and associated inflation. In each of the five cases tabulated, the reform package is calculated to generate an equilibrium domestic deficit which can be financed by a roughly similar rate of inflation tax as the pre-reform deficit. This requires the foreign exchange denominated value of the deficit to fall, since the value of expenditure, and hence required real money balances (also denominated in foreign exchange), are lower in the new equilibrium. However, in the absence of increased capital inflow, in each case the deficit initially rises before it falls. This has the effect of accelerating the inflation rate temporarily, after the initial period of grace because of the substantial fall in the price of importables. Thus in Table 10.5, the consumption inflation rate drops to 4.2 per cent in the first year of reform and then jumps to 17.1 per cent, 14.7 per cent and 13.0 per cent during Years 2, 3 and 4, respectively. The fully-employed representative agent in the model would presumably be mollified by the welfare gain that accompanied this inflationary surge. However, in practice, with substantial redistributions taking place and very incomplete information about what is happening, high rates of inflation may be very damaging both to a reform's credibility and to its political acceptability. In consequence, it is not unreasonable for governments to wish to minimize the inflationary consequences of reform.

To the extent that the pattern of Tables 10.5, 10.6, 10.8 and 10.9 is typical, there are two options available. Either the government can engage in a temporary tightening of fiscal policy, or it must obtain increased capital inflows. Since trade policy reform may already be a politically fragile option – because it threatens the interests of the elite – fiscal measures that have an impact on the population at large may be very unattractive. It is natural therefore that a government pressurized to implement a trade reform should seek additional transitional aid. Table 10.7 repeats the simulation of Table 10.5, with the addition of a temporary injection of aid during the first two years. It has sometimes been suggested that aid-assisted liberalization is very problematical, because it slows the resource reallocation.[8] However, in the present case it appears to be remarkably successful. The disruption it causes to the necessary process of resource reallocation is minimal – the real figures for Year 4 are almost indistinguishable for Tables 10.5 and 10.7, and the earlier years differ very little. On the other hand, the inflation sequence is altered radically. The unproblematical first year is marginally reduced to 3.3 per cent but the rates for years 2 and 3 are more than halved, to 8.1 per cent and 6.4 per cent, respectively. The consequence is that the inflation rate falls below the norm for the first three years of the programme, rising to only a little above it (temporarily) thereafter.

The fourth feature of the tables to be stressed is how remarkably consistent they are in respect of these major features. If a trade and fiscal reform were competently designed for long-run compatibility, then, in the circumstances portrayed by the model of Appendices 1 and 2, the transitional path would probably involve very substantial labour movements, increased budget deficits, accelerating inflation, and an investment collapse. It is hardly surprising that many liberalizations are aborted in practice well before completion.

Fiscal structure, economic structure and liberalization

The previous section analyzed the dynamic aspects of liberalization, concentrating on packages that were compatible in comparative static terms, and using a stylized model of the Kenyan economy as a vehicle for the analysis. In this section we turn briefly to consider the circumstances in which liberalization packages might or might not have the property of comparative static compatibility. For this purpose, we continue to use the model of Appendix 1, but now concentrate on the static features, and use arbitrary coefficients for the comparison. The deterioration or improvement in the budgetary position is fully covered by a change in the level of foreign financing, so no fiscal adjustment is required. While this is normally a poor way in which to close this type of model, it is appropriate in the present case, since it enables us to track the extent of the 'pure' fiscal consequences of liberalization. The alternative assumptions of exogenous foreign finance or limited accommodation would force endogenous budget adjustment, obscuring the pure effects.

Before providing illustrative calculations, it is helpful to consider the following highly stylized liberalization. Trade policy in the initial equilibrium consists entirely of quota restrictions. Liberalization takes the extreme form of abolishing quotas without introducing tariffs, and allowing the exchange rate to equilibrate the balance of payments. The question is whether this package needs to be accompanied by fiscal reform. In other words, were the quotas in any way substituting for a tighter fiscal stance? Economies often end in a quota-ridden equilibrium, having started with an excessive fiscal deficit that spilled over into a balance-of-payments problems which was countered by the adoption of quantitative restrictions on imports. However, other policy changes, including fiscal ones, will also have been undertaken during this process.

In a very simple model,[9] where government spending on importables and non-tradables exhibits the same (constant) elasticity of substitution as private spending, it turns out that for equilibrium to have been achieved, it is analytically as plausible that the fiscal regime has become tighter than would be required for free trade as that it remains too lax to be consistent with it. The reason is that quotas do not remove the excess purchasing power in the hands of the private sector, given the government's spending. They simply re-route it away from imports towards import substitutes and non-tradables, drawing resources out of the export sector. Whether this process helps to make the original fiscal laxity sustainable, or whether it exacerbates it, depends on the elasticity of substitution in consumption between importables and non-tradables, and on the pattern of the budget. If government revenues are more concentrated on tradables than government expenditures, and if tradables and non-tradables are net complements in consumption, then some fiscal tightening (an increase in taxes or a reduction in spending) must accompany the removal of quotas. The same is true if revenue is relatively more concentrated on non-tradables, and the goods are net substitutes. On the other hand, if revenue is derived relatively more from tradables (non-tradables) and the goods are net substitutes (net complements), the removal of quotas could be accompanied by fiscal relaxation.

While it is relatively common for governments to obtain a high proportion of their revenue from the tradable sector, and to devote a high proportion of their expenditure to non-tradables, there does not appear to be any obvious presumption as to the substitutability of those goods in consumption. In consequence, there is no strong a priori presumption that a liberalizing government will need to generate additional revenue to make the liberalization feasible.

This argument has been constructed for a very stylized case. In practice, the conclusion is likely to be reinforced. Typically, there are tariffs in place and these are usually higher on the most quantitatively restricted goods, as in the Kenyan case described in the previous section. Hence, additional revenue is generated automatically as the volume of imports expands, the composition shifts towards more heavily taxed goods and the domestic price of imports rises. However, the actual budgetary impact of a liberalization will depend on the broad structure of the budget and of the economy in question.

Illustrative calculations

In all the calculations reported here, unless explicitly noted otherwise, the capital intensities (measured by the profit share in profit and wage income) of the three production sectors are proportional to: 4 (importables), 0.3 (non-tradables), and 0.2 (exportables) with equality holding in the undistorted equilibrium. Returns to capital and labour combined are 0.8 and the elasticity of substitution between them is 0.5. The distribution of private expenditure in the undistorted state is 36 per cent on importables, 54 per cent on non-tradables, and 10 per cent on foreign goods. There are no direct taxes on wages, profits or rents. The elasticity of substitution in consumption is 1 between importables and non-tradables, and 0.2 between this composite and foreign goods. The government purchases equal quantities of the three consumption goods, and 15 per cent of labour services. The output of these services does not enter into production or private consumption. The indirect tax regime is stipulated in each set of calculations.

In Table 10.10, column (1) gives the equilibrium of the economy under non-distortionary taxation, provided by $t_m = t_n = tt_f$, which is tantamount to a uniform sales tax. This provides a benchmark against which

Table 10.10 Trade liberalization, illustration with exports highly elastic[1]

	(1)	*(2)*	*(3)*	*(4)*	*(5)*	*(6)*	*(7)*	*(8)*	*(9)*
t_q	0	0.8	0	0	0	0	0	0	0
tt_m	0	0.3	0.3	1.34	1.34	0.98	1.12	1.10	0
t_m	0.2	0	0	0	0	0	0	0	0
t_n	0.2	0	0	0	0	0	0	0	0
t_x	0	0.2	0.2	0.2	0	0.2	0.2	0.2	0
tt_f	0.2	0.2	0.2	0.2	0.2	0.2	0.2	0.2	0
Q_m	0.097	0.450	0.294	0.460	0.433	0.440	0.450	0.448	0.078
Q_n	0.769	0.856	0.838	0.842	0.842	0.839	0.840	0.840	0.912
Q_x	0.582	0.043	0.295	0.044	0.100	0.083	0.064	0.067	0.466
E_m	0.480	0.498	0.497	0.489	0.490	0.488	0.488	0.448	0.586
E_n	0.719	0.806	0.788	0.792	0.792	0.789	0.790	0.790	0.862
E_f	0.133	0.228	0.132	0.223	0.225	0.189	0.202	0.200	0.171
$E_m - Q_m$	0.383	0.048	0.203	0.029	0.058	0.048	0.038	0.040	0.509
L_m	0.047	0.329	0.194	0.338	0.313	0.321	0.330	0.329	0.035
L_n	0.431	0.506	0.494	0.496	0.495	0.495	0.496	0.496	0.533
L_x	0.373	0.015	0.163	0.015	0.042	0.033	0.024	0.025	0.282
K_m	0.031	0.200	0.118	0.205	0.191	0.193	0.199	0.198	0.024
K_n	0.185	0.198	0.193	0.194	0.195	0.192	0.193	0.192	0.229
K_x	0.093	0.003	0.037	0.003	0.010	0.008	0.005	0.006	0.071
K	0.309	0.401	0.347	0.403	0.395	0.393	0.397	0.397	0.323
g_{exp}	0.150	0.180	0.149	0.180	0.181	0.168	0.172	0.172	0.155
g_{wag}	0.150	0.222	0.137	0.220	0.225	0.187	0.200	0.198	0.159
d_{rev}	0.000	0.000	0.000	0.000	0.000	0.000	0.000	0.000	0.000
i_{rev}	0.266	0.069	0.146	0.092	0.123	0.101	0.096	0.097	0.000
Def	0.034	0.333	0.140	0.308	0.283	0.254	0.276	0.273	0.314
gdp	1.599	2.683	1.583	2.672	2.699	2.264	2.421	2.398	1.709
u_e	1.332	1.511	1.415	1.483	1.487	1.455	1.466	1.465	1.619
w	1.000	1.478	0.912	1.468	1.499	1.248	1.332	1.320	1.058
P_a	1.000	1.607	0.987	1.592	1.618	1.358	1.448	1.435	1.103
Def (%)[2]	2.1	12.4	8.8	11.5	10.5	11.2	11.4	11.4	18.4

Notes:
1 $G_m = G_n = g_f = 0.05$.
2 Def (%) is deficit as percentage of GDP.

equilibria can be measured. At the given parameter values the budget deficit is 0.034, or 2 per cent of GDP at factor cost, so this might be regarded as a sustainable equilibrium.

Column (2) portrays a highly illiberal fiscal/trade regime. Apart from the 20 per cent tariff on the foreign goods (tt_f) there is now 20 per cent tax on exports (t_x), a 30 per cent tariff on importables (tt_m) and, a fairly savage quota on importables having a tariff equivalent of 80 per cent. Since this is over and above the tariff of 30 per cent, the full tariff equivalence of the two combined is 1.34 (1.8 × 1.3 – 1). All revenues are now generated by trade taxes: because of the high elasticities involved, revenues are very low (competitive imports have fallen from 0.383 to 0.048 and exports from 0.582 to 0.043, offset partly by increased imports of the foreign good from 0.133 to 0.228); however, expenditures have risen, reflecting the rise in prices of importables and non-tradables, and of wages. The deficit, in consequence, is 0.333, or more than 12 per cent of GDP.

We now consider a variety of liberalization measures. In column (3), the quota is simply abolished, leaving all other taxes in place. Total private imports are substantially, up to (0.203 + 0.132 in place of 0.048 + 0.228), as is the tariff yield. There is a large gain in export volume (up from 0.043 to 0.295). Coupled with the very substantial decline in prices, the budget improves to a deficit of 0.140. In this case, the abolition of quotas is substantially beneficial to the budget as well as to resource allocation.

Column (4) illustrates the consequences of replacing the quota with an equivalent tariff rate of 1.34. Interestingly, this hardly improves the budgetary position from the illiberal regime of column (2) and, if anything, worsens the allocative outcome. (Resources move yet further into the importables sector.) In this case, the budgetary consequences of replacing a quota with a tariff are unambiguously worse than simple abolition.

Column (5) combines quota replacement with a tariff and abolition of the export tax. In the present case this has remarkably little revenue impact; since exports are so small, nor does it lead to any substantial recovery of exports.

It is apparent from the table that there are at least four different meanings of 'tariff equivalence of a quota'. The usual meaning is the one underlying column (4), that yields an equivalent elevation of domestic producer prices over the world price. However, it does not necessarily imply the same level of imports, the same scale of domestic output of importables, or the same level of employment in that sector. In the present case, the 'equivalent tariff' leads to a substantially more severe contraction of imports (0.029 against 0.048). Column (6) gives the tariff rate (absent quotas) which yields a similar degree of import compression – namely, a tariff rate of only 98 per cent. Similarly, column (7) gives a rate (112 per cent) which yields the same level of production of importables: and column (8) the rate (110 per cent) which yields the same level of employment in the importable sector. Column (9) shows that abolition of all taxes as well as quotas yields a smaller absolute value of the deficit than the quota ridden equilibrium of column (2).

How dependent are these results on the high degree of elasticity of export supply? Table 10.11 gives comparable computations when this is very low. In particular, the elasticity of output with respect to the variable factors in the exportable sector is now set at 0.1 instead of 0.8. The same tax variations are considered.

Once again, column (1) gives the non-distortionary benchmark, and column (2) the illiberal equilibrium. As can be clearly seen, the quantity

Table 10.11 Trade liberalization, illustration with exports highly inelastic[1]

	(1)	(2)	(3)	(4)	(5)	(6)	(7)	(8)
t_q	0	0.8	0	0	0	0	0	0
tt_m	0	0.3	0.3	1.34	1.34	0.36	0.43	0
t_m	0.2	0	0	0	0	0	0	0.0973
t_n	0.2	0	0	0	0	0	0	0.0973
t_x	0	0.2	0.2	0.2	0	0.2	0.2	0
tt_f	0.2	0.2	0.2	0.2	0.2	0.2	0.2	0.0973
Q_m	0.092	0.153	0.121	0.283	0.233	0.136	0.152	0.040
Q_n	1.282	1.313	1.300	1.146	1.198	1.285	1.269	1.371
Q_x	1.102	0.992	1.053	1.011	1.030	1.051	1.049	1.075
E_m	0.788	0.790	0.789	0.655	0.696	0.774	0.759	0.888
E_n	1.182	1.213	1.200	1.046	1.098	1.185	1.169	1.271
E_f	0.219	0.405	0.230	0.307	0.336	0.233	0.236	0.277
$E_m - Q_m$	0.696	0.637	0.668	0.371	0.463	0.638	0.607	0.847
L_m	0.044	0.083	0.062	0.183	0.142	0.072	0.083	0.015
L_n	0.718	0.737	0.732	0.630	0.663	0.723	0.713	0.767
L_x	0.088	0.031	0.056	0.037	0.045	0.055	0.054	0.068
K_m	0.029	0.056	0.041	0.118	0.093	0.048	0.055	0.011
K_n	0.308	0.321	0.312	0.262	0.280	0.306	0.300	0.349
K_x	0.022	0.008	0.014	0.009	0.011	0.014	0.013	0.018
K	0.359	0.385	0.367	0.389	0.384	0.367	0.368	0.378
g_{exp}	0.300	0.408	0.322	0.371	0.382	0.323	0.325	0.326
g_{wag}	0.150	0.313	0.181	0.258	0.275	0.183	0.186	0.193
d_{rev}	0.000	0.000	0.000	0.000	0.000	0.000	0.000	0.000
i_{rev}	0.438	0.470	0.457	0.761	0.688	0.487	0.518	0.270
Def	0.012	0.250	0.046	–0.132	–0.031	0.020	-0.006	0.250
gdp	2.626	4.195	2.761	3.687	4.028	2.790	2.832	3.040
u_c	2.188	2.363	2.219	1.980	2.098	2.191	2.162	2.431
w	1.000	2.086	1.207	1.723	1.831	1.220	1.242	1.288
P_n	1.000	2.079	1.216	1.706	1.817	1.231	1.253	1.263
Def(%)[2]	0.005	0.060	0.017	–0.036	–0.008	0.007	–0.002	0.082

Notes:
1 $G_m = G_n = G_f = 0.1$
2 As Table 10.10 above.

shifts are much more muted, with the fall in export volume being 10 per cent instead of 93 per cent. Despite this dramatically less responsive economy, the rest of the story is remarkably similar. In particular, abolition of the quota (column 3), dramatically improves the budget deficit (0.250 to 0.046). In this case, however, replacement with an equivalent tariff is still more beneficial, column (4) yielding a budget surplus of 0.132. The cost of this further budgetary gain is a dramatic worsening in resource allocation, with a very large further increase in the level of resources going to the importables sector, and a very sharp reduction in imports. Indeed, the tariff having an equivalent compressive effect on imports would only be a little over the existing 30 per cent rate at 36 per cent, while that sustaining an equivalent level of domestic output would be around 43 per cent (column 7). Finally, column (8) shows the reduced uniform sales tax rate (9.7 per cent) which would maintain the budget deficit at a level equivalent to that generated by the illiberal trade regime of column (2). In both cases, the abolition of quotas markedly improves the budget deficit. This is not, in the case of Table 10.11, because tariffs and quotas combined have reduced the level of imports below the revenue-maximizing level. It is caused partially by the gain on export duties, but very substantially to the fall in the public-sector wage bill associated with the large fall in P_n and w.

These calculations have two main implications. First, they show that the large potential fiscal gains from liberalization discussed in the previous section depend neither on very high tariff rates within the protected sector, nor on the presence of very elastic export supply. Second, they raise difficult questions concerning tariff equivalence. Replacing a composite of tariffs and quotas by a tariff regime which is equivalent in the sense of elevating domestic prices to the same extent $[(1 + tt_m)^2 = (1 + tt_m)(1 + tt_q)]$ is far more severe than the alternative definitions, which include: (i) maintenance of a similar degree of import compression; (ii) maintenance of the same level of domestic production of the importable; (iii) maintenance of the same level of employment in domestic production of the importable; and (iv) revenue neutrality. In particular, any attempt to preserve equivalence defined by price neutrality is likely to involve significant overshooting by the other criteria. This is likely to be inefficient and may even threaten the implementation of the reforms.

Conclusions

Developing country governments are often resistant to pressures from international agencies and others to liberalize their trade regimes. There are two distinct types of reason for this. First, the government may be associated with or dependent on elites who benefit directly from the rents associated with illiberal trade regimes. Reduction or removal of these rents poses a real problem in political economy. Second, even if the government is able and willing to confront these political difficulties, it may be concerned that liberalization will be problematic in more narrowly economic terms.

The particular problem on which this chapter focused is that liberalization may exacerbate the government's already difficult fiscal circumstances, and lead to larger deficits and accelerating inflation. One reason for the prevalence of this concern lies in the historical evolution of the trade regime itself. A quota-ridden equilibrium has often arisen, not so much from concerns to protect domestic industry as from some initial fiscal laxity spilling over into a balance-of-payments disequilibrium. Since the gradual imposition of tighter quotas was originally a response to a fiscal problem, it is natural to worry that quota relaxation will lead to the re-emergence of the deficit. However, it is clear from the earlier discussion in the chapter that quota relaxation may just as well ease the government's fiscal situation as worsen it. This conclusion can still hold even when the liberalization package includes tariff reductions as well as quota reductions, and when the government is a net purchaser of foreign exchange. In short, there is no presumption that liberalization requires fiscal tightening to be rendered compatible in the long run.

However, it also emerges from the simulations reported in earlier in the chapter that the dynamic path of adjustment may be more problematical. This has two aspects. First, there is likely to be a temporary deterioration in the budget deficit and hence in the foreign financing requirement or domestic inflation rate, even when the long-run consequences of the programme are sustainable. This may lead to severe political difficulties for a reforming government, and there may be a substantial role for an aid-assisted package. Second, in an uncertain world, these temporary phenomena may call into question the credibility of the entire programme. It may wrongly be assumed that the adverse transitional characteristics imply that the programme is not, in fact, compatible in the long run. Alternatively, it may be assumed – perhaps correctly – that they imply the government will be unable politically to sustain the programme, so that, even though feasible, it becomes incredible.

This leaves the government facing a real dilemma. It may be necessary to overshoot the long-run equilibrium, by tightening the fiscal system by more than is economically justified to ensure political implementation. This would involve an inefficient set of signals, and resource allocations, and may make the whole reform programme unacceptable. On the other hand, a feasible (and politically acceptable) programme may have transitional characteristics that soon undermine its credibility, or that of the government's continued resolution.

Appendix 1: structure of the model

The model distinguishes four goods: three produced, and three absorbed into the country:

(i) *Export good*, indexed by x. This is produced in the country, but not consumed or invested.
(ii) *Non-tradable good*, indexed by n. This is produced and absorbed into the country, with absorption limited to what is produced domestically.
(iii) *Competitive importable good*, indexed by m. This is produced and absorbed into both the country and the rest of the world. In principle, it could be exported or imported, but attention is restricted here to the case where the country is a net importer.
(iv) *Foreign good*, indexed by f. This cannot be produced domestically, and domestic absorption has to be sustained by imports.

World prices are given. There are no intermediate goods; production in each sector is a CES function of capital and labour and also depends on a fixed factor which is supposed to enter in a multiplicative (Cobb–Douglas) way (Equation 10.1). Labour is homogeneous and is assumed to move freely between sectors, but is limited in aggregate to the given domestic labour force. All markets are supposed to clear continuously, including the labour market (Equation 10.3). Capital is assumed to be supplied elastically (in the long run) at the given rate r^*. Firms are supposed to act as price takers, since their share of the fixed factor (which determines their efficient size) is sufficiently small (Equation 10.2). Consumption is determined by a utility function defined over the three consumption goods, here indexed by i, j and k (Equations 10.15 and 10.16).

The pair i, and j are modelled as having a direct relationship within the sub-utility function u_1, which then enters the utility function u_2, along with good k. The purpose of this construction is to retain the relative tractability of the CES function while allowing the substitutability between the goods to differ. Notice that the special relationship between i and j does not necessarily imply that they are closer substitutes for each other than for the third good, that is, that $\sigma > \epsilon$. The relationship could involve, instead, a high degree of complementarity between i and j, with the composite being more substitutable for k, that is, $\sigma > \epsilon$. Of course, if $\sigma = \epsilon$, it reduces to a standard CES function in the three goods.

In consequence, it is not appropriate to pre-assign any specific pair of goods to be nested within the subutility function u_1. For notational convenience, this structure will be denoted as $(i, j, ..., k)$. Thus $(m, n, ..., f)$ indicates that the importable and non-tradable goods are intimately related in consumption via σ, with the composite related to the foreign good via ϵ.

The government has two sorts of expenditure: on goods (G_m, G_n and G_f, respectively); and on wages. It is sure to employ some fraction L_g of the labour force, and to pay the going wage. It may employ a wide variety of tax instruments, all at constant rates. Direct taxes may be levied on wages, profits on capital, rents to the fixed factor, and rents arising from quotas, the rates being t_w, t_p, t_{pr} and t_r, respectively. Indirect taxes may take the form of sales taxes on importables (t_m, t_f) or non-tradables (t_n), tariffs on importables (tt_m and tt_f) and an export tax (t_x).

The remaining instrument of trade policy is a quantitative restriction on imports of the competitive importable, which is set at a level having a tariff equivalent value of t_q. (Thus the producer price of importables is $(1 + tt_m)(1 + t_q)$ times the world price, and the consumer price is $(1 + t_m)$ times the producer price.) The rents arising from these restrictions accrue to the private sector. It is assumed that there are no QRs on imports of the foreign good; in other words, the original motivation is protection of domestic producers.

Following liberalization, revenues and expenditure alter automatically following the changes in prices, incomes and expenditure. It is assumed for concreteness that the volume of the government's spending is invariant to these changes, so that no substitution takes place from categories that have become relatively more expensive to those that have become cheaper. This assumption puts the fiscal impact of liberalization in the least favourable light, since, in practice, at least limited substitution would be feasible.

The government is assumed to exempt its own purchases of the importable from the quantitative restriction; this applies only to imports for private purposes. (The importance of this point is simply that the government does not pay quota rentals to the private sector in respect of its own purchases.)

In stationary equilibrium, the private sector has net savings sufficient to just maintain capital labour ratios, given the growth of the labour force. Money is held only for transaction purposes, and velocity (*vel*) is constant so that money demand is proportional to the value of private expenditure. Domestic currency is the private sector's only financial asset. The domestically-financed component of the budget deficit is therefore financed by a combination of seignorage and the inflation tax. In the long run, private savings are elastic at some given rate of return (r^*), so that current private consumption will fall short of its steady-state level when rates of return to capital are high, and vice versa.

Production

$$Q_i = b_i\left[a_{ik}^{1/\theta} K_i^{1-1/\theta} + (1 - a_{ik})^{1/\theta}\, L_i^{1-1/\theta}\right]^{\frac{1-a_i}{1-1/\theta}}, \quad i = m, n, x \tag{10.1}$$

$$\frac{Q_i^{1-a_{ij}\theta}}{[L_i/(1 - a_{ik})]^{1-a_{if}}} = b_i^{1-\theta}\left[\frac{w}{p_i(1 - a_{if})}\right]^{\theta(1-a_y)}, i = m, n, x \tag{10.2}$$

$$\Sigma L_i + L_g = \overline{L} \tag{10.3}$$

Balance equations

$$Q_m = E_m + G_m - M_m \tag{10.4}$$

$$Q_m = E_n + g_n \tag{10.5}$$

$$Q_x = X \tag{10.6}$$

$$M_f = E_f + G_f \tag{10.7}$$

$$E_i = C_i + I_{gi}, \quad i = m, n, f \tag{10.8}$$

Prices
(a) Producer prices

$$P_x = (1 - t_x)P_{xw}/e \tag{10.9}$$

$$P_m = (1 + tt_m)(1 + t_q)P_{mw}/e \tag{10.10}$$

(e, P_n, w are endogenous)

(b) Consumer prices

$$P_{mc} = (1 + t_m)P_m \tag{10.11}$$

$$P_{tc} = (1 + t_f)(1 + tt_f)P_{fw}/e \tag{10.12}$$

$$P_{nc} = (1 + t_n)P_n \tag{10.13}$$

(c) Average prices for private expenditure

$$P_{ia} = (1 + (1 - s)t_i)P_i, \; i = m, n, f \tag{10.14}$$

Private sector

$$u_1 = \left[d_i^{1/E}E_i^{1-1/\sigma} + (1 - d_i)^{1/E}E_j^{1-1/E}\right]^{\frac{1}{1-11_E}}, \quad E \neq 1, D_I \leq 1 \tag{10.15}$$

$$u_2 = \left[d_k^{\frac{1}{\sigma}}E_k^{1-\frac{1}{\sigma}} + (1 - d_k)^{\frac{1}{\alpha}}U_1^{1-\frac{1}{\sigma}}\right]^{\frac{1}{1-\frac{1}{\alpha}}}, \quad \sigma \neq 1, d_k \leq 1 \tag{10.16}$$

$$E_i/E_j = \frac{d_i}{1 - d_i}(P_{jc}/P_{ic})^{\epsilon} \tag{10.17}$$

$$E_k/E_j = \frac{d_k(P_{jc}/P_{kc})^{\sigma}\left[(1 - d_i) + d_i(P_{jc}/P_{ic})^{\epsilon-1}\right]^{\frac{\epsilon-\sigma}{\epsilon-1}}}{(1 - d_k)(1 - d_i)} \tag{10.18}$$

i, j, k equal *m, n, f* in some order.

$$\begin{aligned} Y = {} & (1 - t_w)W\overline{L} + [(1 - t_p)r_{av} + \delta]P_kK + (1 - t_{pr})\Sigma a_{if}P_iQ_i \\ & + (1 - t_r)\frac{P_mt_q}{1 + t_q}[E_m - Q_m] + TRANF/e \end{aligned} \tag{10.19}$$

$$Y = P_{ma}E_m + P_{na}E_n + P_{fa}E_f + (MS_{t+1} - MS_t) \tag{10.20}$$

$$MS = E_{xt}/Vel \tag{10.21}$$

Government

$$G_i = G_{if} + g_{iv}E_i \quad i = m, n, f \tag{10.22}$$

$$GEX = P_nG_n + P_{fw}G_f/e + P_mG_m \tag{10.23}$$

$$GWAG = WL_g \tag{10.24}$$

$$DREV = t_wW\overline{L} + t_pr_{av}P_kK + t_rt_q(1 + tt_m)P_{mw}(E_m - Q_m)/e + t_{pr}\Sigma a_{if}P_iQ_i \tag{10.25}$$

$$\begin{aligned} IREV = {} & t_{na}P_nE_n + (t_{fa} + tt_f(1 + t_{fa}))P_{fw}E_f/e + t_xP_{xw}Q_x/e \\ & + [tt_m(E_m = Q_m) + t_{ma}(1 + tt_m)(1 + t_q)E_m]P_{mw}/e \end{aligned} \tag{10.26}$$

$$DEF = GEX + GWAG - DREV - IREV - AID/e \tag{10.27}$$

$$MS_{t+i} = MS_t + DEF \tag{10.28}$$

Investment

$$r_i = \frac{P_i q_i(1 - a_{if}) - wL_i}{K_i p_K} - \delta \qquad (10.29)$$

$$K_{i,t+1} = K_{i,t}[(1 - \delta) + MAX\{0, (gro + \delta + \tau(r_i/r^* - 1))\}] \qquad (10.30)$$

$$I_{gi,t} = K_{i,t+1} - K_{i,t} + (1 - \delta) \qquad (10.31)$$

$$r_{av} = \sum \frac{[P_i Q_i(1 - a_{if}) - wL_i]}{P_k \sum k_i} - \delta \qquad (10.32)$$

$$S = \Sigma P_k I_{gi}/E_{xk} \qquad (10.33)$$

Exogenous variables

a_{ik}, a_{if}	Technical coefficients determining sectoral capital intensity, and the sectoral joint returns to capital and labour, $i = m, n, x$.
b_i	Productivity parameter, $i = m, n, x$.
θ	Elasticity of substitution between capital and labour, all sectors.
$\overline{L}$, L_g	Total labour force, government employment.
d_i, d_k	Distribution parameters in utility function, $i = m, n$, or f; $k = m, n$, or f, $k \neq i$.
ϵ, σ	Elasticities of substitution between i and j and between composite i/j and k, respectively.
t_a	Implicit tariff equivalent value of initial quota.
tt_m, tt_f	Tariff rates on competing and non-competing imports.
t_m, t_n, t_x, t_f	*Ad valorem* tax rates on competing importables, non-tradables, exports and non-competing imports, respectively.
t_w, t_p, t_r, t_{pr}	Direct tax rates on income from wages, profits, fixed factor rentals, and rents arising from trade restrictions, respectively.
G_{if}	Fixed volume component of government spending on good i, $i = m, n, f$.
g_{iv}	Ratio of variable component of government spending on good i to private spending on i, $i = m, n, f$.
AID	Net capital inflow to government.
TRANF	Net capital inflow to private sector.
r^*	Required real rate of return.
δ	Annual depreciation rate
gro	Annual growth of labour force.
vel	Velocity of circulation.
τ	Speed of adjustment of capital stock to discrepancy in required and historic rates of return.
p_{iw}	World prices, $i = m, x, f$.

Endogenous variables

Q_i	Output in sector, i, $i = m, n, x$.
E_i	Real private expenditure, $i = m, n, f$.
G_i	Real government expenditure, $i = m, n, f$.
L_i	Employment, $i = m, n, x$.
K_i	Capital stock, $i = m, n, x$.

I_{gi}, I_{ni}	Gross and net investment, $i = m, n, x$.
r_i, r_{av}	Realized rate of return, $i = m, n, x$, and for economy as a whole.
e	Exchange rate (foreign currency purchased per unit of domestic currency).
w	Wage rate.
P_n	Producer price of non-tradables.
GEX	Government spending on goods and services.
GWAG	Government wage bill.
DREV	Revenue from direct taxes.
IREV	Revenue from indirect taxes.
DEF	Domestically-financed component of the budget deficit.
X	Volume of exports.
M_m, M_f	Real imports of competing and non-competing goods.
MS	Money supply.
Y	Private income.
GDP	Gross domestic product at factor cost.
GDPW	Gross domestic product at world prices.
E_{xk}	Total private expenditure at producer prices ($\Sigma E_i P_i$).
E_{xc}	Total private expenditure at consumer prices (ΣE_iP((ic}).
E_{xt}	Total private expenditure at market prices ($\Sigma E_i P_{ia}$).
I_{nf}	Rate of inflation (rate of change of P_c).
u_2	Level of instantaneous utility if all expenditure consumed.
u_c	Level of utility generated by current consumption.
P_k	Price of capital goods (E_{xk}/u_2)
P_c	Price of consumption, cost of living (E_{xc}/u_2)
S	Share of gross private investment in total private spending at producer prices.

Appendix 2: calibration of the Kenya model

The model was calibrated on national accounts data for 1989, and the fiscal data for that year obtained by averaging, as described in the text. Where there was a discrepancy between these two sources of data, the national accounts figures were adjusted for consistency, as noted below. The tradable sector is taken to comprise monetary agriculture, forestry and fishing; mining and quarrying; and manufacturing. After deducting government services, the residual (including non-monetary agriculture) is taken to comprise the non tradable sector.

In any exercise of this kind, a number of heroic assumptions must be made in the light of data inadequacy, data inconsistency, the discrepancy between the conceptual basis underlying the data and that underlying the model, and the imperfect observability of various model parameters. This appendix describes the particular set of assumptions used in the base model discussed in the text, but some variations are noted. The most important general limitation of the model which should be stressed is that it is a value-added model, and makes no use of input – output data. While this inevitably imposes some deformation on the data, this class of models is of considerable interest, since they can quickly be constructed even for countries with relatively poor databases, can handle quite complicated specifications of the policy structure, and can trace a range of relative price and quantity responses in a consistent way.

The model is normalized so that in the base case the exchange rate, wage rate, producer price of non-tradables and world prices of tradables are all equal to one, and the total labour force is also set equal to one. Units of capital are chosen relative to units of output so that the unit capital rental also equals one. Then Table 10.A2 derives the production parameters of the three sectors with each being assumed to take the Cobb – Douglas form in capital, labour and a fixed factor, with output elasticities a_{ik} $(1 - a_{if})$, $(1 - a_{ik})(1 - a_{if})$ and a_{if} respectively in sector i.

Production

Gross private capital formation in 1989 (Government of Kenya (1991) *Economic Survey 1991*, table 2.10) was K£372.21 million in tradables, as defined above, and K£765.22 million in non-tradables, excluding dwellings. Hence, normalized as in Table 10.A2, gross investment in tradables was $372.21 \times 1.747421/7426.19 = 0.087583$, and that in non-tradables was $765.22 \times 1.747421/7426.19 = 0.180060$.

The economy is assumed to be in balanced growth at the time of calibration at the rate *GRO*, and depreciation is uniform across sectors at the rate *DELTA*. Hence the ratio of gross investment to capital stock in each sector is (*GRO* + *DELTA*). Meanwhile, the gross rate of return to capital in equilibrium (*R1* + *DELTA*) is common between sectors and given for sector i by $a_{ik}(1 - a_{if})Vi/P_kK_i$ where V_i is

Table 10.A1 GDP at factor costs, 1989 (K£ millions)

	Value-added	*Labour costs*	*Adjusted value[1] added*	*Adjusted labour[2] costs*
Tradables	3083.17	627.34	3083.17	1483.58
(of which)				
Exportables[3]	1997.68		1997.68	1015.73
Importables	1085.49		1085.49	467.85
Government services	1166.55	1157.35	896.00	896.00
Non-tradables	3176.47	1415.09	3447.02	1870.22
Total	**7426.19**	**3199.78**	**7426.19**	**4249.80**

Notes:

1 Government services in production accounts comprise almost entirely labour costs, but these are larger than those given in Table 10.1 of this text (which refer to central government only); in the adjusted value-added figures, government services are set equal to central government labour costs, an dthe excess is allocated to non-tradables.

2 The share of labour costs in agricultural value added is unreasonably low (9.0% in the monetary sector, 1.1% in the non-monetary sector). This is replaced arbitrarily by 50%, increasing the labour cost in tradables from K£627.34 million to K£1483.58 million. Importables are assumed to have the same share of labour costs as manufacturing (43.1%), which is then substracted to leave K£1015.73 million, or 50.8% as the share of labour costs in exportable valued-added. The share of labour costs in Government Services is set by assumption at 100%, leaving that in non-tradables as K£1870.22 million or 54.3%.

3 It is assumed that all exportable production is actually exported. Hence the value of exports is set equal to exportables' value-added, and the residual of tradables is allocated to importables.

Source: Government of Kenya (1991) *Economic Survey 1991*, tables 2.3 and 2.6; and Table 10.1 of this volume.

Table 10.A2 Derivation of production parameters

	Normalized value-added[1]	*Share of*[2] *Labour Force*	$(1–a_{ik})$ $(1–a_{if})^3$	a_{if}[4]	a_{ik}
Exportables	0.470063	0.239007	0.508457	0.446383	0.081573
Importables	0.255422	0.110088	0.431004	0.1	0.521107
Government	0.210833	0.210833	—	—	—
Non-tradables	0.811102	0.440072	0.542561	0.1	0.397154
Total	**1.747421**	**1.000000**			

Notes:

1 From the third column of Table 10.A1 normalized so that total labour cost equals 1.

2 From the fourth column of Table 10.A1, giving the share in efficiency units, so that an individual earning twice the average wage is treated as two units of average labour.

3 Column (2) divided by Column (1).

4 For importables and non-tradables, the elasticity of output with respect to the variable factors is arbitrarily set equal to 0.9. This is intended to pick up some effects associated with quality and/or differential labour, and not be relevant to secular growth. The derivation of the coefficients a_{ak}, a_{xf} is described in the text.

value added in sector *i*, K_i is the capital stock in sector *i*, and P_k is the price of a unit of capital.

Hence $$\frac{GRO + DELTA}{RI + DELTA} = \frac{P_k I_i}{a_{ik}(1 - a_{if})V_i} \qquad (10.A1)$$

where $P_k I_i$ is the value of gross investment in sector *i*. We have that $P_k I_n = 0.180060$, and from Table 10.A2, $V_n = 0.811102$, $a_{nk} = 0.397154$, $a_{nf} = 0.1$.

Hence $$\frac{GRO + DELTA}{RI + DELTA} = 0.621070$$

Setting *DELTA* as 0.05 and *GRO* at 0.0365 (which equals the population growth rate: that is, this assumes no secular real income growth at the time of calibration) yields an equilibrium value of the net rate of return RI = 0.089276. Substitution into Equation (10.A1) for the importable sector yields $P_k I_m = 0.074399$. Substitution of this from the total gross investment in tradables of 0.087583 yields investment in exportables of 0.013184. Application of Equation (10.A.1) once again yields a_{xk} $(1 - a_{xf}) = 0.013184/(0.470063 \times 0.621070) = 0.045160$.

Since we have $(1 - a_{xk})(1 - a_{xf}) = 0.508457$ from the adjusted labour share in value-added, this yields the values $a_{xf} = 0.446383$ and $a_{xk} = 0.081573$ given in Table 10.A2.

Expenditure and taxation

It is assumed that government imports are free of quotas and tariffs, and that government expenditure generally is free of indirect taxation. For the computations carried out in the text, it is also assumed that the volume of government spending on each category of goods is invariant, as is the share of the labour force employed by the government.

From Tables 10.1 and 10.A1, private spending on non-tradables at producer prices is 3447 – 490 = 2957. Public spending on domestically-produced importables (Table 10.1) is 476 – 142 = 334. Hence private spending on these goods is 1085 – 334 = 751. From Government of Kenya (1991) *Economic Survey 1991*, table 7.1, the resource balance was 495. Hence imports were 1998 + 495 = 2492. Subtracting 142 for direct government imports, private imports were 2351.

In 1989, the Kenyan trade regime consisted of five schedules. Two of these, Schedules IIIB and IIIC, covered imports that competed with domestic production. The first, restricted only by tariffs, accounted for 11 per cent of all import items and 5 per cent of the value of imports in 1986/7; the second, where restrictions included quotas, accounted for 29 per cent of items, and 7 per cent of the value of imports. A series of surveys, carried out at the time[10], found that the average nominal rate of protection over a fairly wide range of Kenyan manufacturing industry was 119.9 per cent, 53.9 per cent accounted for by tariffs, the residue attributable to quantitative restrictions. (For comparison, the World Bank[11] computed a production-weighted tariff for 1989/90 of 61.8 per cent, compared to an import weighted tariff of 24.5 per cent.)

On this basis, total private imports of 2351 are partitioned into the 12 per cent (282) which are competitive with domestic production – that is, are in the importable category indexed in the model by m – and the 88 per cent (2069) that are non-competitive – that is, are in the pure import category, indexed by f. With a tariff rate of (tt_m) 53.9 per cent on category m, duty of 152 is realized. This leaves 285 – 152 = 133 to be levied on category f, implying a tariff rate (tt_f) of 6.4 per cent. In addition, the quota restrictions yield rents of 186 (t_q = 42.9 per cent) which accrue to the private sector.

Hence, total private expenditure at producer prices is 2069 + 133 = 2202 on pure imports; 282 + 152 + 186 = 620 on competing imports; 751 on domestically-produced importables; and 2957 on non-tradables. Total private expenditure at producer prices is therefore 6530. The share of gross private productive investment expenditure in this is 1137/6530 = 0.174184. It is assumed that the sectoral composition of investment expenditure is common between investing sectors and the same as the sectoral composition of consumption expenditure. In other words, the sectoral composition of expenditure is sensitive to relative prices, but not to intertemporal choices. Indirect taxes have been in transition to a value-added form; gross investment expenditures are assumed to be exempt.

Private consumption expenditure on non-tradables and domestically-produced importables is (1 – 0.174184)(2957 + 751) = 3062. On this base, the excise and domestic sales tax raise 143 + 338 = 481, yielding a domestic tax rate of 0.157072. We assume that the same rate is applied to competing imports, yielding a revenue of 80, and leaving the residue of the sales tax on imports (277 – 80 = 197) to be levied on pure imports at the average rate 0.108105. This procedure therefore sets $t_m = t_n = 0.157072$, $t_f = 0.108105$. The total value of private expenditure at market prices is then 7288, with the share of non-tradables being 0.458364, that of pure imports being 0.329051 and that of other importables being 0.212585.

Given the assumed invariance of government expenditure in volume terms, it is a matter of indifference how government imports are allocated between the two categories. For simplicity, it is assumed that they are entirely of the non-competing variety, so that government purchases of other importables come entirely from domestic sources.

The remaining budgetary items in Table 10.1 consist of direct taxes, other revenues, transfers and financing. Taking the domestic component first, these are aggregated into an equivalent uniform direct tax on all income (which is neutral in the model). The government has outgoings of 515 (domestic interest 323, transfers 192) and incomings of 366 (other revenues, including the very small export tax revenue for completeness). This net domestic transfer to the private sector of 149 is deducted from income tax revenue of 556 to yield a composite direct tax of 407. The tax base for this is factor income net of depreciation plus rents, or 7426 – 657 + 186 = 6955. Hence the composite direct tax ($t_w = t_p = t_r = t_{pr} = t_y$) is at 0.058520. The depreciation figure of 657 is derived as the proportion *DELTA*/(*GRO* + *DELTA*) or 0.578035 of gross investment, 1137.

As regards the financing and foreign exchange flows, the overall resource balance, as noted before, was 495. The government accounts in Table 10.1 shows a net capital inflow to government of 294 (external grants 202 + net borrowing 251 – foreign interest payments 159). This would imply direct flows to the private sector of 201 or, more probably, amounts borrowed under the aegis of government and lent on (for example, to parastatals). However, the partitioning of government financing between net foreign and net domestic financing is usually fragile in Kenya (it is often subject to spectacularly large revisions). Hence the procedure here is to split the total capital inflow of 495 between central government (*AID*) and the rest of the economy (*TRANF*) in such a way as to leave the domestically-financed component of the budget deficit (assumed all monetized) at a level consistent with steady inflation (*INF*) at 9 per cent p.a., the Kenyan average throughout the 1980s.

To implement this, it was necessary to compute an appropriate measure of the velocity of circulation. The procedure here was to derive a proxy for high powered money at year end by subtracting private sector loans from the sum of money and quasi-money (Government of Kenya (1991) *Economic Survey 1991*, table 5.3). Private transactions for the following year were proxied by taking total resources for domestic investment and consumption (from Government of Kenya (1991), *Economic Survey 1991*, table 2.6) and adjusting these to private expenditures only (using the 1989 share of government spending on goods and services derived from Table 10.1). The average value of the velocity of circulation between these two concepts during the 1980s was 10.8. Hence domestic financing of the budget deficit at a rate equal to a fraction (1 + *INE*)(1 + *GRO*) – 1/10.8 of private expenditure is consistent with inflation at the rate of *INF*. With *GRO* = 0.0365, *INF* = 0.09, domestic financing would have to equal around 1.2 per cent of private spending and about the same percentage of GDP at factor cost (K£7426 million in 1989, compared to private spending at market prices of K£7288 million).

As is apparent from the text, the fiscal/economic structure described so far in this appendix ensures that the budget is very favourably affected by trade liberalization. This is very substantially a consequence of the trade policy regime, where the highest tariffs are levied on a group of imports that are powerfully compressed by quantative restrictions. When the QRs are relaxed, the expansion of imports in this competing category generates substantial additional tariff revenues. These are sufficient to ensure favourable budgetary outcomes, even if other components of the system are altered radically (for example, assigning all the net foreign exchange flows to the private sector, adopting very different speeds of adjustment of the

Table 10.A3 Parameter values at calibration

	Base case	*Alternative case*
a_{mk}	0.521107	As base
a_{nk}	0.397154	" "
a_{xk}	0.081573	" "
a_{mf}	0.1	" "
a_{nf}	0.1	" "
a_{xf}	0.446383	" "
s_n	0.458364	0.448998
s_f	0.329051	0.342755
s_i	0.174184	0.170221
t_q	0.429	1.199
tt_m	0.538854	0.0
tt_f	0.064295	0.137775
t_m	0.157072	0.156322
t_n	0.157072	0.156322
t_f	0.108105	0.100637
t_y	0.058520	0.057268
g_{mf}	0.035768	As base
g_{nf}	0.115300	" "
g_{ff}	0.033343	" "
l_g	0.210833	" "
l_m	0.110088	" "
l_n	0.440072	" "
l_x	0.239007	" "
AID	0.054100	0.035466
TRANF	0.062303	0.080937
RI	0.89276	As base
DELTA	0.05	" "
VEL	10.8	" "
GRO	0.0365	" "

Notes:

1 Numbers derived from computations described in text.

2 Tax rates expressed relative to appropriate tax base (t_x and tt_i).

3 Labour shares as fractions of unity (l_k).

4 Government expenditure, AID and TRANF relative to numeraire that total wage bill equals 1 (g_f).

5 s_n, s_f share of private spending on non-tradables and non-competing imports in total private spending at market prices.

6 s_i share of gross private investment in total private spending at producer prices.

capital stock, and/or depreciation rates, or varying the assumed labour content of agricultural value-added).

One variant utilized in the text is the high depreciation case, where *DELTA* is set at 0.20 instead of 0.05. Other parameters remain as in the base case, with these exceptions: the net rate of return *RI*, using Equation (10.A1) is now raised from 0.089276 to 0.180794; and the partitioning of net capital inflow between *AID* and *TRANF* to maintain *INF* at 9 per cent is slightly altered, from 0.054100/0.062303 to 0.058290/0.058113.

To examine a rather different set of circumstances, an alternative trade policy regime is now outlined, which generates a similar expenditure and fiscal pattern prior to liberalization, but a very different path following it. It should be stressed that this structure is not consistent with the evidence for Kenya, but is designed as a counterfactual case. It is now assumed that all tariff revenue is raised on imports that are non-competing, and not constrained by QRs. The 12 per cent of imports that are quantity constrained now have all their nominal protection from this source: that is, $t_q = 1.199$, $tt_m = 0$. The duty of 285 is levied entirely on the non-competing category so that $tt_f = 285/2069 = 0.137775$. Rents on competing imports are now 338; in consequence, the base for income tax is slightly altered, as is total private expenditure. The following table gives the parameter values derived for the base case discussed earlier, and for the alternative case, following the same procedures, given these alternative assumptions.

As noted in the text, the Kenya model adopts a Cobb–Douglas specification for all production activities ($\theta = 1$) and a constant elasticity specification of the utility function symmetric over the three arguments ($\sigma = \epsilon = 0.7$).

Notes

1. See, for example, the massive study co-ordinated by Papageorgiou *et al.* (1991).
2. See, for example, Newbery and Stern (1987), or Gillis (1990).
3. Exceptions include Pinto (1989); Greenaway and Milner (1990); Mitra (1990); Seade (1990); Bleijer and Cheasty (1990); Bevan *et al.* (1990) and Thomas *et al.* (1991).
4. We assume that transfer payments will increase in line with the wage rate, and that excise taxes are adjusted where necessary to maintain their *ad valorem* rates.
5. Income tax is the sum of personal income tax (mainly PAYE) which would be expected to rise roughly in line with wages, and taxes on companies. To the extent that trade liberalization would reduce corporate rents, revenues from companies would be affected adversely. Recent breakdowns of income tax are not published, so no estimate of this effect is made.
6. This is the estimated share of non-tradables in aggregate spending on non-tradables and domestically-produced importables. See Appendix 2.
7. See, for example, Mosley *et al.* 1991.
8. See, for example, Collier and Gunning (1992).
9. This case is analyzed in Bevan *et al.* (1990).
10. Maxwell Stamp Associates (1989).
11. World Bank (1992).

References

Bevan D. L., P. Collier and J. W. Gunning (1990) *Controlled Open Economies* (Oxford University Press).

Bleijer, M. and A. Cheasty (1990) 'Fiscal Implications of Trade Liberalization', in V. Tanzi (ed.), *Fiscal Policy in Open Developing Economies* (Washington, DC: IMF).

Collier, P. and J. W. Gunning (1990) 'Aid and Exchange Rate Adjustment in African Trade Liberalizations' *Economic Journal*, vol. 102.

Gillis, M. (ed.) (1989) *Tax Reform in Developing Countries* (Durham, North Carolina and London: Duke University Press).

Government of Kenya (1990) *Statistical Abstract 1990.*

Government of Kenya (1991) *Economic Survey 1991.*

Greenaway, D. and C. Milner (1990) *The Fiscal Implications of Trade Policy Reform: Theory and Evidence*, mimeo, (CREDIT, University of Nottingham).

Maxwell Stamp Associates (1989) *Study in Support of ISAC Trade liberalization Programme*, mimeo.

Mitra, P. (1990) 'The Co-ordinated Reform of Tariffs and Domestic Indirect Tax Rates', *World Bank Country Economies Department Working Paper*, WPS 490.

Mosley, P., J. Harrigan and J. Toye (1991) *Aid and Power: The World Bank and Policy-Based Lending* (London: Routledge).

Newbery, D. and N. Stern (eds) (1981) *The Theory of Taxation for Developing Countries* (New York: Oxford University Press for the World Bank).

Papageorgiou, D., M. Michaely and A. M. Choksi (eds) (1991) *Liberalizing Foreign Trade* (Oxford: Basil Blackwell).

Pinto, B. (1989) 'Black Market Premia, Exchange Rate Unification and Inflation in Sub-Saharan Africa', *World Bank Economic Review*, vol. 3, no. 3.

Seade, J. (1990) 'Tax Revenue Implications of Exchange Rate Adjustment', in V. Tanzi (ed.), *Fiscal Policy in Open Developing Economies* (Washington DC: IMF).

Thomas, V., J. Nash and Associates (1991) *Best Practices in Trade Policy Reform* (Oxford University Press for the World Bank).

World Bank (1989) *Kenya: Public Expenditure Issues* (Washington DC: World Bank).

11
The Fiscal Impact of Trade Reforms in Tanzania in the 1980s

William Lyakurwa

Introduction

While many developing countries implemented structural adjustment programmes throughout the 1980s, and these often included trade reform measures, the need for trade policy reform continues and is likely to intensify during the 1990s. There is now a greater appreciation by developing countries that trade reform means more than simply export promotion and increased foreign-exchange earnings. The opening up of an economy provides an array of benefits and economic stimuli in both the short and long term. Greater access to imports enables exporters to become more competitive in world markets and can also motivate local producers, resulting in greater efficiency of production. Openness also implies a more favourable environment for the transfer of both technology and human resources, and greater opportunities for trade in services, goods, and foreign direct investment flows.

Recent events have given a new impetus to trade liberalization, and a broad consensus has emerged on the importance of a greater market opening. Eastern European countries have rejected the closed command economy and are moving, albeit gradually, towards more open, competitive markets. Among the developing countries, Peru, Tanzania, and Uganda – to cite just a few examples – are closely following on the heels of earlier trade reformers such as Chile, Ghana, Indonesia, Mexico and Turkey. However, even where there may be a convergence of views on the desirable direction of reform, differences abound concerning the trade-offs between various policy options and the specific sequencing of reform measures as a country moves from a relatively closed to a relatively open economy.

Many developing countries rely heavily on trade taxes as a principal source of government revenue. The fiscal impact of trade policy measures is thus an important consideration for the reform process. The revenue and expenditure aspects of protection can often be an important consideration for governments in deciding whether or not to change their trade policies. In similar manner, the consequences of a liberalization for the budget balance, if they have not been anticipated and accompanied by complementary macro policies, may greatly complicate the process of implementation of trade reforms.

During the 1970s the Tanzanian economy was beset with a number of problems: the first oil shock of 1973/4, the war with Uganda in 1978, the second oil shock of 1979, drought in 1979/80, stagnating and declining export production, and severe decline in the terms of trade beginning in 1978. All these problems put tremendous pressure on the government budget which, together with foreign exchange constraints, resulted in high rates of inflation and declines in output in almost all sectors of the economy (Lyakurwa, 1988). Since the early 1980s the government has initiated a series of efforts to restore the economy and break the vicious circle of economic deterioration. The most recent was the Economic and Social Action Programme, (ESAP) in 1989, but the most far reaching of these programmes was the Economic Recovery Programme (ERP) during 1986–9. With steps being taken under the ERP to adjust the exchange rate, give greater emphasis to agricultural development, initiate schemes that allow exporters to retain part of their foreign exchange earnings and liberalize imports, there has been a gradual change in the economy. The trade policy changes have had implications on the fiscal stance. The principal aim of this chapter is to evaluate the fiscal impact of these trade policy reforms in Tanzania in the 1980s with some emphasis on government revenue.

The next section reviews the trends in the Tanzanian budget and describes how it differs from its neighbours. The following section presents the details of the predicted fiscal effects of specific trade policy reforms, while the fourth section presents the actual trade policy reforms implemented in Tanzania and the subsequent budgetary effects. The paper ends with some concluding remarks drawing on the lessons learned and implications for future policy.

A fiscal profile of Tanzania

During the early 1970s Tanzania's fiscal stance was fairly conservative with total revenue about equal to total expenditure at about 20 per cent of GDP. In 1978, the overall deficit jumped to about 10 per cent of GDP, largely because of expenditure on the Uganda War, which represented an increase of about 40 per cent over 1975/6 levels. Continuous efforts have been made to contain the size of the deficit through improved tax collection procedures, raising taxes and holding down expenditure, which was contained at an average of about 22 per cent of GDP for the entire period of the 1980s.

Development expenditure was maintained at between 10 and 14 per cent of GDP between 1970 and 1977, and after 1980 expenditure declined to an average of 6.6 per cent of GDP (1980–1988/9). The overall deficit of 7.4 per cent during the economic crisis in 1984 rose to 12.3 per cent in 1988/9. However, bank borrowing as a percentage of the deficit declined sharply during the ERP period and was in fact positive in 1988/9, indicating the government's commitment to the fulfilment of the conditionality implicit in the ERP. The budget deficit was financed by foreign inflows. The primary reason for the high deficits in the last year of the ERP was the growth in expenditure in the form of transfers to cover the operating losses of the then Crop Parastatals (now Marketing Boards) and the National Milling Corporation, which bears the cost of a subsidy to producers of food grains and to urban consumers. Trends in the fiscal account indicate that the Government used the budget as a major instrument of adjustment policy. Thus the budget has borne the brunt of trying to raise producer prices and cushion the decline in urban consumption levels. This was done to mitigate the income distribution effects of adjustment.

Tanzania's tax system, like that of most of its East African neighbours, employs a combination of taxes, including individual income taxes, company taxes, sales taxes, excise taxes, property taxes, and duties on international trade. As Table 11.1 illustrates, central government tax revenues as a share of gross national product (GNP) appear to be roughly in line with those of its neighbours, at 15.2 per cent. This is somewhat higher than the tax share of other countries at similar stages of economic development, which average 11.7 per cent. Relative to other countries, the composition of revenues in Tanzania, however, is very distinctive. The share of domestic indirect taxes exceeds that of all of its neighbours and amounts to twice the figure for the average of all low income countries.

This point is reinforced by the figures presented in Table 11.2, which show the changing composition of revenues in Tanzania over the 1980s. Total indirect taxes accounted for about 75 per cent of total tax revenues and increased in relative importance. Income taxes, in contrast, fell as a share of total revenue, from more than 35 per cent at the beginning of the 1980s, to around 25 per cent in the fiscal year 1990. Furthermore, the dominant share of revenues, which accounted for over 40 per cent of all

Table 11.1 Composition of central government revenue in Tanzania and selected countries, fiscal years 1980–9 and total revenues as percentage of GNP, 1988

	Domestic indirect taxes	*International indirect taxes*	*Income taxes*	*Other revenue*	*Total*	*Total revenue as % GNP (1988)*
Tanzania	55.6	15.2	24.5	4.7	100.0	15.2
Kenya	41.2	18.9	28.5	11.4	100.0	21.5
Uganda	24.4	69.6	6.0	0.0	100.0	8.2
Malawi	33.0	16.0	33.7	17.3	100.0	20.6
Zaire	14.6	42.5	26.8	16.1	100.0	15.3
Other low income countries (excluding India and China)	28.0	19.3	27.4	21.3	—	11.7

Source: Policy Economics Group (1991), 'Indirect Taxation Reform Study for Tanzania' (February).

revenues and 75 per cent of sales tax revenues is collected from sales tax on domestic production (Policy Economics Group, 1991).

The reasons for the relatively high concentration of the sales tax system on domestic production are threefold. First, foreign-exchange shortages during the mid-1980s limited Tanzania's ability to import goods, thereby limiting the amount of duties and sales taxes collected on imports. Second, the specific structure of the sales tax as a suspension system allows many goods used as inputs to be imported free of tax, with the producers paying tax only on their final production. Third, the majority of the tax is collected from very few industries, which engage primarily in production for the domestic market. Beer, soft drinks, tobacco, textiles and petroleum products account for over two-thirds of the tax.

In recent years, however, the share of revenues from import duties more than doubled, reaching 15 per cent of total revenue in fiscal year 1989, while the sales tax collected on imports increased fourfold, to 13 per cent of revenue, in fiscal year 1989. With the increased availability of foreign exchange, imports expanded and so have the revenues from taxes and customs duties on imported goods. The increase in customs duties can be attributed to the increase in the value of imports, particularly after 1986, when the value of imports, increased from US$1047.5 in 1986 to US$1363.5 in 1990; a change in the nominal exchange rate which depreciated from an average of TShs 38.15 to the dollar in 1986 to TShs 195.33 to the dollar in 1990; and to the change in the average collection

Table 11.2 Composition of recurrent government revenue, fiscal years 1980–90 (%)

	1979/80	*1980/1*	*1981/2*	*1982/3*	*1983/4*	*1984/5*	*1985/6*	*1986/7*	*1987/8*	*1988/9*	*1989/90*
Tax revenue	100.0	100.0	100.0	100.0	100.0	100.0	100.0	100.0	100.0	100.0	100.0
Income taxes	35.3	33.5	35.0	33.8	29.8	27.8	32.9	24.9	22.7	23.9	23.9
Total indirect taxes	64.7	66.5	65.0	66.2	70.2	72.2	67.1	75.1	77.3	76.1	76.1
Domestic Taxes on goods and services	44.8	54.6	56.5	56.8	61.9	60.8	57.8	59.3	63.4	56.5	59.6
Sales tax – local	40.2	48.3	47.5	46.5	46.8	51.2	45.2	42.0	42.7	38.8	24.9
Sales tax – imports	3.0	5.0	7.8	7.7	10.9	7.4	3.8	12.4	13.1	12.0	10.5
Excise taxes	0.0	0.0	0.0	0.0	0.0	0.0	0.0	0.0	0.0	0.0	0.0
Hotel levy	0.0	0.0	0.0	0.0	0.0	0.0	0.6	0.5	0.8	0.8	1.0
Stamp duty	0.8	0.3	0.2	1.2	2.3	0.9	2.7	3.2	3.8	3.4	3.8
Other	0.8	1.0	1.1	1.4	1.8	1.4	5.5	1.2	3.0	1.6	2.0
Taxes on international trade	18.7	10.7	7.5	6.6	7.1	8.9	7.7	13.8	13.7	13.0	14.8
Import duties	11.9	8.1	7.3	6.5	7.0	8.8	7.7	13.8	13.7	13.0	14.8
Export duties	6.8	2.6	0.2	0.1	0.1	0.1	0.0	0.0	0.0	0.0	0.0
Other taxes	1.2	1.1	1.0	2.8	1.2	2.5	1.6	2.1	0.2	6.6	1.7

Note: Income tax revenues have been assumed to maintain same relationship to total revenues in 1989/90 and 1988/9 because of lack of data.
Source: United Republic of Tanzania, Economic Surveys and Annual Plans – Various Issues.

Table 11.3 Value of imports, customs duty, nominal exchange rate and average tariff rate, 1986–90

Year	*Import duty revenue US$m (current prices)*	*Value of imports US$m*[2] *(current prices)*	*Average nominal exchange rate Tshs/US$*[1]	*Average tariff rate*[3] *(collection) (%)*
1986	106.61	1047.5	38.15	10.18
1987	80.21	1150.0	68.65	6.97
1988	81.95	1192.4	103.45	6.87
1989	104.60	1230.0	154.27	8.50
1990	112.13	1363.5	195.33	8.22

Sources:
1 Bank of Tanzania (1989) *Economic and Operations Report* (June).
2 ERB (1991) *Tanzanian Economic Trends*; vol. 4, no. 2 (July 1991); and vol. 5, no. 2 (July 1992).
3 Computed by the author.

tariff rate which increased from 6.97 per cent in 1987 to 8.22 per cent in 1990 a reflection of the decrease in the scheduled tariff rates in 1989 and 1990, which induces compliance and less frequent recourse to exemptions.

Predicted fiscal effects of specific trade reforms

How will trade policy reforms affect the government budget? We consider this question for changes in import duties, the exchange rate and export taxes separately.

Import duties

Within the standard Heckscher–Ohlin trade model and under perfect competition, trade taxes disrupt the free flow of goods among countries and create a welfare loss. When the assumption of perfect competition is relaxed, and monopoly, monopsony or other market power is introduced at the international level, trade taxes could exploit this market power, using the optimal tariff argument.

It has been shown that the revenue importance of import taxes is a function of (1) the average tariff rate (import duties/total imports), (2) the openness of the economy, represented as a ratio of imports to GNP, (3) a measure of the sophistication of the tax system, defined as the ratio of domestically collected taxes to GNP, (4) the level of economic development as represented by per capita income, (5) the fiscal deficit in relation to GDP, (6) the trade deficit in relation to GDP, (7) the rate of inflation, and (8) the real effective exchange rate index. It has also been shown that across certain levels of development, the share of trade taxes in total tax revenue is related (negatively) to a country's level of economic development (as proxied by a GDP measure) and is positively related to its openness to international trade as measured by the size of its foreign trade sector (exports plus imports/GDP) (Gemmell, 1993). In theory, import duties should not be used as a major tax revenue source because of their non-neutral effects. In practice, however, duties often play such a role if the exchange rate is overvalued and if a basic level of protection is justified. When used as such, a duty should be levied at a uniform, *ad valorem* rate on all imports. In such a case, import duties would have the same revenue-generating properties as a general sales tax: they would be collected without lags and an adjustment of the rate would immediately translate into more or less revenue.

More appropriately, a limited number of carefully designed import duties could be justified to provide temporary protection to domestic industries that the government wishes to encourage. In this regard, import duties should not play an important role in raising revenue. In fact, extremely high rates of duty that are completely effective in protecting a domestic industry would not raise any revenue whatsoever, since a substantially high rate on a particular good would result in zero imports of that good (and therefore zero duty). In Tanzania, protection is provided by both tariff and non-tariff barriers. Until the early 1970s, tariffs were more prominent in determining the protection structure. However, with the emerging shortage of foreign exchange in the late 1970s and early 1980s, QRs became more prominent. With the introduction of trade liberalization measures in early 1984, and especially through the introduction of 'own funds' imports and imports through retained export earnings, QRs have been eased and tariffs now have a bigger role to play (Lyakurwa, 1991).

Difficulties in tax administration and the lack of a well-developed business sector often force a government to rely more heavily on import duties and excise taxes than would otherwise be desirable. Such a focus is subject to a number of potential problems. First, an over-reliance on import duties can cause unwanted bias against free trade and offer domestic industries a higher degree of protection than is appropriate. Second, a heavy reliance on excise taxes, almost by their very nature, results in a heavy reliance on a limited number of items where a high degree of physical controls can be exercised.

The narrow base not only limits the ability of the tax system to raise additional revenues without becoming confiscatory, but also, as a result of the frequent use of specific rate taxes, leaves the system open to the risk of a rapid erosion of tax revenues during periods of even moderate inflation.

A heavy reliance on either import duties or excise taxes also increases the degree of economic distortion that leads to an inefficient allocation of the country's resources (Policy Economics Group, 1991). It has also been pointed out (Greenaway and Milner, 1991) that high tariff rates have a tendency to encourage the search for reducing tax liability, even for recorded imports, quite apart from smuggled or unrecorded imports, as well as creating an opportunity for bribery, all of which lead to reduced government revenues.

Exchange rate

Exchange-rate depreciation would have the same effect on revenue as an increase in *ad valorem* import tariffs. The relationship between the exchange rate and the budget deficit in an African setting has been explored by Chhibber *et al.* (1989). Exchange-rate movements affect both the revenue and expenditure sides of the budget. With devaluation, both external debt and debt service payments in domestic currency are raised. Similarly, devaluation raises the domestic currency value of government imports. The net effect of a devaluation on the volume of imports is a function of the price and income elasticity of demand. But changes in the level of imports affect revenue realized from customs duties.

On the supply side, devaluation stimulates the production of exports, raises the incomes of exporters and subsequently increases revenue generated from taxes (Corden, 1989). Recent empirical reviews by Chhibber and Mansour quoted by Seade (1990) showed that for Chile the large devaluation of 1982–4 hurt the profitability of investment through the increase in the replacement price of capital. But over time the profitability of the expanding export and import competing sector led to a revival of investment. Growth in investment would lead to high output growth and hence high tax revenue. For Indonesia it was observed that an overvalued exchange rate is beneficial only in the short-run. The lower growth of exports because of the overvaluation, lowers overall growth and reduces investment in the long run and *hence lowers tax revenue.* The effect of the exchange rate change on the fiscal deficit will depend on its net effect on government revenue and expenditure and the accompanying macroeconomic policies.

Export taxes

Export taxes are a means of taxing agricultural and rural producers who are difficult to reach through income or land taxes. However, over the last decade the use of export taxes has declined, from 7 per cent of total recurrent revenue in 1973, to 3 per cent in 1980/1. Export taxes were eliminated over the 1981/83 period as part of the National Economic Survival Programme of encouraging exports by reducing anti-export bias.

The 1970s and early 1980s witnessed growing macro instability and balance of payments pressure. Increasing overvaluation of the official exchange rate led to the imposition of import and exchange controls to restrain the current account deficit to levels consistent with available resources and external financing. Administered producer prices for export crops were insufficiently adjusted in the face of inflation. Thus exports came to be thrice taxed: first through direct export taxes; second, through the overvalued exchange rate and, third, by falling real producer prices. Hence the policy induced incentive regime discriminated against tradeables and exports. While the elimination of export taxes removed explicit taxes on exports, the implicit taxes remained. Taking 1984 as an example, the implicit tax on coffee exports as a result of the overvaluation of the exchange rate would be approximately US$114.4 million.[1] The evolution of the parallel market in Tanzania dates back to the 1978 war, when the government increased substantially the money supply to finance the war, the 1979 oil price shock, and the 1980 failure by the government to reach agreement with the IMF on structural adjustment measures.

If one examines the variables that affect government revenue, these could be categorized as exogenous variables (world market prices of exports and imports, other inflows and aid flows); endogenous variables (volume of exports); and policy instruments (exchange rate, export tax and import tax). The effect on the government revenue of changes in these variables can then be analysed over three time periods: pre-reform (1980–4); reform period (1984–7) and post-reform (1987–90) (see Table 11.4).

The direction of change of the implicit taxes (subsidies) is governed by changes in policy instruments as well as in the exogenous variables. Changes in these variables also indicate the predicted direction of change of government revenue.

While explicit taxes on exports were eliminated in the 1981/2 period, implicit taxes rose during the pre-reform period but declined in the post-reform period as a result of the continuous adjustment of the exchange rate which reduced the overvaluation of the shilling. Similarly, while the implicit subsidy on imports rose during the pre-reform period, the post-reform period shows that such subsidies have been declining.

Given that over 70 per cent of all imports are government imports, it is clear that during the pre-reform period, the government was heavily subsidized, and given that government imports were brought into the country free of import duty, this contributed to the worsening of the budget deficit. The direction of change of the budget in the post-reform

Table 11.4 Policy instruments and other variables that influence government revenue (pre-reform, reform and post-reform periods)

Variables	*Pre-reform 1980–4*	*Major reform period 1984–7*	*Post-reform, 1987–90*	*Predicted effect on government revenue*
1 Policy instruments				
(i) Exchange rate	rising	rising	declining	+
(ii) Export Tax (tx)	declining	eliminated	eliminated	–
(iii) Import Tax (tm)	rising	rising	declining	+
2 Exogenous variables				
(i) Export prices ($)	constant	constant	declining	–
(ii) Import prices ($)	constant	constant	constant	+
(iii) Other inflows (own funds)	declining	rising	rising	+
(iv) Aid flow (imports - [exports + own funds])	declining	rising	rising	+
3 Endogenous variables				
Volume of exports	declining	constant	rising	+
4 Tax revenue				
(i) Exports – explicit tax	declining	eliminated	eliminated	–
– implicit tax	rising	declining	declining	+
(ii) Imports – explicit tax	rising	rising	declining	+
– implicit tax/subsidy	rising	rising	declining	+

period arising from policy changes is upwards. Thus the fiscal implications of the exchange rate change is a higher increase in revenue, hence a decrease in the budget deficit if expenditures remain at about the same levels.

There has been some improvement in export volumes during the post-reform period which should have a positive influence on the budget deficit. A reduction of the tariff rate would have a positive impact on the budget deficit depending on the relative impacts of the exchange rate change and the change in the volume of imports. Overall, the impact should be positive if it is coupled with an increase in compliance as well as broadening the tax base through elimination/reduction of exemptions.

Trade policy reforms and subsequent budgetary effects

Policy reforms

Since the outset of the economic crisis in 1977/8, Tanzania has tried several stabilization and/or structural adjustments either on its own or with the support of the IMF/World Bank. Although a number of programmes were adopted not all were implemented because of inertia in implementing domestic policy changes.

The first stabilization programme was initiated in 1979 with expected IMF support, but it could not be implemented as agreement with the IMF was not reached. The second programme was the National Economic Survival Programme (NESP) adopted in 1981. This focused on crisis management of the external sector imbalance via exhortation. It has been described as being long on targets but short on policy instruments to achieve them (Lipumba, 1984). An important trade policy instrument implemented during this period was the elimination of export taxes and the introduction of an export compensation scheme in the form of export rebates as a measure to promote exports. However, the rebate rates, which ranged from 0–25 per cent of the fob value of exports were too low to produce the intended results given the very high overvaluation of the shilling.

The third was the Structural Adjustment Programme (SAP). This was a comprehensive adjustment programme covering a three-year period, 1982/3–1984/5. It was designed to restore balance in the government and external sector accounts, contain inflation, and restore output to pre-crisis levels while maintaining social services and the expansion of economic infrastructure. With respect to the fiscal stance, the programme recognized that there was a budgetary imbalance which resulted in high monetary growth rates which fuelled inflation.

Overall, however, the experience during the period shows that SAP failed to redress the fiscal imbalance. Although during the first year both recurrent and overall deficits declined, they both increased during the subsequent years, reaching high levels of Shs 5499.0 million and Shs 11 541 million, respectively, in 1985/6. This situation resulted in excessive borrowing by the government from the banking system, reaching a record figure of Shs 4925 million in 1985/6. These developments contributed greatly to the high inflation rate of about 30 per cent that prevailed during the period.

It was against this background, therefore, that the government launched the Economic Recovery Programme (ERP) in June 1986. ERP was a three-year comprehensive programme deepening government efforts to achieve structural adjustment. Among the objectives of ERP was the restoration of internal and external balance by pursuing prudent fiscal, monetary and trade policies.

Following the trade liberalization in June 1984, the country's policies assumed new dimensions. In 1985 the Sales Tax Act was amended and the Registered Dealers Certificate (RDC) was introduced. From 1985. import duty and sales tax rates were gradually reduced, and a more significant rate reduction and rationalization occurred in 1988 and 1990 in respect of import duty and sales tax, respectively. Excise duty was reintroduced in 1989 to facilitate rationalization and simplification of sales tax structure and administration (Osoro, 1990).

So far, implementation of ERP has yielded encouraging results. Improved budgetary discipline combined with higher economic growth has resulted in improved revenue collection. Although the overall deficit increased from 35.7 per cent of total expenditure in 1985/6 to 38.2 per cent in 1988/9, bank borrowings (which had reached a record level of Shs 4925 million in 1985/6 declined to a net repayment level in 1988/9. The proportion of government borrowing from the banking system to total expenditure declined from 15.2 per cent in 1985/6 to 3.3 per cent in 1987/8, and disappeared in 1988/9. However, movements towards achieving the ERP targets have been enhanced by foreign inflows.

Import support financed 35 and 62.3 percent of the recurrent deficits in 1986/7 and 1987/8, respectively. This implies that had it not been for import support, the impressive performance in bank borrowing would not have been feasible. In the short run this phenomenon is not harmful, because financing recurrent deficits with import support is not inflationary. However, it might be questioned whether it is wise to allocate such a large proportion of external assistance to support the recurrent budget. This makes the basic activities of the government vulnerable to donor conditionality pressures, and cannot be sustainable.

Table 11.5 Predicted fiscal effects of specific trade policy reforms

Reform episode	*Relevant trade policy reforms*	*Predicted effect on govt revenue*
1 National Economic Survival Programme (NESP) 1981/2	Elimination of export taxes, Institution of export compensation scheme (rebates)	–
2 Structural Adjustment Programme (SAP) 1982/3-1984/5	Trade liberalization, own funds imports, export retention schemes, removal of confinement policy	+
3 Economic Recovery Programme (ERP) 1986-9	Exchange rate adjustment. Reduction of scheduled tariff rates and sales tax rates. Institution of excise tax on domestic production as well as on imports	–

Although there have been encouraging developments under ERP, there are still problems that continue to limit economic growth. Among these are: inadequate domestic savings; a high rate of inflation; weaknesses in the agricultural marketing system and the resultant pressures on a financial system affected by structural weaknesses; and the poor state of social services. In order to tackle these problems the government launched a three-year Economic and Social Action Programme (ESAP) in 1989/90 as a successor to ERP. With respect to government finance and fiscal balance, ESAP sought to reduce significantly dependence of the budget on import support by the end of the programme in 1991/2 and progressively to reduce government involvement in activities which can be undertaken by other agencies so as to concentrate on infrastructure and social services. It is also the Government's intention under ESAP to strengthen the tax system. This had led to the recent appointment of the Tax Commission. The results of all these efforts can only be evaluated against the lapse of time. It should be noted that even after the launching of ESAP, about 70 per cent of the recurrent budget and 95 per cent of the development budget are foreign-financed. This compares to previous levels of 40 and 70 per cent, respectively (Osoro, 1990). The predicted effects of these policy changes on government revenue are summarized in Table 11.5.

Effects of reforms on the budget

Active exchange rate policy

It has been argued by Collier and Gunning (1991) that although trade liberalization does not inevitably worsen the balance of payments, it seems likely to do so. Trade liberalization lowers the domestic price of importables, thereby reducing the demand for money. The resulting excess supply of money manifests itself as a payments deficit. Collier and Gunning (1991) argue further that to maintain payments balance, the demand for money must be maintained (or its supply reduced). One way to achieve this is by offsetting the reduction in importables prices brought about by trade liberalization with an exchange rate depreciation. The domestic price of importables is related to the exchange rate and trade restrictions through

$$P_d = P_w e(1 + t)$$

where P_d is the domestic price of the importable, P_w the international price (in dollars), e the exchange rate (units of domestic currency per dollar), and t the nominal rate of protection (tariffs plus the tariff-equivalent of quotas).

Over the decade of the 1980s, a large number of Sub-Saharan African countries, including Tanzania, have pursued a rather active exchange-rate policy. Ndulu (1991) has pointed out that more than fifteen out of thirty countries not operating under a fixed-peg arrangement depreciated their nominal effective exchange rates (measured in foreign currency terms) by more than 50 per cent during 1982–8 in an effort to regain external viability. In Tanzania, the real effective exchange rate was depreciated by 67 per cent between 1982 and 1988. Ndulu (1991) has observed that movements of RER over the 1966–90 period display three distinct phases: 1966–73 was characterized by relative stability of RER; 1973–85 saw a strong trend of RER appreciation, mainly as a result of expansionary macroeconomic policy, a rapid increase in the taxation of imports and intensified use of exchange controls; and during 1986–90, a steep depreciation of the RER was effected which can be translated into a real depreciation of the shilling.

As indicated above, the main link between fiscal policy and trade is the exchange rate. Generally, excessive fiscal deficits are at the root of overvalued exchange rates. As fiscal deficits increase, additional pressure on domestic demand drives wages up. Over-reliance on money creation for financing the deficit also results in inflation. Increased domestic prices relative to the prices in a country's trading partners leads to overvaluation in the real exchange rate.

It has been argued that, in the majority of developing countries, a devaluation is likely to raise government revenue since it shifts taxable value-added towards the foreign trade sector, where tax bases are more easily taxable (Seade, 1990). Tanzania began to pursue an active foreign exchange policy during the Economic Recovery Programme. As a result of the policy measures introduced with the programme, recurrent revenue increased from 14.7 per cent of GDP in 1985/6 to 19.8 per cent in 1988/9, while recurrent expenditure increased from 18.6 per cent of GDP to 27 per cent over the same period (Economic Research Bureau (ERB), 1992). Active exchange rate policy may not necessarily rid the fiscal deficit in the short run. On the contrary, the fiscal deficit may in fact worsen before it improves. Supplementary fiscal and monetary policy measures are essential in order to attain significant reductions in the fiscal deficit.

Rationalization of import tariff rates

In a large number of countries, including Tanzania, forced import compression was implemented via quantitative restrictions. Exchange control and trade restrictions rather than exchange-rate adjustment were the main instruments of balance-of-payments management.

Some analysts have argued that the fiscal deficit and inflation should be reduced before trade policy changes are introduced. One issue is possible inconsistency with stabilization efforts: tariff reductions may reduce revenue, devaluation may fuel inflation, and liberalization may exacerbate balance of payments deficits. It has, however, been shown that, in practice, significant trade policy reformers have also generally managed to reduce the fiscal deficit, inflation and the balance of payments more than have the weaker reformers (Nash, 1990).

A variety of trade reforms complement the fiscal adjustment. Eliminating non-tariff barriers – especially converting them to equivalent tariffs – and eliminating tariff exemptions are revenue enhancing. This has been shown to be the case for Kenya, Jamaica and Mauritius (Nash *et al.*, 1990). Reducing tariffs and harmonizing them can be revenue-neutral or revenue-enhancing if the lower tariff rates are offset by a large depreciation of the exchange rate. And reducing very high tariff rates can increase trade tax revenue if tariff evasion rates fall or if import demand is price elastic (that is, if actual tariff rates exceed maximum-revenue tariff rates). This has been shown to be the case in Tanzania, where tariff reduction coupled with exchange rate depreciation led to increases in customs revenue (Table 11.3). It has further been shown that in a sample of countries that primarily reformed non-tariff barriers without lowering tariffs, tariff revenue increased from 2.7 to 3.4 per cent of GDP. But in a sample of countries that reduced tariffs as well as implementing other reforms – among them Mexico, Morocco, the Philippines, and Thailand – revenue fell on average from 2.8 to 2.3 per cent of GDP (Nash *et al.*, 1990). In general, if tariff reform exacerbates the fiscal deficit and if that deficit is unduly high, offsetting fiscal measures are necessary. Measures to reduce expenditure or enhance revenue from other sources (such as consumption taxes) may need to be implemented. Trade and internal reforms are best carried out simultaneously because of their complementary effects; the benefits of trade policy reforms are usually greater when accompanied by internal reforms. Bleijer and Cheasty (1989) have pointed out that even if trade reforms produce clear improvements in the fiscal balance in the long run, short-run effects, as well as the process of adjustment to more open trade, may be costly for the government. However, as pointed out above, the short-term costs could be countered by taking appropriate internal fiscal measures.

Own funds imports and export retention schemes

The promotion of non-traditional exports which are not in the realm of manufacturing is one of the avenues towards export growth that several African countries have discovered recently (Siggel, 1990). Getting the exchange rate right is insufficient, on its own, for successful development of such niche markets. New types of market information, dynamic entrepreneurship, risk capital as well as financial and other incentives are necessary.

Since 1984, Tanzania has been trying to reverse the trend of inward-looking policies with the introduction of trade liberalization measures which allow 'own funds' imports and exporters to retain a portion of the foreign exchange earned. Own-funds imports, and imports from retained export earnings, now account for about 30 per cent of the total import bill. The policy measures mentioned above have probably been the most powerful instruments for the promotion of non-traditional exports. As a proportion of total exports, non-traditional exports rose from 25 per cent in 1985 to 45 per cent in 1988 (Bagachwa *et al.*, 1990, p. 33). This increase is partly due to the officialization of part of the parallel export flows. The increase in imports as a result of own-funds imports and imports paid for from retained export earnings has had a significant impact on government revenue through import duty, sales tax on imports, and excise duty introduced in the 1988/9 budget. As a proportion of total recurrent revenue, total taxes on imports increase from 8.4 per cent in 1984/5 to 11.8 per cent in 1988/9 (Economic Research Bureau (ERB), 1990 and 1992).

Increases in export earnings would be reflected in the budget through increases in income tax. However, given the narrow base of income tax in Tanzania, and given that non-traditional exports are not sufficiently well-organized for income tax purposes, increases in non-traditional exports may not filter through to the government coffers. As a proportion of total recurrent revenue, revenue from income tax declined from 26.4 per cent in 1984/5 to 24.9 per cent in 1988/9 (Economic Research Bureau (ERB), 1990 and 1992).

International trade taxes have been greatly affected by the extent of tax exemptions on imports. Taking the year 1989 as an example, total exemptions on imports represented about 30.5 per cent of total recurrent revenue. The government introduced a number of trade policy measures, which included the 1988/9 extensive tariff reform, and the 1989/90 sales tax reform, plus the introduction of excise duty, the Open General Licence (OGL) of 1988/9 and the 1990 Investment Promotion Centre. All these measures had a significant impact on the government budget, particularly on the revenue side. All except the Investment Promotion Centre have a positive impact on the recurrent revenue, but this can only be assessed fully with the passage of time.

While there has been substantial progress towards revenue enhancement, there has been inertia on the part of the government in reducing expenditure, particularly in respect of the loss-making parastatals that have for a long time acted as a drain on the government coffers.

Concluding remarks and lessons learned

The macroeconomic prospects of the Tanzanian economy following the liberalization process can be characterized as good, with GDP estimated to be growing at 5 per cent, agriculture at 4 5 per cent, industry at 6 per cent, and services at 4 per cent. However, even with official exports projected to grow at 9 per cent in volume terms, the balance of payments situation is likely to remain a critical constraint. From the perspective of public finance, the implications of this macroeconomic scenario are that prospects for the revenue base performing better than during the 1980s would be brighter. However, while this should improve public finances over the long term, the process is likely to be a relatively slow one.

In the long run, given the improvement in national income that follows trade liberalization, there is no reason why the budget balance should be worse than when the economy was protected. However, several possible shortcomings of the tax structure could prevent the economy's revenue potential from being realized, and these need to be addressed by adjustments in policy.

In Tanzania, not all incomes are taxed, particularly incomes from the emerging export sector which has been greatly stimulated by the liberalization process. There is also the prevalence of numerous exemptions in the tax system, some of which are statutory. For the budget to capture the income gains associated with liberalization, it is important for the tax system to be broadly based. There is, therefore, the need to redefine and broaden the tax base as an important complement to the trade liberalization exercise.

Two revenue-related costs of liberalization, which tend to reduce the budget balance, appear to be unavoidable, even under the most prudent of policy regimes. First, although both export and import volumes increase after liberalization, revenue from these sources falls. First, because export taxes were eliminated, and second, imports are not as heavily taxed as before the liberalization. Hence trade liberalization implied a shift from traded goods in the tax base to traded goods 'outside' the tax base. Second, while both exports and imports are relatively easy to tax, to collect revenue from income and domestic consumption taxes requires a relatively sophisticated accounting system which at present is lacking. Hence some of the income arising from trade liberalization may go untaxed or may go to tax collectors outside the government system.

With regard to tax policy, the greater significance of the domestic tax base in a low-tariff economy will make it more crucial that the tax system be broad and neutral. It is also necessary to streamline the domestic tax system to control its overall administrative costs and corruption. If these steps are not taken, the revenue potential of the economy will not be realized through the tax system and government might be tempted to reverse the liberalization process in a bid to curb declining revenues.

Notes

* The author wishes to express his gratitude to the African Economic Research Consortium for a 1992 research grant for the preparation of the paper from which this chapter was prepared, and to Paul Collier, Ibrahim Elbadawi and two anonymous referees for some very useful comments. All errors and omissions are entirely the responsibilities of the author.

1. Implicit export tax calculated as export earnings multiplied by the differential between average official exchange rate and the average parallel market exchange rate for that year, divided by the parallel market exchange rate.

References

Bagachwa, M. G. D., N. E. Luvanga and G. D. Mjema (1990) *A Study on Non-traditional Exports in Tanzania – A Report*, January.

Bank of Tanzania (1989) *Economic and Operations Report*, June.

Bleijer M. I. and A. Cheasty (1989) 'The Fiscal Implications of Trade Liberalization', in V. Tanzi (ed.), *Fiscal Policy in Open Developing Economics* (Washington DC: IMF).

Broden, P. (1990) *The Seed Capital Revolving Scheme, A Report* (Dar-es-Salaam).

Cheasty, A. (1990) 'The Fiscal Implications of Reducing Trade Taxes', *Finance and Development*, March.

Chhibber, A. J. *et al.* (1989) 'Inflation, Price Controls and Fiscal Adjustment in Zimbabwe', *World Bank Working Papers*, WPS 192, April.

Collier, P. and J. W. Gunning (1991) 'Trade and Development: Protection Shocks and Liberalization', Centre for the Study of African Economies, Oxford University, mimeo, October.

Corden, W. M. (1989) 'Macroeconomic Adjustment in Developing Countries', *The World Bank Research Observer*, vol. 4, pp. 51–64.

Diaz, A. C. (1976) *Foreign Trade Regime and Economic Development in Colombia* (New York: National Bureau of Economic Research).

Economic Research Bureau (ERB) (1990) *Tanzania Economic Trends, A Quarterly Review of the Economy*, vol. 2, no. 4, January 1989; vol. 2, no. 3, October, vol. 4, no. 2, July 1991.

Economic Research Bureau (ERB) (1992) *Tanzanian Economic Trends*, vol. 5, no. 1, April; and vol. 5, no. 2, July.

Evans, D. (1989) 'Visible and Invisible Hands in Trade Policy Reform', mimeo, July.

Gemmell, N. (1993) 'Fiscal Dependence on Trade Taxes and Economic Development', *Scottish Journal of Economics*, vol. 40, pp. 56–68.

Greenaway, D. and C. R. Milner (1991) 'Policy Appraisal and the Structure of Protection in a Low-Income Developing Country: Problems of Measurement and Evaluation in Burundi', *Journal of Development Studies*.

IMF (International Monetary Fund) (1988) *A Review of Tanzania's Tax System*, Report, August.

Hitiris, T. (1990) 'Tax Structure, Trade Taxes and Economic Development. An Empirical Investigation', in V. Tanzi, *Fiscal Policy in Open Developing Economies* (Washington DC: IMF), ch. 2

Linn, J. F. and D. L. Wetzel (1990) 'Public Finance, Trade and Development: What Have We Learned?', in V. Tanzi (ed.) *Fiscal Policy in Open Developing Economies* (Washington DC: IMF), ch. 1

Lipumba, N. I. H. (1984) 'The Economic Crisis in Tanzania', in Lipumba, Msambichaka and Wangwe (eds), *Economic Stabilization Policies in Tanzania*, (Dar-es-Salaam: Department of Economics and ERB).

Lyakurwa, W. M. (1987) *Export Development Strategy for Tanzania, A Report.*

Lyakurwa, W. M. (1988) *Structural Adjustment Programmes in Africa: The Case of Tanzania, A Report*, September.

Lyakurwa, W. M. (1991) 'Trade Policy and Promotion in Sub-Saharan Africa: A Review of Issues and Experiences', African Economic Research Consortium, Special Report no. 12, May.

Nash, J. (1990) 'An Overview of Trade Policy Reforms with Implications for Sub-Saharan Africa' (Washington DC: World Bank, Trade Policy Division).

Nash, J., V. Thomas and K. Martin (1990) *Lesson in Trade Policy Reform*, Policy and Research Series no. 10 (Washington DC: World Bank).

Ndulu, B. J. (1990) 'Growth and Adjustment in Sub-Saharan Africa', Paper prepared for the African Economic Issues Conference Nairobi, 5–7 June.

Ndulu, B. J. (1991) *Exchange Rate Policy and Management in the Context of Economic Reform in Sub-Saharan Africa: Tanzania as an Illustrative Case*, June.

Osoro, N. E. (1990) 'The Revenue Generating Potential of the Tanzanian Tax System, *Tanzania Journal of Economics*, vol. 1, pp. 53–62.

Policy Economics Group (1991) *Indirect Taxation Reform Study for Tanzania*, Report KPMG Peat Marwick, February.

Rhee, Y. W., K. Katterback and J. White (1990) 'Free Trade Zones in Export Strategies', mimeo.

Seade, J. (1990) 'Tax Revenue Implications of Exchange Rate Adjustment', in V. Tanzi (ed.), *Fiscal Policy in Open Developing Economies* (Washington DC: IMF), ch. 4.

Siggel, E. (1990) 'A Case for Technical Assistance in Trade Policy Reform for Sub-Saharan Africa', Paper prepared for the UNDP/World Bank Trade Expansion Programmes, April.

Takacs, W. E. (1989) *Alternative Transitional Measures to Liberalize Quantitative Restrictions: Implications for Developing Countries.*

United Republic of Tanzania (1989) *National Accounts of Tanzania* (Dar-es-Salaam: Bureau of Statistics).

United Republic of Tanzania (1991) *Budget Speech by the Minister of Finance* (Dar-es-Salaam: Government Printers).

United Republic of Tanzania (various dates) *Economic Survey* (Dar-es-Salaam: Government Printers).

World Bank (1989) *Tanzania: Public Expenditure Review, A Report*, May.

World Bank (1990) *Uganda: An Agenda for Trade Reform*, UNDP/World Bank Trade Expansion Programme, Country Report, April.

Ziba, F.-L. and M. Katz (1989) 'Fiscal Dimensions of Trade Policy', in M. I. Bleijer and K.-Y. Chu (eds), *Fiscal Policy Stabilization and Growth in Developing Countries* (Washington DC: IMF), ch. 11.

12

Portfolio Responses to Trade Policy Incredibility

Paul Collier and Jan Willem Gunning

Introduction

This chapter analyzes the causes of incredibility in trade reform and its consequences for portfolio choices. It takes as its context Africa, where portfolio choices have been highly distinctive. Private investment is currently lower in Africa as a share of GDP than in any other developing region, and foreign direct investment is negligible – despite remarkable growth in other developing areas, Africa's share is currently lower than at any time since the mid-1980s (Miller and Sumlinski, 1994, pp. 6 and 30). Zambia provides an illustration of domestic portfolio choices: during the liberalization of 1985–7, three-quarters of investment consisted of inventory accumulation as opposed to gross fixed capital formation (Bates and Collier, 1993). The high degree of policy uncertainty that has surrounded African liberalizations may be an important reason for these portfolio choices.

Most African countries had long periods of control regimes in which exchange-rate over-valuation was made compatible with the balance-of-payments constraint by quantitative restriction of imports. This had consequences for portfolio choice. Because domestic returns on capital were low, foreign assets were preferred, manifested by capital flight and negligible inward investment. Domestic investment was skewed towards tradable capital goods because these were implicitly subsidized by exchange-rate overvaluation, and towards the import-substitute and non-tradable sectors. Since the mid-1980s, many of these countries have liberalized trade, but around half of these attempts have subsequently been reversed (Foroutan and Nash, 1994). Both liberalizations and reversals were to some extent anticipated by private agents. We first consider the causes of incredibility in implementation, and then turn to the portfolio consequences. Since the effects of fully credible pre-announcement and incredible implementation of trade liberalization are symmetrical, both involving an anticipated change in trade policy, the analysis is applicable to both situations.

Policy credibility

We begin with an analysis of the determinants of credibility once a liberalization has been implemented. The sufficient conditions for policy reversal to be predictable follow from the necessary conditions for a liberalization to be sustainable: *time consistency*, the absence of *systematic forecastability* and *macroeconomic compatibility*, the last subdividing into fiscal and balance-of-payments impacts.

We illustrate the application of time inconsistency to trade liberalization in the context of a two-period game between the government and the private sector. The government must choose an export tax on coffee in each period, t_{x1} and t_{x2}. The private sector has two decisions to make, both of which must be taken in the first period. It must decide whether to plant coffee trees and whether to use 'fertilizer' in Period 1. 'Fertilizer' in this story has the effect not so much of raising yields as of shifting them between time periods: if fertilizer is applied in Period 1, it raises the yield in Period 1 at the cost of reducing it in Period 2. The problem worrying the government is that by levying an export tax it discourages the planting of coffee trees. This is socially inefficient and reduces its own revenue in Period 2. The 'first best' would be if the government could fool the private sector into expecting that the export tax would be zero. The private sector would plant coffee and the government could then tax it, since the planting is, by assumption, irreversible. The government might in this situation be tempted to liberalize trade in Period 1 (that is, set $t_{x1} = 0$), in the hope that private agents would then expect that the policy would be maintained in Period 2. If this strategy worked it would be superior to setting the export tax at the same positive rate in both periods ($t_{x1} = t_{x2} > 0$), which could therefore be described as the 'second-best' strategy. However, private agents know the structure of the game, also that the government has no incentive to maintain the export tax at zero in Period 2. The trade liberalization in Period 1 is therefore incredible, because the maintenance of the policy would be against the government's own interests. If the government ignores the problem of time inconsistency and sets $t_{x1} = 0$, then private agents know that in Period 2 the export tax will be positive. Knowing this, they not only have an incentive not to plant coffee, but they also have an incentive to use 'fertilizer'. The 'fertilizer' enables private agents to bring their output forward from Period 2 to Period 1, thereby avoiding the anticipated Period 2 tax. However, since the 'fertilizer' merely shifts output intertemporally, it is socially costly. The government's attempt to achieve the 'first-best' has therefore resulted in the 'third-best': no coffee planting and excessive fertilizer.

A second reason why African trade liberalization may be time inconsistent is if it is supported by programme aid. The game is now between the government and donors. A government which does not intend to liberalize can still benefit from implementing it in order to get programme aid, after which policy will revert to trade restrictions.

The systematic forecastability of macroeconomic policy is familiar through the Lucas model. In Africa it has been common for governments to ration foreign exchange according to its availability. This variation in implicit tariffs has been termed an *endogenous trade policy*. Policy is then predictable to the extent that the events which influence the supply of foreign exchange to the central bank are predictable. Although shocks such as droughts and coffee booms are not predictable, once such a shock has occurred it is sometimes reasonably clear that it will not persist. The operation of an endogenous trade policy rule makes pre-announcement redundant in the early stages of a commodity boom, and reversal predictable in the late stages.

Trade liberalizations can be incompatible through their effects on either the balance of payments or the budget. The impact on the balance of payments depends on the structure of the trade restrictions. If there is no export tax ($t_x = 0$) while there is an import restriction ($t_m > 0$), the trade liberalization lowers the price of importables. If the price of imports is permitted to fall then the demand for money falls, producing a payments deficit. By contrast, suppose that trade restrictions are all on the exportables side (there is an export tax, $t_x > 0$, but no import restrictions, $t_m = 0$), and that whatever is raised from the export tax is given to other private agents. Then the trade liberalization raises the domestic price level and so improves the balance of payments. In both cases, overtime, as resources relocate into the export sector, real income in the economy rises, and this raises the demand for money. The trade liberalization therefore has an ambiguous impact effect depending on the structure of trade restrictions, but subsequently tends to improve the balance of payments. Generally in Africa trade restrictions are more severe on the import side than on the export side ($t_m > t_x$) and importables are more important in expenditure than are exportables. As a result, trade liberalization has an impact effect which worsens the balance of payments.[1] Since a liberalization-induced payments deficit is unsustainable, an incompatible trade liberalization will predictably either be reversed or made compatible through exchange-rate depreciation. Thus, if implemented, an incompatible liberalization cannot be fully credible.

Fiscal incompatibility as a source of incredibility in trade liberalization is less sharply defined than payments incompatibility. First, the impact on the budget is obscure. While trade liberalization on the export side is liable to lower government revenue in the short run, reductions in implicit tariffs are ambiguous. For example, the liberalization of quotas can change the composition of imports in favour of revenue-yielding items, while the compensating policy changes needed to maintain payments-compatibility will also have revenue effects. The policy reaction to fiscal incompatibility is also more obscure than that to payments incompatibility. In Africa, policies which produce payments deficits must be reversed, since governments cannot now borrow commercially, whereas policies which produce fiscal deficits may only be reversed once inflation becomes unacceptable. However, if private agents regard a trade liberalization as fiscally costly, and the government does not include offsetting measures in the reform package, then the liberalization is unlikely to be fully credible.

Portfolio responses to credible pre-announcement and incredible implementation

Recall that there is an element of symmetry in the effects of credible pre-announcement and incredible implementation: in both, agents anticipate a change in trade policy. We consider the consequences of an anticipated change in trade policy first on savings and then on investment.

The pre-announcement of trade liberalization has been advocated by Edwards and van Wijnbergen (1986), who describe their result as being 'of great policy importance' (p. 147). They argue that pre-announcement will raise domestic savings temporarily, and these are suboptimal because of financial repression.[2] Their model has two periods and two consumer goods, an import subject to tariffs, and an export. An investment good is duty-free in Period 1 and produces output in Period 2. In Period 1, the removal of the tariff in Period 2 is pre-announced. The economy is subject to foreign borrowing constraints which can be set at zero for each period without altering the model. The increased inducement to save as a result of pre-announcement is a substitution effect: consumers realise that the relative price of imports will fall.

While the model is technically correct, it is rather misleading. Although tariff reduction directly reduces the domestic currency price of imports, a compatible trade-liberalizing devaluation maintains the demand for money by preserving the price level constant. In terms of the EW model, there is then no intertemporal price effect and therefore no increased inducement to save. Further, if the liberalization is sustainable, private agents will anticipate the increase in real income that the liberalization will eventually bring. This income effect causes a *fall* in savings as a result of pre-announcement. Hence, if the price level is kept constant, there is no intertemporal substitution effect, so that the incoming effect necessarily dominates. In that case, to the extent that the analysis of pre-announcement is indeed 'of great policy importance', the message is the precise opposite of that claimed by Edwards and van Wijnbergen: pre-announcement will, through the income effect, reduce welfare.

For a liberalization to lower the price level, tariffs must be reduced without an offsetting change in the exchange rate. Such a policy conjunction can occur in each of the three circumstances discussed above: the trade liberalization may be incompatible; it may be made compatible by programme aid; or it may reflect an endogenous trade policy rule at the onset of a temporary commodity boom. In each of these circumstances the sustainability of the liberalization is incredible. If pre-announcement is fully credible in these cases it will indeed give rise to a savings boom, since the reduction in the price level with a fixed nominal rate of interest raises the consumer rate of interest. However, once the liberalization is implemented, portfolios will respond to this incredibility as discussed below.

The damage done by a credible pre-announcement of liberalization is not confined to the savings response. In Zimbabwe, the trade-liberalizing devaluation of January 1994 was indeed pre-announced, in November 1993. The response was a large increase in payments for imports and large falls in the receipt of imports and the delivery of exports. By advancing payment but delaying importation, agents could benefit from both the existing overvaluation of the exchange rate and the prospective reduction in tariff rates. By delaying delivery, exporters could benefit from the prospective devaluation. These windfalls were at the expense of the government budget and so were a socially costly outcome of pre-announcement.

The obverse of the Zimbabwean response to the pre-announcement of liberalization is the response to incredible implementation. Calvo (1987) showed that the appropriate strategy during incredible implementation is to borrow from abroad and hoard imports. Here we extend the analysis to show that the most profitable form of import-hoarding depends on the cause of the incredibility.

Recall that if the trade liberalization is payments-incompatible, then imports are temporarily cheap: either the exchange rate will be devalued to make the liberalization compatible, or the liberalization will be reversed. If agents expect an increase in implicit tariffs but no change in actual tariffs or the exchange rate, then hoarding imports in bonded warehouses is the most profitable response, because this defers the payment of import duty. If they anticipate devaluation or tariff increases then there is a case for paying duty in advance of sale and so hoarding in unbonded form. If, by contrast, the diagnosis is of time inconsistency, then imports on average are not temporarily cheap. Once the government reimposes trade restrictions the exchange rate will appreciate. What is anticipated then is not a general increase in the price of imports but a change in their composition: those imports which become scarce will sell for a higher price within the economy, and those that acquire privileged access will become cheaper. Hence, the appropriate response is to stockpile licences for those goods that will be scarce, since holding licences involves negligible cost. Finally, consider a liberalization which is incredible because it is recognized as the response to an endogenous trade policy rule. While with an endogenous trade liberalization imports are indeed temporarily cheap, the policy is sustainable for as long as the terms-of-trade boom lasts. Hence, agents might initially stockpile import licences, only converting them into bonded imports once the terms of trade deteriorate. Reinikka (1994) applies this analysis to the reversed Kenyan trade liberalization attempts of the 1980s and finds evidence that responses varied in accordance with the likely causes of the reversals.

We now turn from the import-hoarding response to that of fixed investment. The effect of credible pre-announcement on investment differs according to the tradability of capital. Agents are told that the implicit subsidy on imported capital purchased with domestic assets will be removed, as will the implicit tax on non-tradable capital purchased with foreign assets. Hence, credible pre-announcement will induce a portfolio shift into tradable capital goods from domestic assets, while there will be a deferral of any substitutions into non-tradable capital from foreign assets. Incredible implementation is the obverse: acquisition of non-tradable capital with foreign assets is urgent, while that of tradable capital with domestic assets should be postponed.

Portfolio response to partial credibility

So far we have considered only a fully credible pre-announcement and a completely incredible implementation. A partially credible pre-announcement may herald either a compatible or an incompatible liberalization. In a partially credible implementation, either a compatible liberalization may be reversed (for example, because of time inconsistency), or an incompatible liberalization may or may not be made compatible by devaluation. All these cases have in common that partial credibility of trade policy creates uncertainty about how relative prices will change.

As Dixit (1989) demonstrated, faced with such uncertainty, agents will defer irreversible investment, and liquid assets will command a premium. We extend this by distinguishing between tradable and non-tradable capital goods.

The consequences of relative price uncertainty depend upon the ease with which investors in aggregate can retrieve their assets. This is determined by three factors: the degree of sector specificity; the degree of physical mobility; and the rate of depreciation. The first of these is particularly problematical in Africa. Fears about policy reversal imply uncertainty about the relative profitability of investment in exports, import-substitutes and non-tradables. Whereas in many countries industries tend to cut across the first two categories, in Africa this is rarely the case. Hence, investments that are technologically industry-specific, are economically sector-specific to a much greater extent than elsewhere. The remaining two mechanisms affect tradable and non-tradable capital goods differently. Rates of depreciation are much lower for non-tradable capital. Typically, buildings depreciate at only around 4 per cent p.a., whereas in African conditions transport equipment, which is the single largest component of tradable capital, may last only a few years. Finally, while non-tradable capital is definitionally country-specific, some tradable capital can, if planned in advance, be removed from the country. In particular, multinational firms may be able to relocate equipment in neighbouring countries. Hence, even where equipment is sector-specific, it need not be subject to policy risk. For example, Mozambique is currently able to attract textile investment despite the fragile and early stage of policy changes.

The Dixit effect of policy risk associated with liberalization is thus likely to be much more powerful with respect to non-tradable capital than tradable capital. Liquid assets will command a high premium relative to non-tradable capital.

Liberalization sequences

Table 12.1 summarizes the portfolio effects of four policy expectations. In the first column there is a credible pre-announcement of a compatible

Table 12.1 The credibility of liberalization and portfolio choice

Asset	*Credible pre-announcement anticipated liberalization is:* *Compatible*	*Incompatible*	*Incredible implementation (incompatible)*	*Policy uncertainty*
Kn	–	+	–	–
Kt	?	+	–	?
Inv.	–	–	+	+
D.F.	–	+	–	+
$	+	+	–	+

Notes:
Kn = Non-tradable capital goods
Kt = Tradable capital goods
Inv. = Inventories of imports
D.F. = Domestic financial assets
$ = Foreign financial assets

trade liberalization. In the second there is a credible pre-announcement of an incompatible liberalization. In the third there is an incredible implementation because of incompatibility. In the fourth we add the effects distinctive to partial credibility of either pre-announcement or implementation. The effects considered are on investment in tradable and non-tradable capital goods, inventories of imports, and domestic and foreign financial assets.

Whether or not pre-announcement is desirable, it can often not be avoided, because the slow pace of government decision making enables well-informed private agents to anticipate the policy change, one example being the devaluation of the CFA franc. Hence, two sequences of trade liberalization are pertinent.

One sequence is of pre-announcement of an incompatible liberalization, followed by a phase in which private agents know that either the liberalization will be reversed, or it will be made compatible by devaluation. In this sequence, the portfolio changes are first those of columns 2 and 4, and then those of columns 3 and 4. Column 4 enters in both phases because there is uncertainty over how the incompatibility will be resolved.

During the pre-announcement phase the policy uncertainty implied by the implementation phase gives rise to a Dixit effect in favour of liquidity. This offsets the relaxation of financial repression. The anticipation of a falling price level raises savings, augmenting the finance for investment, but agents must be wary of locking in to sector-specific investment. There is a Zimbabwe-type inventory effect, since there is an incentive to delay imports.

During the implementation phase, inventory accumulation of imports is reinforced by the conjunction of the Calvo effect and the Dixit effect: inventories benefit from both a liquidity premium and an expectation of appreciation. This sequence thus involves a savings boom–slump and inventories slump–boom cycle, with quite possibly an investment slump in both phases.

The other sequence is of pre-announcement of a compatible liberalization. However, in Africa, once implemented even compatible liberalizations are less than fully credible because of the time-consistency problem.

In the pre-announcement phase of this sequence the portfolio changes combine columns 1 and 4. The pre-announcement reduces saving in domestic financial assets as discussed above, and this in turn reduces investment. However, the knowledge that the subsidy on tradable capital will be removed creates a substitution effect from non-tradable capital into tradable capital, therefore the net effect on the latter is ambiguous. These effects on investment are augmented by the Dixit effect, which similarly reduces fixed investment in favour of liquidity but with a substitution in favour of tradable capital. As in Zimbabwe, imports are pre-paid but not imported, so that inventories are depleted and foreign assets increased.

In the implementation phase, in addition to any changes that a fully credible liberalization might have had, there are changes caused by policy uncertainty, as shown in column 4. Recall that the inherited capital stock has excessive tradable capital and insufficient non-tradable capital, so that a fully credible liberalization might be expected to raise investment in non-tradable capital and reduce it in tradable capital. The limited credibility effect runs counter to this. The net effect may be that investment in tradables falls because of the excessive inheritance, whereas investment in non-tradables remains low because of its illiquidity. Hence, in both phases, there is an investment slump.

The tendency of both these liberalization sequences to lead to investment slumps is consistent with the empirical evidence on the effects of structural adjustment policies (see Bleaney and Greenaway, 1993).

Conclusion

We have considered portfolio responses to the pre-announcement of trade liberalization and to its implementation under limited credibility. We have also considered the circumstances under which liberalization will be incredible. Far from pre-announcement being desirable, as suggested by Edwards and van Wijnbergen, we have shown it to be detrimental. However, given the limited capacity of government to keep policy design secret, pre-announcement may *de facto* be unavoidable. We considered two policy sequences. In one the pre-announced policy is payments-incompatible and so during the implementation phase there is uncertainty as to whether the liberalization will be reversed or made compatible by devaluation. In the other, the pre-announced policy is payments-compatible but may be time-inconsistent. These sequences give rise to a Dixit effect and Calvo effect. The Dixit effect, we argued, in which there is a premium on liquidity, is particularly detrimental to non-tradable capital goods. The Calvo effect (the speculative hoarding of inventories of imports) is symmetrical in credible pre-announcements and incredible implementations. During partially credible liberalization the two effects work in conjunction, producing a powerful substitution from fixed investment into inventories, which may account for the Zambian portfolio response noted in the Introduction.

Notes

1. This is not inevitable. As Mussa (1976) shows, it is possible that the rents from trade restrictions actually rise as the implicit tariff is reduced (at least over a certain range). This tends to raise nominal expenditure and the demand for money. Where trade restrictions are initially very severe and the liberalization is modest, this effect could conceivably dominate.
2. They describe such liberalization as gradualism, though, in fact, the effect would be the same were the liberalization abrupt as long as it was pre-announced.

References

Bates, R. and P. Collier (1993) 'The Politics and Economics of Zambian Economic Policy Reform', in R. Bates and A. O. Krueger (eds), *The Political Economy of Policy Reform* (Oxford: Basil Blackwell).

Bleaney, M. and D. Greenaway (1993) 'Adjustment to External Imbalance and Investment Slumps in Developing Countries', *European Economic Review*, vol. 37, pp. 577–85.

Calvo, G. A. (1987) 'On the Costs of Temporary Policy', *Journal of Development Economics*, vol. 27, pp. 245–62.

Edwards, S. and S. van Wijnbergen (1986) 'The Welfare Effects of Trade and Capital Market Liberalization', *International Economic Review*, vol. 27, pp. 141–8.

Foroutan, F. and W. Nash (1994) *African Trade Liberalization* (Washington DC: World Bank).

Miller, R. R. and M. A. Sumlinski (1994) *Trends in Private Investment in Developing Countries, 1994: Statistics for 1970–92*, Discussion Paper 20, International Finance Corporation, Washington DC.

Mussa, M. (1976) 'Tariffs and the Balance of Payments', in J. Frenkel and H. G. Johnson (eds), *The Monetary Approach to the Balance of Payments*. London, George Allen & Unwin.

Reinikka, R. (1994) 'The Welfare Cost of Speculation During Kenyan Trade Reform', WPS94/11, Centre for the Study of African Economies, Oxford.

Index

Note: page numbers in **bold** type refer to illustrative figures or tables.